Fruit

Fruit

A Connoisseur's Guide and Cookbook

ALAN DAVIDSON
AND
CHARLOTTE KNOX

SIMON AND SCHUSTER

New York   London   Toronto   Sydney   Tokyo   Singapore

Simon & Schuster
Simon & Schuster Building Rockefeller Center
1230 Avenue of the Americas, New York, New York 10020

Editors: Diane Pengelly, Kirsty Seymour-Ure
Designer: Paul Drayson
Production: Ted Timberlake
Managing Editor: Chris Foulkes

Typeset in Garamond ITC by Servis Filmsetting Ltd,
Manchester, England
Color reproduction by Scantrans Pte Ltd, Singapore
Printed in Germany by Mohndruck GumbH, Gütersloh.

10 9 8 7 6 5 4 3 2 1

Library of Congress Cataloging-in-Publication Data

Davidson, Alan, 1924–
    Fruit : a connoisseur's guide and cookbook / Alan Davidson ;
illustrated by Charlotte Knox.
        p.   cm.
    Includes bibliographical references and index.
    ISBN 0–671–72884–9 ; $30.00
    1. Cookery (Fruit)   2. Fruit.   I. Title.
TX811.D38   1991
641.6′4—dc20
                                                                    91–3689
                                                                        CIP

ISBN: 0-671-72884-9

Acknowledgements

from Charlotte Knox

Most of the fruit and nuts illustrated in this book have been painted from fresh specimens, and I would like to thank the following institutions and people in Great Britain who helped me greatly.

Tony Kirkham, Mike Sinnott, David Cook and Dr David Field, all of The Royal Botanic Gardens, Kew, London, supplied me with information and specimens both fresh and dried.

John D Main of The Royal Botanic Gardens, Edinburgh, sent me plant material unavailable in the south of England, and John Winter of the Kirstenbosch National Botanic Gardens sent material from South Africa.

Many of the English apples and pears and the cherry blossom were picked at The Brogdale Horticultural Trust, Faversham, Kent, thanks to the assistance of Russell Williams. Harry Baker at the Royal Horticultural Society Garden, Wisley, Surrey, helped me with many enquiries, as did the staff at the Lindley library at the Society's office in Vincent Square, London. Pippa Sargent put me in touch with flower show competitors including Mr Buller, Gerald Edwards and Andrew Knott who all agreed to donate their show specimens for me to paint. Other fruits were collected thanks to Fiona Crumley at the Chelsea Physic Gardens, London, and Della Connelly at Peper Harow, Godalming, Surrey.

In America Dr Julia Morton, Director of the Morton Collectanea at The University of Miami, whose book *Fruits from Warm Climates* has been an invaluable reference book to me, kindly lent me her excellent photographic slides of such exotic fruit as I could not find – either fresh or dried. Other slides of uncommon and rare exotica were lent by Dr Jonathan Crane of the Tropical Research and Education Center, University of Florida, and J R Brooks & Son Inc also of Florida.

Many English nurserymen, orchardmen and traders have been most helpful in supplying me with fruit, particularly Mr and Mrs Terence Read of Read's Nursery, Norfolk, who sent citrus fruit and figs; Ken Muir of Honeypot Farm, Clacton-on-Sea, Essex, who supplied me with strawberries, blackberries and raspberries; Clive Simms of Stamford, Lincolnshire, who supplied me with nuts and slides of uncommon fruit; John Vanderplank of Greenholm Nurseries, Avon, who sent all the passion fruit, and Mr Harbutt of Rougham Hall Nurseries, Bury St Edmunds, who supplied all the gooseberries. The cherry page was completed thanks to the help of Ken Tobutt of IHR, East Malling; Stuart Malcolm of Barfield Farm, Offam; Jim Worley of Court Lodge Farm, Yalding; and Alan Burbridge of Paynes Farm, Wormshill; all of Kent.

Meg Game of Oldbury Farmhouse, Sevenoaks, Kent, and Marilyn Hamstead of Foxhill Farms, Michigan, both sent me nuts; Anmore Exotics, Havant, Hants, donated the monstera fruit; and Chilton Seeds of Cumbria sent me seeds to grow for artist's reference.

Other people who have supplied fruit and helped me in my enquiries are: Ron and Dave of Something Tropical, Winchester Place, Ridley Road, London, who import an enormous selection of tropical fruit from the Caribbean; Sri Owen, Elizabeth Schneider, Claudia Close, Mrs Davidson and Judy Cassell.

I would also like to thank Tom Maschler of Jonathan Cape for giving me permission to reuse and expand on some of my fruit paintings originally commissioned for *Exotic Fruits and Vegetables* by Jane Grigson (1986).

I would finally like to thank my brothers-in-law Dr Tom Earle and Charles Earle, who helped proofread the foreign names, as did my husband Joe Earle. Joe must also be thanked for his patience and tolerance, as well as for having lived for over a year in fear of eating any fruit in the house in case I had not finished painting it.

from Alan Davidson

I echo many of Charlotte Knox's thanks, since the kindness shown by people who supplied her with specimens or information almost invariably helped me too.

My own special thanks are due to all the numerous colleagues who generously allowed me to use or adapt recipes from their published works (see Bibliography) or unpublished repertoire. All, including also some non-professional contributors, are mentioned in the recipes they provided.

Many of the recipes were tested by Barbara Yeomans, Elizabeth Gabay and Russell Harris, the last two of whom worked with me on other aspects too, such as the foreign names of fruits. Helen Saberi not only provided recipes from her own charming book on food and cookery in Afghanistan but also contributed many ideas for other recipes and many practical suggestions arising out of tests and tastings (we all tasted each other's dishes). Laura Mason, specializing in confectionery and in the historical approach, was equally fertile in suggestions and contributions.

I was considerably helped in dealing with questions of taxonomy and nomenclature by amiable experts and amateurs in many parts of the world, notably Professor Richard Hosking at Hiroshima; Philip Iddison at Bangkok; Joe Roberts in India; Dr Astri Riddervold in Norway and both Anna-Maija Tanttu and Dr Annikki Palmén in Finland (all of these especially for berries); Dr Joan Morgan for everything to do with apples; John Vanderplank at the National Collection of Passiflora for all to do with the passion fruit family; and Charlotte Knox herself, who was so diligent in pursuing enquiries about the fruits she was painting that her knowledge often outstripped mine.

Thanks such as the above are to be expected in a book such as this one. But there are also thanks of a less usual nature. It happened that on the evening of the day on which I had, as I saw it, put the finishing touches to the book I suffered a heart attack (not cause and effect, just a coincidence), which stranded me in hospital and left my editor, Diane Pengelly, without an author at the very moment when she had the maximum number of questions to resolve and a dense array of deadlines to meet. Moreover, what I had perceived as the "finishing touches" were not quite that – there were still some loose threads and rough edges. She coped valiantly with the unexpected problem; and I must also thank most warmly my wife Jane and my daughter Caroline for their vital help in tidying everything up. I thank likewise Philip and Mary Hyman in Paris, who volunteered at short notice to constitute a first-aid team for some recipes which still needed expert attention.

Finally, I hope that it will not seem too self-indulgent if I murmur a word of appreciation to Dr Emma Vaux at the Roehampton Hospital, who started my heart beating correctly again with mere seconds to spare, and thus enabled me to see the results of all this devoted activity.

cooking mangos

Contents

Introduction

Fruits include some of the most beautiful foods there are. Anyone familiar with Italian Renaissance paintings and with Dutch still lives of the 17th century will know how strongly they have attracted painters, and with what exquisite results. The same applies to more recent times: the beauty and monumental character of a bowl of apples painted by Cézanne are, though in quite a different way, still breathtaking.

So, when Charlotte Knox decided that, after two years' painting seafood she would spend two painting fruits, and that these would be fruits from all round the world and would include nuts, I was very ready to be her partner a second time and provide the prose.

There was just one potential problem. Fruits have inspired poets as well as painters, and might seem to demand prose of a more romantic character than mine. However, thought I, just as the glowing fruits in Dutch still lives were often set, and suitably so, on a dark or otherwise undistracting background, so Charlotte's paintings could be effectively matched by sober prose of the sort I write.

Like Jane Grigson (who said that, among all her books, the one she had most enjoyed composing was that on fruit), I have found the subject a rich source of pleasure. Besides bread and seafood, fruits are what I eat most; and a valid reason for eating even more than usual has been welcome. Also, besides eating them, I had been studying their history and taxonomy for the purposes of a quite different and separate book for over ten years.

These studies and my fruit-shopping expeditions at home and abroad have made me well aware of the astonishing changes which have taken place in the last two decades in the availability of what were formerly – from the point of view of, say, a New Yorker or a Londoner – exotic fruits. Many fruits to which I thought I had said goodbye when leaving South-East Asia in the 1970s now confront me in our British supermarkets. Even the durian, which, because of its great weight and offensive smell, had always seemed to be the South-East Asian fruit least likely to be imported, has recently arrived in great piles in London's Chinatown. It quickly enlarged its range to embrace the more polyglot of London suburbs, and has penetrated north to Leeds (1989) and to Scotland (1990).

So, to describe the fruits of the world is no longer a task which involves leaving a great deal to the imagination of most readers. To be sure, there are fruits which stay put in the regions where they grow. But the general picture is one of fruits in unprecedented motion, from one hemisphere to another, from one established cultural setting to other new ones.

It is also true that the art of growing fruits and of developing new varieties of particular fruits has been progressing faster than ever before. Great advances were made in Europe in the 18th and 19th centuries, and, a little later, in North America. Yet what has been happening in the last few decades, when the science of genetic engineering in food plants has really blossomed, is something else again.

Not every new variety that is acclaimed is equally welcome. Some are developed to meet the convenience of the markets rather than please the palates of consumers; the quest for the square tomato is a joke, but behind it lies the reality of tomatoes that travel better, have a longer shelf-life, behave themselves beautifully as a "commodity", but do not have a good flavor, indeed may not have any flavor at all. However, as I see it, the general trend is towards producing what really are finer fruits for eating; and it is accompanied in many countries by a healthy interest in old and flavorful varieties.

Having mentioned tomatoes gives me my cue to explain what I mean by a fruit. Botanically, the tomato is a fruit. But in ordinary parlance it is not; it is a vegetable. The way most people speak of fruits and vegetables, which is determined by how they are used rather than by botany, is the way I have followed. Hence sweet melons and watermelons are in this book, but the oriental melons used for pickling or as vegetables are not. Nor are avocados, nor plantains. This seems to me the best course to take in a book intended for the general reader. A strictly botanical approach would produce too disconcerting an assemblage, including for example the peppercorns which are the fruits of *Piper nigra*.

I have followed a similar course in dealing with nuts. What people call nuts are what I treat as nuts, although some, such as the peanut are not true nuts.

Although so many people are making the acquaintance of so-called new fruits, they may feel a lack of information about them. Indeed, they may also lack knowledge of fruits that have long been familiar. My aim in writing about the fruits and nuts so beautifully painted by Charlotte has been to supply some such information; neither too much, I hope, nor too little.

Another intention of mine has been to treat the subject in a global way, in accordance with my belief that what has been happening in the last decades of the 20th century makes this both more appropriate and less difficult than it used to be. The point is not one that is peculiar to fruits. Their movements, to which I have already referred, are not unique, since vegetables, cereals, herbs and fungi also leap from continent to continent in harvested form or as introduced plants.

But it is not just a matter of movements and availability. There are also the relationships and connections which have only begun to be fully apparent since our world began to "shrink". Knowing how fruits from different parts of the world are related is not just a source of intellectual satisfaction but can also be of practical use in the kitchen. And interesting new ideas are apt to emerge when a foodstuff which used to belong exclusively to one corner of the world is now translated into other corners where traditions of preparing and cooking are quite different.

A Note about Names

I have also taken pains to supply on a generous scale the names of the fruits and nuts in other languages, besides giving their latinized botanical names. The latter consist normally of two words, such as *Citrus sinensis* (the orange). Of these, the first word indicates the genus while the second identifies the species within the genus.

Of course, there are higher categories too, again with latinized names. In this book it has not seemed necessary to introduce Classes or Orders, but the families are stated in every instance. Nuts are grouped in more familiar categories according to the way they are most often used. In almost all cases, however, family names appear at the top of the left-hand column of a page of text facing a painting. The attentive reader will notice that a few families account for a large number of the fruits we eat: notably the citrus family (Rutaceae) and the rose family (Rosaceae). A glance at the list of contents (beginning on page 6) shows this most clearly.

These botanical names for species change from time to time, sometimes at a speed which must be disconcerting even for botanists. Some of those given here may already have the skids under them, scheduled for replacement before long by less familiar names. Fortunately, obsolete names have a sort of afterlife, continuing to enjoy some currency for a decade or more after they have been replaced. So there should be no doubt about which fruit I mean.

Doubts there would be in plenty, for certain fruits, if only the common names which are in everyday use were given; even cursory study of how names like "custard apple" have been applied in different parts of the world is enough to demonstrate that.

These common names, whether in English or another language, are themselves of considerable interest – they may tell us much, for example, about how exotic fruits were first perceived by Old World settlers in the New World – and are often of great charm.

A Note about the Recipes

These have their own introduction, beginning on page 144. However, on the assumption that some readers will skip over that, let me mention three points here.

First, the choice of recipes is a personal one, with a certain emphasis on traditional and simple dishes; I do not stray into the territory of haute cuisine whose heights are more accessible to professional chefs.

Secondly, they are recipes in which fruits or nuts are the principal ingredient; they do not include the manifold ways of using fruit in other branches of cooking, notably in savory dishes.

Thirdly, a recipe is intended to serve four people unless otherwise indicated.

A Note about Sources

The Bibliography starting on page 189 indicates the other published material that I have consulted. I should, however, pay a special tribute to certain books, both recent and older. Dr Julia Morton's vast work on *Fruits of Warm Climates* became at once, on its publication in 1987, the standard reference; and it seems likely to remain so. Previously, Wilson Popenoe's *Manual of Tropical and Sub-tropical Fruits* had been both my introduction to the subject and my chief reference for many years; a learned and friendly book which it is always a pleasure to read. The citrus fruits were not covered by Popenoe, but for them we have that astonishing and inspirational study, *Hesperides*, by Tolkowsky (1937). Coming back to more recent years, Elizabeth Schneider's *Uncommon Fruits and Vegetables* (1986) is a work of considerable substance, pleasantly written, soundly based, a good and reliable companion.

Alan Davidson

Apple

family ROSACEAE

Other Names for *APPLE*

French: *pomme*
German: *Apfel*
Italian: *mela*
Spanish: *manzana*
Basque: *sagar*
Catalan: *poma*
Portuguese: *maçã*
Dutch: *appel*
Danish: *aeble*
Norwegian: *apal*
Swedish: *apel*
Finnish: *omena*
Russian: *yabloko*
Czech: *jablko*
Slovak: *jáblon plǎňǎ*
Hungarian: *alma*
Romanian: *mǎr*
Serbo-Croat: *jabuka*
Bulgarian: *yabulka*
Greek: *melon*
Turkish: *elma*
Hebrew: *tapuaḥ*
Arabic: *tuffāḥ*
Persian: *seb*
Afghanistan: *saib*
Indian languages: *sev* (Hindi), *tsoonth*
(Kashmir)
Chinese: *ping guo*
Japanese: *ringo*
Indonesian: *apel*

The **APPLE**, *Malus pumila*, one of the first fruits to have been cultivated, is now the most important fruit in Europe, North America and other temperate regions in both northern and southern hemispheres. There are about 7–8,000 named varieties, although only a few of these are of commercial or historical importance. Some interesting ones are listed on pages 183–6.

The familiar large, sweet apple is essentially a cultivated product, much changed from the tiny, sour crab apples which were its wild ancestors. An apple tree should, in order to propagate itself most effectively, produce hundreds of tiny fruits instead of fewer, wastefully large ones. The apple's wild relatives in the rose family, for example the rowan and hawthorn, all do this. The development of the cultivated apple must have consisted in the selection of trees with unusually large fruits and persuading them to evolve against their natural bent to give ever larger apples. The very largest apples available today – coarse Gravenstein cooking apples from Italy and other relatively warm regions – weigh well over 1 pound each.

The main ancestors of the modern apple were *M sylvestris* (the common crab apple) and *M pumila* var *mitis*, a native of the Caucasus where it still grows wild. There is evidence that such apples were being eaten 8,000 years ago or more, and it is thought that some success had already been achieved by 2000 BC in coaxing the unpromising trees to yield larger and fleshier fruits. The first written mention of apples is usually said to be by Homer, in his *Odyssey*. But the word he used, melon, was applied by the Greeks to almost any kind of round fruit which grew on a tree. Thus the legendary apples of Greek myth – given by Paris to Aphrodite, or growing in the Hesperides – may have been other kinds of fruit, or no particular kind at all. Similarly, the apples with which the Shulamite in the Song of Solomon asked to be comforted were probably quinces. (It is true that the quince, being sour, is not a comforting fruit to eat, but its smell was deemed agreeable.) Nor is the Bible specific about the nature of the Tree of the Knowledge of Good and Evil. The notion that this was an apple tree came much later.

During classical times it was discovered how to produce apples of a consistent variety: by taking cuttings (scions) of a good tree and grafting them on to a suitable rootstock, where they grow into branches producing the desired fruits. The process is described in Cato the Elder's De Agricultura (2nd century BC). This was a fundamental requirement for systematic apple-growing, since, as Behr (1989) has put it:

> Unless an apple blossom is intentionally sealed off and then fertilized with selected pollen – as is done today with the tip of a camel's-hair brush – the second parent can only be guessed at. In the open, each seed may have been fertilized by a different parent, and in any case each produces a tree with a unique combination of characteristics. Without the techniques of grafting (or of rooting a branch), each tree in the world would constitute its own variety, distinct from every other.

It is possible that two or three varieties of apple known to the Romans have survived until present times. One is the Lady apple, known in French as "Pomme d'Api" and said by Pliny to have been bred by a man called Appius. It is a small, hard, well-flavored winter apple, yellow with a red cheek. Another, known in France as the "Court pendu plat", is a small apple with a delicate flavor.

After the fall of the Roman Empire the Arabs, who belonged to hot regions unsuitable for apples, were not in a position to do anything about apple growing. However, apples continued to be grown in Europe, and certain distinct types were recognized. In medieval England the two leading kinds were the Costard, a large variety, and the Pearmain.

Grafting was reintroduced and became systematic by the 16th century. Good new varieties of apples were developed, including the first Pippins and the

Key to the Painting

top left: Jester;
top right: Ashmeads Kernel;
center: two Pitmaston Pine apples, with Decio above and a crab apple, Red Siberian, below;
bottom left: James Grieve;
bottom right: Laxton's Superb

Tips for the Cook

Do not take too seriously the distinction between eating and cooking apples. The choice of apples for cooking depends on the dish being prepared. For some, apples which disintegrate (for example, Bramleys) are best; while for others it is suitable to use apples which hold their shape.

Key to the Painting

center: Reverend W Wilks;
top left: Charles Ross;
top right: Golden Noble;
bottom left: Howgate Wonder;
bottom right: Lord Derby

Reinettes. ("Reinette", from the Latin "renatus" meaning reborn, originally meant an apple propagated by grafting, while a Pippin was grown from a pip; but these meanings were soon forgotten.)

Emigrants to America at first took apple pips rather than scions, which would have died on the voyage, in order to establish the domestic apple in the New World. This procedure gave rise to entirely new varieties, which were further diversified by interbreeding with native American crab apples. As a result American apples became and remain a distinct group. For example, the famous Newtown Pippin is quite different from and juicier than any European Pippin.

The spread of apple cultivation in America was encouraged by a notable eccentric, Johnny Appleseed, born John Chapman in Leominster, Massachusetts, in 1775. He collected large numbers of apple seeds from cider mills and journeyed up and down the country planting them wherever he went.

Apples could also be grown successfully in some parts of the southern hemisphere, and new varieties were developed there too. For example Bismarck, a brilliant crimson cooking apple, was bred in Tasmania. South Africa, Australia, New Zealand, and Chile are now all major exporters of apples to the northern hemisphere, taking advantage of the reversed seasons to sell when local apples are scarce. Japan also produces apples, and has contributed the variety Mutsu to the international repertoire.

In Britain apples are divided clearly into eating and cooking varieties, a distinction which is much less rigid in other countries. (An English cooking apple disintegrates to a purée when cooked. This effect is brought about by a high content of malic acid.) As regards eating apples, the British are catholic in their taste. It may still be possible to discern traces of the effects produced by the Victorian and Edwardian custom of taking dessert with port; this prompted enthusiasm for apples with a nutty flavor which would complement the port. It was also partly responsible for a small tide of gastronomic prose about apples which washed over England in the late 19th and early 20th centuries, and which embodied language which resembled writing about fine wines. But none of this had much effect on the vast majority of British people. They now accept the imported Golden and Red Delicious, but their favorite is still the Cox; and they are not deterred by the curious appearance of the Russets, which has caused these to be neglected in other countries.

In the USA apples are judged more by their appearance, and red varieties are preferred. While some deep red apples are good, there are also insipid kinds such as Rome Beauty which sell on their looks alone. There are also popular varieties of other colors: Golden Delicious is of American origin. Most kinds sold are dual-purpose, for eating or cooking.

From early times apples were preserved by drying. The usual method in medieval Europe was to peel and core the apples and dry them whole, threaded on strings. One unusual method was the preparation of Norfolk Biffins. These were Pippins of an already hard and dry variety. They were dried, whole and unpeeled, in warm bread ovens so that they shriveled into a form like roundish, red prunes. The partial cooking helped to preserve them. They were close packed in layers as they dried.

Apple butter, which is apple sauce concentrated by boiling it down with cider, was a traditional European product associated especially with the Dutch. It was they who introduced it to America, now its principal stronghold.

All the old preservation methods were made less necessary at the beginning of the 20th century by the introduction of chilled storage. The keeping life of apples may be extended several times over by storing them just above freezing point. More recently, inert nitrogen storage has become widespread. Nitrogen, which makes up three quarters of the atmosphere, is harmless to fruit. It is only the oxygen in the air which contributes to spoilage; so, if this is removed, keeping time is much prolonged.

Many dishes made with apples are of medieval origin. Culinary texts of the 14th century give recipes for apple sauce, fritters, rissoles and drinks.

Before the introduction of the domestic oven, apples were roasted whole in front of an open fire. Practical difficulties in cooking them evenly led to the development of more complicated apple roasters. These were metal racks incorporating curved tinplate reflectors to heat the far side of the apples.

Apple Pie, perhaps the most famous apple dish, appears with at least a dozen other recipes for this versatile fruit in the recipe section at the back of the book.

Pear

family ROSACEAE

Other Names for *PEAR*

French: *poire*
German: *Birne*
Italian: *pera*
Spanish: *pera*
Portuguese: *pêra*
Dutch: *peer*
Danish / Norwegian: *pære*
Swedish: *päron*
Finnish: *päärynä*
Russian: *grusha*
Polish: *gruszka*
Czech / Slovak: *hruška*
Hungarian: *vadkörte*
Serbo-Croat: *kruška*
Romanian: *pară*
Bulgarian: *krousha*
Greek: *achládi*
Turkish: *armut*
Hebrew: *agas*
Arabic: *kummathrā*
Persian: *amrūd*
Chinese: *li*
Japanese: *yōnashi*
Indonesian: *buah pér*

Tips for the Cook

Pears, generally, can be cooked like apples. Unripe dessert pears can be cooked just as well as cooking pears; they are best poached in syrup.

Pears, like apricots, go well with rice.

The flavor of cooked pears is often improved by the addition of, for example, red wine, almonds or vanilla. Pears also associate happily with chocolate.

Recipes

Key to the Painting

top row (with stalks), left to right: Joséphine de Malines and Louise Bonne de Jersey, with the lower part of Red Anjou above center;
2nd row: Red Williams and Beurre Hardy;
3rd row: Beurre Superfin and Glou Morceau;
4th row: Japanese pear (nashi), with Packman's Triumph;
5th row: Merton Pride;
bottom row: Doyenne de Comice and Williams Bon Chrétien

Writing about the **PEAR**, Edward Bunyard remarked with his usual felicity: "As it is, in my view, the duty of an apple to be crisp and crunchable, a pear should have such a texture as leads to silent consumption."

Whether the epicures of ancient and classical times ate their pears noiselessly, we do not know. But it is certainly true that the pear was then considered a better fruit than the apple. Thus the Chinese, during the Sung dynasty (700 years ago) had only one kind of apple, but many sorts of pear. The ancient Greeks also had a high opinion of the pear, "the gift of the gods," as Homer put it; and in the 2nd century AD Pliny the Elder described 41 varieties known to the Romans.

The pear, *Pyrus communis* and other *Pyrus* species, originated in the general region of the Caucasus (as did its cousin the apple), and both fruits were spread by the Aryan tribes from that area as they migrated into Europe and northern India.

The original wild pear has been developed into what are now nearly 1,000 varieties, after a certain amount of interbreeding with other native wild pears of Europe and Asia.

In the 17th century, pear growing in France was at its height and many new varieties were developed. Louis XIV was particularly interested in fruit and vegetables and the pear was one of his favorite fruits.

The most notable pear growers of the 18th century were, however, both Belgian. Nicolas Hardenpont of Mons (Bergen) bred the first of the juicy, soft pears called Beurre (butter). These represented a real advance, so different were they from former pears, and so much more delectable. The work of Hardenpont was carried forward by Dr van Mons.

Meanwhile the pear had been introduced into North America in 1629. Because the first American pears were raised from seed which, like that of the apple, does not breed true to variety, American pears became even more diverse than their European ancestors and many good, purely American strains arose.

The following are some notable varieties.

Anjou (full name **Beurre d'Anjou**) is the principal winter pear of North America. It is a broad and lopsided pear, yellowish green marked with russet. It originated in France or Belgium in the 19th century, and now exists in several forms, including the handsome Red Anjou.

Bartlett is the name used in the USA and Australia for the English Williams. Named after the American grower Enoch Bartlett, it was first raised in 1770 in Berkshire, England, by a schoolmaster called John Stair and was renamed Williams when it arrived in London. It was later taken to America by Enoch Bartlett and renamed again. The season for these pears begins early, in late summer. The original variety, Williams Bon Chrétien, is dull green with a red blush; there are now also clear green and red kinds (for example, Red Williams). The flavor is generally musky.

Beurre varieties (they should really be called "Beurré", but the correct spelling has largely evaporated) are particularly soft and juicy, with little of the gritty texture which some others exhibit. They include two good winter eating varieties: Beurre d'Anjou (see under Anjou, above); and Beurre Bosc (see Bosc, below).

Bosc (full name **Beurre Bosc**), is a winter pear, aromatic in flavor, juicy, described as "buttery but not melting". This variety is unmistakable by reason of its long, tapering neck. The color is dark yellow overlaid with russet.

Clapp Favorite, an early-ripening dessert pear of fair quality, but rather granular, is broad and dull greenish yellow with some russeting.

Comice is short for **Doyenné du Comice**, which means top of the show. Many would agree with this boast. It is a broad, blunt pear, greenish yellow marked with russet or a red blush. The texture is unequaled: very juicy, and not even faintly gritty. The flavor is sweet and aromatic.

Conference, a widely sold English winter variety, is easily recognized by its long, thin shape and russet skin; like a parsnip in khaki battledress, someone said

Classification of Asian Pears

It seems to be accepted at present that there are two species, *Pyrus pyriformis* and *P ussurensis*. Fruits of the former are mostly apple-shaped (not pear-shaped, as the specific name suggests); while those of the latter are not globose. What is perhaps more to the point is that there are very many varieties and cultivars and hybrids, and that no one description comes any-where near fitting the lot. Shape, size, color all vary greatly. The variety most popular in Japan and the USA in the 1980s was Twentieth Century (or Nijisseiki), a round fruit which is quite sweet and very juicy.

Tips for the Cook

(For ordinary pears, see the preceding page.)

Asian pears need to be cooked for a long time.

If they are to be cut up raw for use in fruit salads, remember that they are so crisp that they can be sliced very thinly; and that the flavor of most of them is so faint that it will be quite overpowered by other fruits with a strong flavor.

Key to the Painting

left: Black Worcester;
right: Pitmaston Duchess with leaves;
bottom: Winter Nelis with leaves

unkindly – but flavor and texture can be good.

Glou Morceau, a pear which dates back to the 18th century, is also called Beurre d'Hardenpont, after the Belgian priest, the Abbé Nicolas Hardenpont of Mons, who was the first true breeder of pears. He gave the world half a dozen pears of the new "melting" kind, four of which, including Glou Morceau, enjoyed high esteem and popularity well into the present century.

Jargonelle, a fine old French pear dating from about 1600, is a dessert or cooking fruit with a distinctive aroma (roughly imitated in the traditional British sweets called pear drops: the main component of the fragrance is amyl acetate).

Joséphine de Malines, a 19th-century pear of Belgian origin, is still grown commercially in the southern hemisphere. Malines is a town of Flanders which, according to one writer, enjoyed "a repose bordering on stagnation" as well as a sheltered location, clear skies and favorable rains – everything a pear could wish for. The pear was named by Major Espéren, an unsystematic but indefatigable grower, in commemoration of his wife; and it is the only important pear to have pink flesh. The scent is said to resemble that of the hyacinth.

Louise Bonne de Jersey is a pear to be picked towards the end of September, but not until it has what Brooke calls "a painted, varnished look; the red must be shining red, and the greener portion must be turning yellow."

Merton Pride, an English pear whose history extends back only to the 1950s, has a yellowish skin which covers very juicy, soft flesh, with a good strong pear flavor.

Olivier de Serres, an old French variety often seen in southern Europe, is a good dessert pear which ripens very late. Dull greenish brown in color, it is so squat and short-necked that it might be mistaken for a green russet apple.

Packham's Triumph has achieved popularity during the 20th century. It seems to be better when grown in the southern hemisphere.

Passe crasanne (Passacrassana, if it comes from Italy), a late winter pear suitable mainly for cooking, is common in southern Europe. It is big, broad, dull greenish brown, and well flavored, but rather coarse in texture.

Seckel is a small American pear with a good spicy flavor, but a rather granular texture. It is quite distinct from any European variety, and takes its name from the man who acquired the land in Delaware where the original tree was discovered. A Seckel pear is brownish yellow, and russeted, often with a red blush.

Wardens, often referred to by Shakespeare and Parkinson, were cooking pears – it seems that, in those times, pears were mainly for cooking. For centuries Warden was the pear most commonly grown. It originated at the Cistercian Monastery of Wardon in Bedfordshire, England.

Williams, called Bartlett in the USA and Australia.

Winter Nelis, a long-keeping pear in season from late autumn to late spring, has an excellent spicy flavor and a fair texture but is less popular than it once was, partly because of its small size and rough skin, and partly because it tends to go bad if stored.

Asian pears (see note in left-hand column) are of different species. The development of these pears is proceeding rapidly, the number of varieties appearing in shops in Europe and North America is increasing, and my experience of them, gained in Asia in the 1970s, is obsolescent. What can be said with confidence is that they all have crisp flesh, disconcerting to anyone expecting something which melts in the mouth, but (in the better varieties) with an appeal of its own.

Reverting to ordinary pears, these can generally be picked before they are fully ripe, though not too long before. They will ripen in a fairly cool place. Without this useful characteristic it would be impossible to market them, for a ripe pear is not only soft and easily damaged but also passes through its period of perfect ripeness in a short space of time, and then quickly begins to spoil. There is an old saying that one must sit up at night to eat a pear – meaning that it is essential, but tricky, to eat a pear at precisely its ripest moment. (Ripening can be slightly slowed by refrigeration, but this suppresses flavor. Return the fruits to room temperature before eating them.)

Pears are commercially canned on a large scale. Oddly, the processors take care to avoid the development of a pink color when the pears are heated in the can, whereas domestic cooks and professional chefs are pleased to achieve this effect.

Italians eat fresh pears with parmesan or pecorino cheese, a good marriage of flavors.

Plum, Bullace, Damson, Greengage, Mirabelle, Cherry Plum, Sloe

The **PLUM**, the fruit of *Prunus domestica* and other *Prunus* species, has a particularly close relationship with cherries, the distinction between them being mainly one of size. In the Middle Ages, "plum" meant virtually any dried fruit, and this usage underlies names such as plum pudding and plum cake. Deciding what is a plum and what is not is still no easy matter: bullaces, damsons and greengages are all plums in a general sense, although usually called by their own names. The fruits of *P cerasifera* may be called cherry plums or myrobalans.

The earliest cultivation of plums took place in China. The fruit was noticed by Roman authors in the 1st century AD. Plums were certainly cultivated in the gardens of medieval monasteries in England. In about 1369 Chaucer described a garden with "ploumes" and "bulaces".

Plums can be picked slightly before they are ripe and will reach perfect ripeness in a warm room. Refrigeration slows the process but does not stop it.

The dried plums known as prunes are the subject of an Appendix, page 182.

The **BULLACE**, *P instititia*, occurs wild in Europe and bears small round fruits, often but not always black.

The **DAMSON**, a small plum believed to have derived from the bullace (and therefore called *P instititia* var *syriaca* by some authorities), was even in Roman times considered to be a product of the Near East.

The astringency of the fruit generally prescribes cooking with plentiful sugar. Dorothy Hartley's description of damson cheese, "crimson in a pool of port wine on a gold-washed dish", is a vivid celebration of the sumptuous fare once relished at British tables.

GREENGAGE is the English name for a group of especially good plums, usually green, which derive from the bullace. The original type is thought to have come from Armenia. The fruit reached France during the reign of François I (1494–1547) and is still known there as "Reine Claude" after his wife. The English name is that of Sir Thomas Gage, who received stocks from France early in the 18th century. One of the oldest varieties is the Transparent Gage, whose qualities were vividly evoked by Bunyard:

> If there is a better gage than this, I know it not, and certainly there is none more beautiful. Its French name, Reine Claude Diaphane, exactly describes its clear, transparent look; a slight flush of red and then one looks into the depths of transparent amber as one looks into an opal, uncertain how far the eye can penetrate.

Greengages, being the finest of dessert plums, should be enjoyed in their natural state. They also make the most luxurious of plum jams.

The **MIRABELLE** plums (a French speciality, but also grown elsewhere) are closely allied to the damsons and bullaces. They are usually classified as a variety of *P instititia*, although some regard them as hybrids (*P cerasifera* × *P domestica*) The kind known as Mirabelle de Nancy is believed to have come from the East to France in the 15th century and is still rated highly. The Mirabelle de Metz was first recorded in 1675.

The **CHERRY PLUM**, or myrobalan, occurs in various forms and is associated particularly with the region of the Caucasus.

The **SLOE**, or blackthorn, *P spinosa*, a common wild hedgerow bush throughout Europe and western Asia, bears small, black fruits of mouth-puckering astringency. They make a fine jam.

Cherry

family ROSACEAE

Other Names for _CHERRY_
(names with asterisks are for the sour cherry)

French: _cerise_
German: _Kirsche_
Italian: _ciliegia_
Spanish: _cereza_
Portuguese: _cereja_
Dutch: _kers_
Danish: _kirsebaer_
Swedish: _körsbör_
Norwegian: _kirsebaer_
Finnish: _kirsikka; hapankirsikka*_
Russian: _chereshnya; vishnya*_
Polish: _czereśnia; wiśnia*_
Hungarian: _cseresznyepiros_
Romanian: _cireaşă; vişină*_
Bulgarian: _cheresha; vishna*_
Serbo-Croat: _trešnja; višnja*_
Greek: _kerasiá_
Turkish: _kiraz; vişne*_
Hebrew: _dudevan_
Arabic: _kurayz_
Persian: _gīlās_
Chinese: _ying tao_
Japanese: _sakurambo;_
suminomizakura*
Indonesian: _buah céri_

Other Cherries

The mahaleb or St Lucy's cherry (so named because it was planted at a convent dedicated to that saint), _P mahaleb_, is native to Asia Minor but now grows throughout Europe. Its kernels provide a Turkish sweetmeat generally known as "crème de noyau".

And see also cornelian cherry, page 54, and ground cherry, page 64.

Tip for the Cook

If you pit cherries, do so over a bowl which will catch the juice.

Recipes

Key to the Painting

top row: the two wild ancestors, the gean or sweet cherry (_Prunus avium_), the sour cherry (_P cerasus_), and then Waterloo and Gaucher;
2nd row: Early Burlat, (Napoleon in Britain) Royal Ann, Roundel, and Bing with blossom;
3rd row: Stella with blossom, Van, Merton Glory with blossom, and Bradbourne Black;
4th row: Noir de Guben, May Duke with blossom, Black Tartarian, and Sunburst;
5th row: Rainier, Montmorency with blossom, Morello with blossom, and Lambert

The **CHERRY** is a fruit for painters and poets as well as for eating. Dutch still-life painters of the 17th century captured its beauty to perfection. Of the poets who have incorporated the street cry "Cherry-ripe" in amorous poems, Herrick is the best known, although he was not the first.

True cherries belong to the genus _Prunus_, which also includes plums, peaches, apricots, and almonds, all in the rose family. Cultivated cherries are descended from two wild species, native to western Asia: _Prunus avium_, ancestor of the sweet varieties; and _P cerasus_, from which sour cherries come.

The wild sweet-cherry tree is a handsome one which grows higher than its cultivated descendants are trained to do. The fruits are small, usually dark red, and either sweet or bitter, but never sour. The wild sour cherry, _P cerasus_, is a smaller but hardier tree which has spread further north, for example in Scandinavia, than sweet cherries can. Again, the fruit is small and usually dark red.

Both sweet and sour cherries were cultivated in the Mediterranean area in times BC. The classical Greek name was "kerasos", from which "cherry" is derived. By the 1st century AD, Pliny the Elder was able to record that eight varieties of cherry were under cultivation in Italy, and that the fruit was grown as far away as Britain.

However, after the fall of the Roman Empire cultivation declined; indeed the fruit had to be reintroduced into England in the early 17th century, around the time when colonists were taking it to New England. By 1640 two dozen named varieties were being grown in England, mainly no doubt in Kent, which has always been the principal cherry county; and the number has increased ever since. Parallel developments have taken place in France and Italy, the two principal European producers, and in the USA, especially California and Washington. The number of cultivated cherry varieties, worldwide, is now estimated to be about 900 for the sweet and 300 for the sour cherry.

Sweet cherries have often been classed into two main groups: "bigarreau" with firm, dry flesh; and "guigne" (an old English name, gean, is a version of this) with soft, juicy flesh. However, hybridization has blurred this distinction. Sweet cherries of the firmer sort include the justly popular Royal Ann (light red and yellow, but called White Napoleon in Britain), and the Black Schmidt. Softer varieties include Black Tartarian and Bing, which is red.

Sour cherries (which might better be called acid, but it's too late now to put this right) are classified into two groups: "amarelle" or relatively light-colored, with clear juice; and "griotte", dark or black, with colored juice. Montmorency is a famous variety of amarelle; and Morello the best known griotte.

Sweet-and-sour cherries, a third category, often go under the name Duke. This kind of cherry came to England from Médoc, which name was adapted to May Duke and then abbreviated.

Sweet cherries are usually eaten raw as dessert fruit. Sour cherries have a good flavor when cooked and adequately sweetened, and are preferred for making cherry pies and other dishes. Meat dishes with sour cherries exist in many cuisines from England to Persia and the Caucasus. The cherry soup which is popular in parts of northern Europe is made with sour cherries.

The black Morello cherry is essential for black cherry jam, Black Forest gâteau, Kirschstrudel (cherry strudel), and the white spirit Kirsch.

The small, very sour Marasca or Maraschino cherry was originally grown near Zara, the capital of Dalmatia (now in Yugoslavia), where it was made into maraschino liqueur, now also made in Italy. The special flavor of this drink is due to the pits being crushed to release the almond taste of the kernels, in contrast to Kirsch, where the pits are left whole. Cherry brandy is made by infusing cherries in spirit.

Maraschino cherries in syrup are prepared by pitting and bleaching the cherries, then adding syrup, bitter almond oil, and red or green coloring.

Quince, Medlar, Loquat

family ROSACEAE

Other Names for *QUINCE*

French: *coing*
Basque: *irasagar*
German: *Quitte*
Italian: *cotogna*
Spanish: *membrillo*
Portuguese: *marmelo*
Dutch: *kwee*
Danish: *kvæde*
Swedish: *kvitten*
Norwegian: *kvede*
Finnish: *kvitteni*
Russian: *ayva*
Polish: *pigwa*
Serbo-Croat: *dunja*
Romanian: *gutuie*
Bulgarian: *dyulya*
Greek: *kydoni*
Turkish: *ayva*
Hebrew: *ḥabush*
Arabic / Persian: *safarjal*
Chinese: *wen po*
Japanese: *marumero*

Other Names for *MEDLAR*

French: *nèfle*
German: *Mispel*
Italian: *nespola*
Portuguese: *nêspera*
Danish / Norwegian / Swedish: *mispel*
Finnish: *mispeli*
Russian: *mushmula germanskaya*
Polish: *niesplik*
Serbo-Croat: *mušmula, mešpola*
Romanian: *mosmon*
Bulgarian: *moushmoula*
Turkish: *muşmula*
Hebrew: *sheseq germani*
Persian: *ālū'i dashti*
Japanese: *seiyōkarin*
(the medlar also has some less
respectable names; for example, the
Dutch "apenaars", meaning monkey's
arse)

Other Names for *LOQUAT*

French: *nèfle du Japon*
German: *japanische Mispel*
Italian: *nespolo del Giappone*
Spanish: *nispero*
Portuguese: *ameixa do Japão*
Chinese: *pi pa*
Japanese: *biwa*

Tip for the Cook

The Spanish quince paste called "carne de
membrillo" (quince meat), popular also in
Latin America, is a fine partner for cheese.

Recipes

Appelmoes met Kweepeer (Apple Sauce
with Quince): page 157
Ayva Tatlisi (Turkish Quince Dessert):
page 156
Medlar Jelly: page 180

Key to the Painting

top: loquats;
center: medlars;
bottom: quinces

Small, twisted **QUINCE** trees, *Cydonia oblonga*, still grow wild in the Caucasus, the region of origin which they share with the apple and pear. The common sort of quince resembles a large, lumpy, yellow pear. It has hard flesh and many pips and is too sour and astringent to eat raw; but it has a delicious fragrance and, when cooked with sugar or honey, develops a fine flavor and turns pink.

Quince cultivation spread to the Levant and South-East Europe before that of the apple. It was known in Palestine around 1000 BC, and the apples mentioned in the Song of Solomon were almost certainly quinces.

The Romans called the quince "melimelum", which comes from the Greek for honey apple; this is because the fruit was preserved in honey to make a kind of jam. Quince is called "marmelo" in Portugal, a corruption of "melimelum", and the Portuguese "marmelado" is a confection of quinces. Hence the French "marmelade" and English "marmalade", words which soon acquired wider meaning.

Meanwhile the Greek name "cydonia" became "cotogna" in Italian (hence the Italian quince preserve "cotognata"), then "coing" in French. Chaucer speaks of coines, which word later became quince.

In Persian cuisine, with its tradition of meat and sour fruits cooked together, there are many recipes for meat and quince stews, and for quinces with meat stuffing. The combination is also common in Morocco and in parts of eastern Europe such as Romania. However, Turkey is the country where the quince is most prized and used. Turks distinguish various kinds (for example, "ekmek ayvasi", a roundish, sweet quince of yellow hue, and "limon ayvasi", a larger, oblong, green variety of sour flavor) and make a wide range of dishes from them.

The most common use for quinces in Britain was in tarts and pies. If quinces were added to an apple pie, they gave it a pink color and interesting flavor. Quince marmalade and jelly remained popular until quite recently.

The quince was still a popular fruit when Europeans began to settle in America, and immigrants soon began to grow it. There was even a quince-canning industry in the USA in the early part of this century. North Americans now have little interest in the quince, but it remains popular in many Latin American countries.

Several oriental quinces, of the genus *Chaenomeles*, have been eaten in China and Japan. Their taste is very tart, but they have the true quince fragrance.

The **MEDLAR** is an unusual apple-like fruit, open at the bottom end, as shown in the painting. The small tree, *Mespilus germanica*, a native of Persia, was grown by the Greeks and Romans, as a useful addition to the then scanty range of late-ripening winter fruits; and it subsequently spread as far north as Scandinavia.

The fruit has a notable peculiarity. Even when fully ripe in autumn, it is hard, green, astringent, and inedible. It is picked at this stage and stored in moist bran or sawdust until it browns and softens, a process called bletting.

The strange taste of medlars ("wineskins of brown morbidity", as D H Lawrence described them) was popular in Victorian Britain. The fruits were brought to table in their bran or sawdust in a dish, and, for a dessert, the brown pulp was scraped out and mixed with sugar and cream. Medlar jelly was made, and so was medlar cheese, made with eggs and butter like the more familiar lemon curd.

The **LOQUAT**, the yellow fruit of *Eriobotrya japonica*, a medium-sized, evergreen tree from China, is pear-shaped and up to 3 inches long, with large, hard seeds. It looks slightly like the medlar, and the two are often confused; indeed the loquat is sometimes called Japanese medlar in English, and that is what its names in most other languages mean.

The ripe fruit has a pleasing, but sour, flavor slightly like that of a cherry, and can be eaten raw. Jams and jellies made from unripe loquats, including the seeds, have an almond-like flavor.

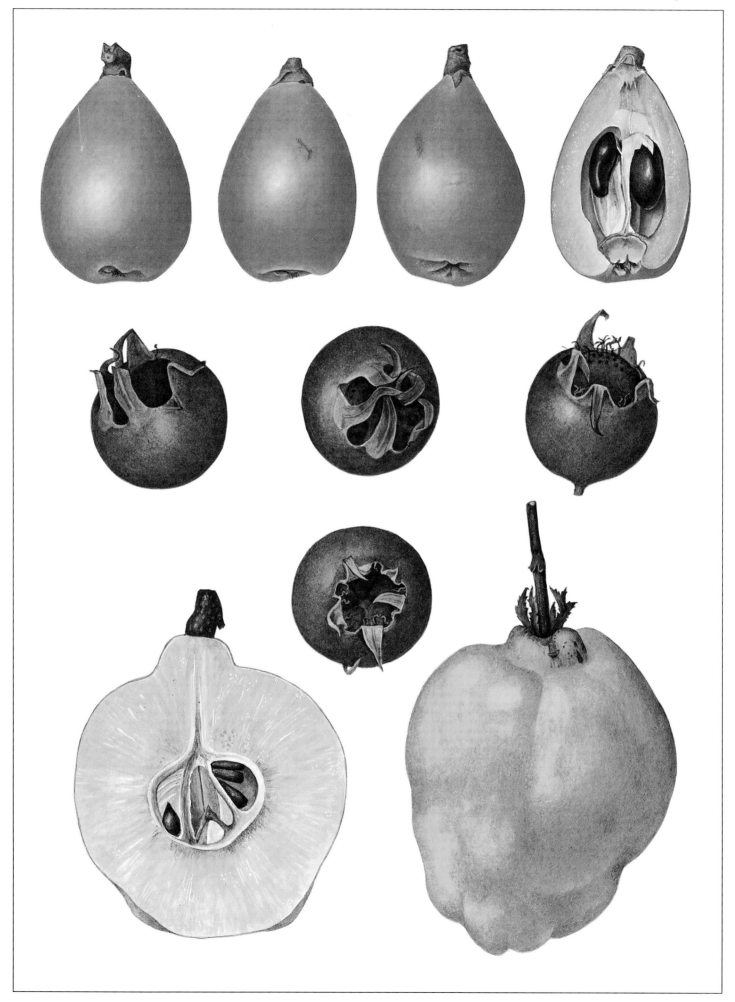

Rowan, Sorb, Rosehip

family ROSACEAE

Other Names for *ROWAN AND SORB*

French: *sorbe*
German: *Vogelbeere*
Italian: *sorbo*
Spanish: *fresno alpestre*
Danish: *røn*
Norwegian: *rogn*
Swedish: *rönn*
Finnish: *pihlajanmarja*
Russian: *ryabina*
Polish: *jarzębina*
Czech: *jérabka*
Slovak: *jerabina*
Hungarian: *veres berkenye*
Serbo-Croat: *oskoruša*
Romanian: *scorusuǎ*
Bulgarian: *ofika*
Greek: *sourbo*
Hebrew: *ḥuzrar*
Japanese: *nanakamado*

Other Names for *ROSEHIP*

French: *gratte-cul*
German: *Hagebutte*
Dutch: *rozebottel*
Swedish: *nypon*
Norwegian: *nype*
Finnish: *ruusunkiulukka*
Polish: *dzika róza*
Bulgarian: *shipka*
Serbo-Croat: *divlja ruža, šipak*
Chinese: *mei gui guo*

Here is a fruitful area of confusion. The rowan and sorb are two distinct sorts of tree in the genus *Sorbus* of the rose family; but the names have been used interchangeably. To compound the confusion, the sorb may also be called service tree in Europe, whereas in America that name is given to a distant relation, the service berry.

The **ROWAN** or mountain-ash, *S aucuparia*, owes its specific name to the practice of bird-catchers in Germany and elsewhere who would trap small birds in hair nooses baited with rowan berries. It grows wild in Europe and parts of Asia, especially in mountainous regions, and is matched by *S americana* in the east of North America.

The fruits are pretty, but have limited use, being much too sour and astringent to be eaten raw. They are best suited to making rowan jelly, which has a fine clear red color and whose pleasing tartness makes it a good accompaniment for venison and other game or fowl. The berries can also be made into a wine or other alcoholic drinks; there is a Scandinavian rowan liqueur of a curious orange color.

The rowan used to have a reputation as a potent antidote to witches; hence customs like making young lambs jump through a rowan-branch hoop, and the hanging of branches over doorways.

The **SORB**, *S torminalis*, tends to grow further south in Europe than the rowan; it is rare in Britain, for example. Its fruits are larger than those of the rowan and are called sorb apples because they are recognizably like small apples or pears, in shape and color. Like rowan berries, they are sour and astringent, although less so after exposure to the mellowing effect of frost. In Britain, where sorb apples used occasionally to be gathered for sale, it was usual to allow them to soften, like medlars, to achieve this mellowing; but even then the fruits were not exactly a treat – not as good as medlars – and would usually be used in tarts. Hulme, whose book *The Fruits of the Countryside* shines with enthusiasm for wild fruits, quotes Gerard ("If they yeeld any nourishment at all, the same is very little, grosse, and cold") and adds ruefully that this "certainly cannot be considered much of a testimonial".

In the south of Italy, the sun ripens the fruits more on the trees, but they still need to be macerated in wine vinegar and sugar before they can be enjoyed. Until recently they could be had, thus prepared, in shops in the Salento.

The fruits of the cultivated sorb, *S domestica*, are, as one would expect, larger, but otherwise the same applies.

ROSEHIPS or haws, the fruit of certain roses, *Rosa* species, have been eaten in Europe, Asia, and by the Native Americans. The vase-like receptacle of the fruit contains seeds covered with irritating hairs (used to good, or rather bad, effect by mischievous schoolchildren to make an itching powder), so it has to be emptied before it is edible. Or the whole fruit can be boiled to make a sweet, slightly perfumed syrup. Species whose fruits are used both in Europe and Asia include *R ponifera*, which has particularly large and tasty fruits; the excellent *R rugosa*; the brier-rose or dog rose, *R canina*, which is made into a tisane; and the eglantine, *R eglantaria* of western Asia. In California the fruits of a related species, *R californica*, are known as macuatas.

During the Second World War, Britain was short of the fruit providing vitamin C. Rosehips contain prodigious amounts of the vitamin, and schoolchildren were sent to gather them, so that they could be boiled down to make a syrup which was issued as a dietary supplement for small children. I was by then past the age to qualify for this, but I observed people in the Yorkshire Dales out gathering them as war work, which was clearly much more pleasant than most such work. Rosehip syrup is no longer given away by the British Government, but it is still sold.

Key to the Painting

above: wild rowanberries;
below: rosehips (*Rosa rugosa*)

Apricot

Tip for the Cook

Buy with care. Appearance can be decep-
tive. For commercial purposes, apricots
are often picked underripe, when they
have already turned orange but before the
full flavor has developed.

Key to the Painting

top: Bergerou plus pit;
2nd row: Bebeco;
3rd row: Super Gold plus pit from Chile

It was probably the Chinese who first cultivated **APRICOTS**, before 2000 BC. Berthold Laufer, in *Sino-Iranica*, gave a plausible account of how the fruit was spread westwards by silk dealers, which resulted in its reaching Persia by the 1st century BC, and Greece and Rome soon afterwards.

The Greeks wrongly supposed the fruit to have originated in Armenia and called it Armenian apple; hence its botanical name, *Prunus armeniaca*. The Romans, impressed by its early ripening, named it "praecocium" (precocious); and from this comes apricot.

The apricot, as a member of the rose family, is closely related to the plum, peach, cherry, and almond. Its original wild ancestor, long since vanished, grew mainly in China, but the fruit is now widely grown in the warmer temperate parts of the world. Partly because it fruits early, it needs highly specific climatic conditions: a fairly cold winter, and moderately high temperatures in the spring and early summer. It can just manage to ripen in the limited sunshine of a British summer. King Henry VIII's gardener brought the apricot to England from Italy in 1542; and in the 18th century real success in growing the fruit was achieved, notably by Lord Anson at Moor Park in Hertfordshire. The variety called Moor Park became famous in other European countries and is still grown.

The main regions of cultivation are: a band stretching from Turkey through Iran and the Himalayas to China and Japan; southern Europe and North Africa; South Africa; Australia; and California. There are many varieties differing in size, color, and flavor. And there are also other species.

The Chinese, and later the Japanese, have cultivated the species *P mume*, known in the West as Japanese flowering apricot, and often misdescribed as a type of plum. Small and sour, it is salted or pickled as a relish, and many Japanese believe that one should be eaten first thing in the morning to cleanse the system.

In China, from at least the 7th century AD onwards, apricots were preserved not only by drying, but also by salting and even smoking. The black smoked apricots of Hupei were famous.

A fresh apricot possesses a potent sensory appeal. It was Ruskin who described it as "shining in a sweet brightness of golden velvet"; and the consumption of freshly picked apricots out of hand is a well-known pleasure. However, most apricots are fated to be dried or otherwise processed.

Apricot jam is not only a good jam but also an important ingredient for the confectioner. It is used as a sweet adhesive in cakes such as Sachertorte; and in diluted form as the apricot glaze which finishes many confections.

In Middle Eastern cookery apricots are used in sweetmeats; for example, pitted and stuffed with almonds or almond paste, the two flavors of the related fruits complementing each other perfectly. Apricots are used in savory dishes too, to give a sweet and sour effect, especially in dishes with lamb, such as the agreeably named mishmishiya (which might be translated as "apricotery").

Apricot kernels are similar to almonds and, like almonds, contain small amounts of prussic acid which is destroyed by roasting them. They cost less than almonds and have many uses. The Italian "amaretti di Saronno", in character between macaroons and biscuits, owe their flavor and texture to apricot kernels.

Dried apricots are perhaps the most successful of all dried fruits in preserving their flavor. Those from Hunza are small but famous, since Hunza people enjoy remarkable health and longevity, both attributed in part to this fruit.

Most dried apricots are prepared by a modern process using sulphur dioxide, which bleaches the fruit, which then has to be recolored with dye. Apricots dried naturally in the sun have a much finer flavor and are, fortunately, available from a number of sources including Turkey and South Australia. Turkey also produces the so-called apricot leather, dried apricot flesh in the form of thin sheets, which the cook melts down for use; these have a highly concentrated flavor.

Peach, Nectarine

Key to the Painting

top left: Flavorcrest, a yellow peach from California;
top right: Dorothée, a white peach from France;
bottom left: Snow Queen, a white clingstone nectarine from California;
bottom right: Independence, a yellow freestone nectarine from USA

PEACH, *Prunus persica*: a fruit distinguished by its velvety skin, to which the Roman poet Virgil drew attention when he wrote of searching for "downy peaches and the glossy plum".

It seems to be widely recognized that the peach, of all fruits, most closely approaches the quality of human flesh, eventually reaching that state expressively described by William Morris as "pinch-ripe". No fruit is more laden with erotic metaphor. The pear is its nearest rival, but its cool, smooth skin cannot compare with the warm nap of a peach. The contrasting names of two varieties, Poire Cuisse-Madam and Pêche Têton de Venus, express the difference.

The peach is a fruit of temperate but warm climates. Wild peach trees still grow in China, their original home. Their fruits are small, sour, and hairy. The process of developing superior strains has been going on for at least 2,000 years. The fruit was the object of a sort of cult from very early times, and for Chinese poets, painters, and sculptors it served as a symbol of immortality.

Cultivation spread westwards through areas with a suitable climate, such as Kashmir, to Persia. It flourished there so well that it came to be regarded as a native Persian fruit; hence the specific name *persica*. It was from Persia that the peach came to Greece, and thence to Rome. It was independently introduced to Spain from the Near East; and it was Spaniards who took it to America in the 16th century.

The two categories of peach, clingstone and freestone, are distinguished by the difficulty or ease with which the flesh comes away from the pit. Each includes fruits with both yellow and white flesh; and varieties of each were known from early times. In England Gerard (1597) described four varieties (white, red, yellow, and d'avant) and added: "I have them all in my garden, with many other sorts."

However, the English climate is not ideal for peaches, and English orchardists have to grow them in sheltered positions. The peach is much more at home in the Mediterranean region and in parts of North America which have a similar climate; and it is American growers, especially in California, who have done most in the 20th century to shape the pattern of world production.

To be at its best, a peach has to ripen on the tree. Freshly picked ripe peaches are so good that it seems a shame to cook them, but they can be poached in wine or made into pies. The most famous peach dessert is Peach Melba, created in the late 19th century to honor Dame Nellie Melba. It is less well known that when Madame Récamier, the famous beauty of the early 19th century, was ill, refusing all food and at death's door, she was tempted to eat and eventually recover by a dish of peaches in syrup and cream.

Peaches survive being canned better than most fruits. The flavor is altered, but still good – or so I think, perhaps because I met canned peaches before fresh ones. The canning industry, which started to grow towards the end of the 19th century, now accounts for much of world production.

In some Mediterranean countries the green fruits (which never ripen fully) of so-called wild peaches are used in cooking and for preserves. These are not true wild peaches (only found in China), but escapees from cultivation.

The **NECTARINE**, *Prunus persica* var *nectarina*, has a smooth skin and a flavor so fine that it is named for nectar, the legendary drink of the classical gods. The flesh is generally yellow and the skin red and yellow, but there is a variety called Blanca del Jalon which is greenish white. Like other peaches, nectarines may be clingstone or freestone.

The origin of the nectarine, first described by a European writer in 1587, is a mystery. It is a true peach, not a cross between a peach and a plum as some suppose. By 1629, according to Parkinson, there were six varieties of it in England and the name nectarine was already in use; but the fruit did not appear in the USA until the 19th century.

Strawberry

family ROSACEAE

Other Names for *STRAWBERRY*
(names with asterisks are for the wild strawberry)

French: *fraise*
German: *Erdbeere*
Italian: *fragola*
Portuguese: *morango*
Spanish: *fresa, freson*
Basque: *arraga, marrubi*
Danish / Norwegian: *jordbær*
Swedish: *smultron*
Finnish: *mansikka; ahomansikka**
Russian: *klubnika; zemlyanika**
Polish: *truskawka; poziomka**
Serbo-Croat: *jagoda; šumska jagoda**
Romanian: *fragă*
Bulgarian: *yagoda*
Greek: *fráoula*
Turkish: *çilek*
Hebrew: *tut sadeh*
Arabic: *farāwla*
Chinese: *cao mei*
Japanese: *ichigo*
Indonesian: *arbéi*

Tips for the Cook

Strawberries should not be washed, unless just before consumption.
The best way to use a glut from the garden is in the form of jam or frozen purée, rather than "bottling".

Recipes

Key to the Painting

top row, left to right: Hautbois (*Fragaria moschata*), Chilean or Pine strawberry (*F chiloensis*), Scarlet Strawberry (*F virginiana*);
2nd row: fraise des bois Baron Solemancher (*F vesca*), Honeyoye (USA) and Bounty (Canada);
3rd row: Shasta (USA), Cambridge Vigour (UK) and Florida 90 (USA);
4th row: Korona (Netherlands), Tenira (Netherlands) and Aromel (UK)

For some people the **STRAWBERRY** is a symbol of the Virgin Mary. For just about everyone it serves to symbolize summer and the delights of summer fruit. As Andrew Boorde put it in the 16th century: "Rawe crayme undecocted, eaten with strawberys . . . is a rural mannes banket."

The strawberry, the fruit of plants of the genus *Fragaria*, has a peculiar and unique structure. It is technically known as a false or accessory fruit. The seeds which, unlike those of any other fruit, are on the outside, are the true fruits of the plant. The fleshy "berry" to which they are attached is an enlarged, softened "receptacle", corresponding to the small, white cone which remains on the stem of a raspberry when the fruit is picked.

The Latin name "fraga" refers to the fruit's fragrance. The English word strawberry refers to the straying erratic habit of the plant.

Wild strawberries are indigenous to both the Old and the New Worlds. It is often said that the flavor of some of these small fruits is better than that of cultivated strawberries. Indeed enthusiasm for them, and for furnishing the markets with what is a costly delicacy, has reached the point at which they are cultivated, to be sold as "fraises des bois". This may be regarded as turning the clock back to the 14th century; for it was then that organized cultivation of strawberries began, and it began, of course, on the basis of the wild fruits. *F vesca semperflorens*, the Alpine strawberry of northern Europe, was popular, in white forms as well as the normal red ones. *F moschata*, the hautbois strawberry, and *F viridis*, the green strawberry, were also grown: small, round fruits, pale and streaked with green, with a special musky flavor.

The next step came with the colonization of the Americas. *F virginiana*, the native wild strawberry or scarlet strawberry, was found growing in North America. So was another species, larger and juicier: *F chiloensis*, the pine strawberry, found on the west coast of both North and South America but associated particularly with Chile. The name pine is for its pineapple flavor. There are red, yellow, and white kinds.

F virginiana was introduced into Europe in the 17th century, and is still a favorite for making jam. *F chiloensis* was brought to France early in the 18th century by a French officer, Frézier, who found the plants growing at the foot of the Andes. They were not sensationally good, but when they began to hybridize naturally with *F virginiana*, the result was of outstanding merit: *F ananassa*, the ancestor of the modern cultivated strawberry.

A major role in the development of strawberries was played by the French botanist Antoine Nicolas Duchesne, who published his *Histoire naturelle des fraisiers* in 1766, when he was only 19 years old. However, one minor result of the French Revolution was to impede the advances being made in France, and the innovators of the 19th century were British. Thomas Andrew Knight pioneered large-scale, systematic strawberry breeding, and produced two famous varieties, the Downton and the Elton. A market gardener called Michael Keens then produced Keens' Seedling, whose remarkable size and flavor caused a sensation when it came into cultivation in 1821. Most modern varieties are derived from it.

There are now hundreds of varieties of strawberry. They exhibit great diversity of size and flavor; but one thing is certain, that any strawberries are best when picked fully ripe. Most people think that they are best eaten raw. Fresh cream is the traditional accompaniment in England; elsewhere in Europe sour cream is preferred, and I myself think that French crème fraîche, with its subtle acidity, is best of all. In France and Italy, red wine is often used instead. Strawberry shortcake is the birthday dessert in our household.

Raspberry, Cloudberry, Arctic Bramble

family ROSACEAE

Other Names for *RASPBERRY*

French: *framboise*
German: *Himbeere*
Italian: *lampone*
Spanish: *frambuesa*
Basque: *martzuka gorri*
Portuguese: *framboesa*
Dutch: *framboos*
Danish: *hindbær*
Norwegian: *bringebær*
Swedish: *hallon*
Finnish: *vattu, vadelma*
Russian / Polish: *malina*
Czech: *malinnik*
Serbo-Croat: *malina*
Romanian: *zmeură*
Bulgarian: *malina*
Greek: *sméouro*
Turkish: *ahududu*
Hebrew: *petel*
Arabic: *farambwāz*
Indonesian: *buah frambus*
Chinese: *mu mei, shan mei*
Japanese: *kiichigo (R parvifolius)*

Other Names for *CLOUDBERRY*

Danish: *multebær*
Norwegian: *molte*
Swedish: *hjorton*
Finnish: *lakka, suomuurain*
Russian: *moroshka*
Chinese: *yun mei*
Japanese: *horomuiichigo*

Other Names for *ARCTIC BRAMBLE*

Norwegian: *åskerbær*
Swedish: *åkerbär*
Finnish: *mesimarja*

Recipes

Fresh Figs with Raspberry Cream: page 153
Summer Pudding: page 157
Raspberry Buckle: page 164
Marjapuuro (Whipped Berry Oatmeal): page 170
Berry Sherbet: page 174
Rødgrøt: page 181

Key to the Painting

top left: red Autumn Bliss and yellow raspberry;
right: cloudberry or baked-apple berry;
below: two Leo raspberries on stalks and flowers; and behind, Arctic bramble;
bottom: wild raspberry and Black raspberry

If it is true that one's taste in fruit is likely to be formed in childhood, then my predilection for raspberries is understandable. My grandmother had them growing in her garden near Glasgow; and Scottish raspberries are among the best of all, because the climate suits them perfectly. Every summer, as a small boy, I would have the task of picking the ripe ones just before supper; and I still think that fresh raspberries and cream are hard to beat.

The **RASPBERRY**, *Rubus idaeus* and other *Rubus* species, grows wild in all the cooler regions of the northern hemisphere, and in some southern parts. The genus also includes the blackberry. One might think that the two could easily be distinguished by color. However, both can be any color from white through yellow, orange, pink, red and purple to black, the difference between them being one of structure (as explained under blackberry, page 34).

The first people known to have cultivated raspberries were the ancient Greeks, who are said to have called the fruit "idaeus" because it grew thickly on the slopes of Mount Ida, as it still does. So it is fitting that *R idaeus* is the modern botanical name of the chief species of both the wild and cultivated raspberry. As for the English name, it comes from the Old English "raspis", of obscure origin, but probably connected with the slightly hairy, "rasping" surface of the fruit.

The common European wild raspberry has a distribution which extends north of the Arctic Circle, and grows also in western and northern Asia. There are red, yellow, and white forms; and the flavor of some wild varieties is outstanding.

Some wild raspberries of northern India and the Himalayas are very dark red or black; for example the Mysore raspberry, *R niveus*, which has an excellent flavor. Another good species, indigenous to the Malay peninsula and southern China, is *R parvifolius*, sometimes called Japanese raspberry or Australian bramble.

Wild American species include what is simply known as the wild red raspberry, similar to *R idaeus* and now thought to be the same species. In the eastern USA and Canada *R occidentalis*, the black raspberry, is common. It is more acid than most raspberries, which makes it particularly good for cooking. The paler, often orange, salmon berry, *R spectabilis*, is named not because of its color but because Native Americans of the North-West often ate it with salmon roe.

Fresh raspberries with cream may be the best raspberry dish, but such simplicity has no place in haute cuisine, where the berries are more apt to appear in the guise of syrups and sauces used as an accompaniment to other fruits such as pears. Raspberry sauce is an ingredient in Peach Melba.

In Yorkshire, England, on a humbler plane, raspberry vinegar used to be served with Yorkshire pudding, before the meat. This vinegar is enjoying a new vogue.

CLOUDBERRY, *Rubus chamaemorus*, is one of the most delicious of all berries and costly, since it is confined to the northern regions of Europe and North America and can be gathered in limited quantities only. In northern Scandinavia, where Finland, Sweden and Norway meet, and the cloudberry thrives, the inhabitants of these otherwise peace-loving countries have been known to engage in "cloudberry wars"; and the Swedish Ministry for Foreign Affairs maintains, or used to, a special section for cloudberry diplomacy. In northern North America, the fruit may also be called the baked-apple berry or just bakeapple.

The berries are golden when ripe, and soft and juicy, so difficult to transport. Although they freeze perfectly, most people encounter them in the form of preserves of one kind or another. Cloudberry jam is outstanding, and a fine accompaniment to ice cream or filling for pancakes.

The **ARCTIC BRAMBLE**, *R arcticus*, is another northern species. Like the cloudberry, it is a low-growing plant. The berries range from red to a deep purple, and are fragrant and delicious.

Blackberry, Loganberry, Tayberry, Boysenberry, Dewberry

family ROSACEAE

Other Names for *BLACKBERRY*

French: *mûre*
German: *Brombeere*
Italian: *mora selvatica*
Spanish: *mora, zarzamora*
Portuguese: *amora silvestre*
Basque: *martzuka*
Dutch: *brammbes*
Danish: *brombær*
Norwegian: *bjønebær*
Swedish: *björnbär*
Finnish: *poimuvatukka*
Russian: *yezhevika*
Polish: *jeżyna*
Czech: *óstružina*
Slovak: *ostružina krovita*
Serbo-Croat: *kupina*
Romanian: *coacăz negru*
Bulgarian: *kupina*
Greek: *batomouron*
Turkish: *böğürtlen*
Chinese: *hei mei*
Japanese: *seiyōyabuichigo*

Other Names for *DEWBERRY*

French: *mûre de la baie*
German: *Ackerbeere*
Italian: *mora di rovo*
Spanish: *zarzamora*
Portuguese: *amora*
Danish: *korbær*
Norwegian: *blåbringbær*
Swedish: *blåhallon*
Finnish: *sinivatukka*
Russian: *yezhevika*
Polish: *jeżyna popielica*
Hungarian: *hamvas szeder*

Recipes

Summer Pudding: page 157
Raspberry Buckle: page 164
Brompton Cemetery Blackberry Fool:
page 170
Berry Sherbet: page 174

Key to the Painting

berries shown with leaves are:
top: blackberry Fantasia;
center left: loganberry;
center right: boysenberry;
bottom: tayberry;
the scattered berries are wild
blackberries

Few fruiting plants are as invasive and prickly as the **BLACKBERRY**. The branches which almost visibly thrust forward in my London garden, annexing any vacant air space or ground, are behaving just like the original blackberries which colonized areas left vacant by retreating glaciers in the very distant past.

The name blackberry usually refers to the common European blackberry, or bramble, *Rubus fruticosus*, but it is also a collective name for a large group of fruits in the same genus which grow throughout the cooler parts of the world, particularly in upland and northern regions. There are said to be over 2,000 varieties, counting both the frequent and naturally occurring hybrids and the cultivated varieties. How many species there are is a question on which botanists disagree.

The genus *Rubus* also includes raspberries. It is not always easy to distinguish between a blackberry and a raspberry, since the shapes and sizes of the fruit, leaves, and thorns vary, and raspberries may be black rather than red. However, there is a sure test. When a blackberry is picked, it comes off the plant with its receptacle, the solid center to which the druplets (the round, black, juicy parts) are attached, and one eats the entire berry; whereas when a raspberry is picked, the cluster of druplets comes away from the receptacle, which stays behind as a hard, white cone on the stem. A good blackberry has druplets which are large in relation to the white inner part.

In western and central Asia blackberries grow as far south as Iran and up to the Himalayas; but the variety which is romantically called Himalayan Giant has been shown to be *R procera*, a species of western Europe.

North American blackberries are highly diverse. The indigenous species vary across regions, and have also been interbred with imported varieties. One common native species is the Pacific blackberry, *R ursinus*, which has large fruits. Another well-known wild blackberry, which arrived from England (via the South Sea Islands!) is the evergreen or cut-leaved blackberry, *R laciniatus*. There is much cultivation of blackberries (and dewberries – see below) in the USA.

Raspberries and blackberries are to some extent interfertile, and hybrids exist, but most have failed to achieve commercial success. If the **LOGANBERRY**, named after Judge Logan of Santa Cruz in California, really is one such hybrid, it is a big exception to the rule. (The Judge certainly believed that it was, but some authorities claim that it was simply a cultivar of the Pacific blackberry). Loganberries are dark red and of a good size. The plants yield well, and the fruits have been canned in large quantities, but their popularity has waned in recent decades. The **TAYBERRY**, which has larger, sweeter and more aromatic fruits, also dark red in color, has meanwhile gained ground.

Two other developments are the **BOYSENBERRY**, the offspring of two blackberry cultivars, and the youngberry, both called after their growers. The youngberry is fairly good, with a large, deep red, sweet fruit. Another cultivar, said to be a cross between the youngberry and the loganberry is the ollalie.

A common relation of the blackberry is the European **DEWBERRY**, *R caesius*, which closely resembles the blackberry, and has a similar distribution; but it bears smaller fruits with fewer and larger druplets, which are covered by a purple bloom. Other dewberries, including *R villosus* and *R canadensis*, are common in North America, where there is some cultivation of them. They tend to be larger than the European ones.

In Scandinavia, northern Europe and Asia blackberries and dewberries are common but there are also species peculiar to the far north. These include the brownish-red rock bramble, *R saxatilis*.

Gooseberry

family SAXIFRAGACEAE

Other Names for *GOOSEBERRY*

French: *groseille maquereau*
German: *Stachelbeere*
Italian: *uva spina*
Spanish: *grosella blanca, grosella verde*
Dutch: *kruisbes*
Danish / Norwegian: *stikkelsbær*
Swedish: *krusbär*
Finnish: *karviaismarja*
Russian: *kryzhovnik*
Polish: *agrest*
Serbo-Croat: *ogrozd*
Romanian: *agrisă*
Bulgarian: *tsarigradsko grozde*
Greek: *ribesion*
Turkish: *bektaşiüzümü*
Arabic: *'inab al-tha'lab*
Japanese: *suguri*

Recipes

Cumberland "Plate Cake": page 161
Greengage Frushie: page 162
Ice Cream: page 172

Key to the Painting

top row: Careless, Lord Derby, Hot
Gossip;
2nd row: Lancashire Lad, White Lion,
Scotch Red Rough;
3rd row: Belle de Meaux, Warrington,
Golden Drop;
4th row: Whitesmith, Greengage, Angler

GOOSEBERRY is a longstanding British slang term for an unwanted third person at a lovers' meeting; and of disparagement generally. But Britain is where the cultivation of gooseberries and the art of cooking delicious dishes with them have been carried furthest. Gooseberry fool, gooseberry tansy, gooseberry pie – all these can be excellent. And so can the kinds of gooseberry grown for eating as dessert – often white, yellow, or red, as well as green.

Gooseberry bushes grow wild in most of the northern temperate zone, flourishing in cool, moist or high regions. Most wild species are thorny, with sour berries; not very promising plants, and it is not surprising that they were late to be taken into cultivation.

The first record is a fruiterer's bill from the court of the English King Edward I, dated 1276, for gooseberry bushes. These, it seems, were imported from France, although the fruit has never been widely popular there. It has, however, been used in northern parts of the country to make a sauce for fish, which explains its French name "groseille maquereau" (mackerel currant). As for the English name:

> Dr Martyun considers the name was applied to this fruit, in consequence of its being employed as sauce for that bird. It is somewhat unfortunate for this derivation that it has never been so used. It seems to me most probably to be a corruption of the Dutch name Kruisbes, or Gruisbes, derived from Kruis, the Cross, and Bes, as Berry, because the fruit was ready for use just after the Festival of the Invention of the Holy Cross; just as Kruis-haring, in Dutch, is a herring, caught after the same festival. (Johnson, 1847)

The *OED*, however adheres to the derivation from goose, in favor of which it may be said that the sharpness of the gooseberry goes well with a fatty or oily meat such as goose (or mackerel).

In southern Europe the gooseberry is largely ignored. Latin languages do not distinguish between it and its near relative the red, white or black currant.

It was in Britain that gooseberries, of which *Ribes reticulata* is the principal cultivated species, became most popular. One 19th-century author thought that Scottish gooseberries were "the perfection of their race", and I would not dispute this. But many of the orchardists responsible for the improved, larger and sweeter varieties worked in England.

In North America, and in Asia too, there are other species, much like those of Europe. One of the best is the American Worcesterberry, *Ribes divaricatum*, with small, almost black berries. Although white settlers, especially those of British origin, made use of North American gooseberries, cultivation of the plants has been discouraged because, like the currant, they act as a host for a disease of timber trees.

A distinction was made between dessert gooseberries, for eating raw, and cooking gooseberries, which are sour but have a superior flavor when cooked. From the late 18th century, and throughout the 19th, amateur gooseberry clubs were set up in the Midlands and the North of England. These held competitions for the best flavored and, more particularly, for the largest fruit. Johnson (1847) points out that extraordinary results were achieved, especially in the vicinity of Manchester, by "the lowest and most illiterate members of society, [who] by continual experience and perseverance in growing and raising new sorts" had tripled the weight of the largest berries.

In England, in the 1980s, fewer than ten such clubs survived, mostly in Cheshire. But the best known is the Egton Bridge Old Gooseberry Society, in Yorkshire. This was founded around 1800, and has held annual competitions, except for one or two years during the First World War, ever since. The sole criterion is weight. A new Egton Bridge record was established in 1985 when the champion berry, of the yellow variety Woodpecker, weighed 1.925 ounces; but the world record, 2.06 ounces, is held by a Woodpecker shown at Marton in Cheshire in 1978.

Red Currant, White Currant, Black Currant

family GROSSULARIACEAE

Other Names for *RED CURRANT*

French: *groseille rouge*
German: *rote Johannisbeere*
Italian: *ribes rosso*
Spanish: *grosella colorada*
Portuguese: *vermelha*
Danish: *ribs*
Norwegian: *rips*
Swedish: *röda vinbär*
Finnish: *punaherukka*
Russian: *krasnaya smorodina*
Polish: *czerwona porzeczka*
Serbo-Croat: *crveni ribiz*
Romanian: *pomusoare*
Bulgarian: *cherveno frensko grozde*
Hebrew: *dumdemanit aduma*
Arabic: *kishmish ahmar*
Japanese: *akafusasuguri*

Other Names for *WHITE CURRANT*

Finnish: *valkoherukka*
Russian: *belaya smorodina*
Bulgarian: *byalo frensko grozde*
Japanese: *shirafusasuguri*

Other Names for *BLACK CURRANT*

French: *cassis*
German: *schwarze Johannisbeere*
Italian: *ribes nero*
Spanish: *grosella negra*
Dutch: *zwarte bessen*
DanishNorwegian: *solbær*
Swedish: *svarta vinbär*
Finnish: *mustaherukka*
Russian: *chornaya smorodina*
Polish: *czarna porzeczka*
Czech: *černy rýbiz*
Slovak: *ribezla čierna*
Hungarian: *fekete ribizke*
Serbo-Croat: *crni ribiz*
Romanian: *agrise negru*
Bulgarian: *kasis*
Greek: *maffro fragkostafilo, kassi*
Hebrew: *dumdemanit shehora*
Arabic: *kishmish aswad*
Japanese: *kurofusasuguri*

The trio of currants are, botanically, just a pair. The black is *Ribes nigrum*; the red *R rubrum*; and the white is just a variety of the red. All are small, round berries which often retain withered remnants of the flower from which they grew at the end opposite the stem.

Wild currants, both red and black, grow worldwide in northern temperate regions, including North America, but the cultivated species all have European and Asian ancestry.

The **RED CURRANT** was first mentioned in European literature in a German manuscript of the early 15th century. It was domesticated in Europe in the 16th century, mainly in the Netherlands and Denmark, and its luminescent beauty soon made it popular with still-life painters.

Red currants, sufficiently dosed with sugar, can be eaten fresh; but their principal use has been in preserves (red currant jelly, to go with lamb or other meat), sauces, Scandinavian fruit soups, and desserts such as the British summer pudding, in which a mixture of red currants and raspberries is of scintillating excellence. Red currant juice is a popular drink in and around Germany.

However, in other parts of Europe, especially the south, currants of whatever color have never caught on. The common Latin languages use the same name for currant and gooseberry. Even when, in Paris in the 18th century, red currant juice enjoyed a vogue, the fruit was known as "groseille d'outre mer" (foreign gooseberry). It is true, however, that the red currant jelly made at and named after the French town of Bar-le-Duc has helped to give these currants a certain standing in France.

WHITE CURRANTS, whose special pearl-like beauty shows up well when they are combined with more colorful fruits, are usually less acid than red currants. Parkinson considered them "more accepted and desired, as also because they are more daintie, and less common" (still true). For most purposes the two can be mixed.

The **BLACK CURRANT**, *R nigrum*, was first cultivated a century later than the red currant, and was long considered inferior despite its greater size (nowadays up to just over $\frac{1}{2}$ inch). Its flavor lacks the brilliance of that of the red currant, especially when the fruit is raw; and it was handicapped by an association with medicine. In Britain, certainly, it was viewed as a cure for sore throats, for which purpose one of the spiced fruit syrups which went by the name "rob" was prepared from it. And, when vitamins were discovered at the beginning of the 20th century, this gave a further boost to its medical reputation, since it is outstandingly rich in vitamin C (half a dozen black currants have more of it than a large lemon).

However, black currants have also been deservedly popular for jam (but note that they need more water than other fruits). And they are good in steamed puddings. A few of them make a welcome addition to mixed fruit salads; and it is feasible to freeze large specimens, picked during the short season, for this purpose. From France the alcoholic cordial crème de cassis, made in Burgundy from locally grown blackcurrants, has won worldwide fame.

A newcomer to the family, the jostaberry, is a hybrid whose parents are black currants and gooseberries. It looks like, and may be treated like, a large black currant, but has a pleasing flavor which is different from either parent. It has largely usurped the place formerly occupied by a similar hybrid, the Worcesterberry.

Key to the Painting

white, red and black currants are shown; plus, bottom center, the jostaberry

Grapes, Raisins, White Raisins, Currants

family VITACEAE

Other Names for *GRAPE*

French: *raisin*
Basque: *mahats*
German: *Traube*
Italian: *uva*
Portuguese: *uva*
Spanish: *uva*
Dutch: *druif*
Danish: *drue, vindrue*
Norwegian: *drue*
Swedish: *(vin)druva*
Finnish: *viinirypäle*
Russian: *vinograd*
Polish: *winogrona*
Serbo-Croat: *grožda*
Romanian: *boabă de strugare*
Bulgarian: *grozde*
Greek: *trapezou*
Turkish: *üzüm*
Hebrew: *'enav*
Arabic: *'inab*
Persian: *angūr*
Thai: *a-ngung*
Chinese: *pu tao*
Japanese: *budō*

One of the undeniable luxuries in which I have indulged was to sit outside our house near Carthage, looking at the blue waters of the Bay of Tunis, to reach up and snip a bunch of **GRAPES** from the vine which cast grateful shade over our lunch table, to dunk them in a huge bowl of iced water and to eat them as dessert.

What grapes were these? I know not, but guess that they were *Vitis vinifera*, by far the dominant species in a world in which grapes constitute the single largest fruit crop. More of them go to make wine than finish up on our tables (a topic recently and admirably covered by Hugh Johnson in *The Story of Wine*); but even so the production of table grapes is very large. The countries which grow most, having the right climate, are Italy, France, Bulgaria, the Soviet Union, the USA, Australia and South Africa. But Belgium has become important too, by producing hothouse grapes of exceptional quality.

When Noah sowed grape seeds on Mount Ararat after the Flood, he showed himself a good horticulturist, since that is the region of origin of *V vinifera*. The grapevine is (or, I should say, was) essentially a plant of temperate zones in the northern hemisphere. In America many native species of vine produce grapes good enough to eat, notably *V labrusca*. The popular black Concord grapes are a cultivated variety of this species.

It is estimated that there are now about 10,000 varieties of *V vinifera*. Yet only a dozen or so of these are important as table grapes. The most important in commerce is Thompson Seedless, which has a clean and refreshing taste. Others include Italia, a large juicy grape with a stronger, and highly agreeable, flavor; and Emperor, Tokay and Perlette.

While the Spanish and Portuguese were establishing the European grape in the Americas, the Dutch took it to the Cape of Good Hope in 1655. Here too there is a native grape of fair quality, *V capensis*, though *V vinifera* is now dominant. Grapes were introduced to South Australia in 1813, and have been grown there successfully ever since. They are also grown to an increasing extent in South America.

Although in modern times grapes are chiefly used for eating or winemaking, various grape products were prominent in earlier times. Sugar syrups, made by boiling down must (fresh unfermented grape juice), were an important ingredient in Roman food. (Grape syrup is still made in the Levant, where it is called "dibs".) Verjuice, the juice of unripe grapes (or sometimes of other fruit such as crab apples), is another grape product of ancient origin, much used as a souring agent in European cookery in Europe until it was ousted by vinegar.

RAISIN is a term of general application, meaning simply dried grape. However, it is not just any grape which is dried to make a raisin. There are certain varieties which are suited to and grown for the purpose. Raisins are often distinguished by the kind of grape used (for example, Muscatel, one of the most usual) or by the place of origin (for example, Malaga and Alicante, both in Spain). The main raisin producers are the USA, Turkey, Greece and Australia. Seedless raisins are the most popular, but ones with seeds may have more flavor.

WHITE RAISINS (or Smyrna raisins, as they used to be called, because most of them were shipped from Smyrna in Turkey) are small raisins, pale golden in color, seedless, sweet, and much in demand for table use and in confectionery.

CURRANTS are small dried black grapes, traditionally best from the region of Corinth in Greece, which provided them with their name. These are seedless.

The term "raisins of the sun", often encountered in English recipes of the 17th and 18th centuries, was used to distinguish ordinary raisins from currants (although all were dried in the sun).

Key to the Painting
the variety shown is Muscat of Alexandria

Pomegranate

family PUNICACEAE

Other Names for
POMEGRANATE

French: *grenade*
German: *Granatapfel*
Italian: *melagrana*
Spanish: *granada*
Portuguese: *romã*
Basque: *grenada*
Dutch: *granaatappel*
Danish: *granatæble*
Norwegian: *granat*
Swedish: *granatäppelträd, granatäpple*
Finnish: *granaattiomena*
Russian: *granat*
Polish: *owoc granatu*
Serbo-Croat: *zranata, šipak, jabuka*
Romanian: *rodie*
Bulgarian: *nar*
Greek: *ródi*
Turkish: *nar*
Hebrew: *rimon*
Arabic: *rummān*
Persian/Afghanistan: *anar*
Indian languages: *anar* (Hindi), *dalim*
(Bengali), *mathalam pazham* (Tamil)
Burmese: *tha-le*
Thai: *thap thi*
Malay / Indonesian: *delima*
Philippines: *granada*
Chinese: *shi liu*
Japanese: *zakuro*
Brazil: *roma, romeira*

Tips for the Cook

Pomegranate seeds (more precisely, the ruby-colored arils which contain the actual seeds) make a wonderful garnish for all sorts of dishes; their sweet-and-sour taste and handsome appearance fit them for almost any company. It is easiest to winkle them out if you first cut off the blossom end, then score the fruit lengthways and break (not cut) it into quarters along the score marks.

The **POMEGRANATE** has an interior of surpassing beauty, like an ovoid Fabergé jewel-case opened to display rubies within. Its native region is a wild and romantic one, embracing Persia (Iran), southern parts of the Soviet Union, and across through Afghanistan to the Himalayas.

Botanists know the small tree which bears these fruits as *Punica granatum*, a name with an interesting origin. Although the fruit was known to the ancient Greeks, it seems to have reached the Romans circuitously, via Carthage in North Africa; so they called it "mala punica" (Carthaginian apple). That explains the generic name *Punica*. The species name *granatum*, the Spanish "granada", and indeed the name pomegranate itself all refer to the many "grains" or seeds. These are distributed by birds, which eat the fruit with relish.

Although the pomegranate has been cultivated and appreciated since remote antiquity (it was well known in ancient Egypt, and Moses had to assure the Israelites that they would find it again in the Promised Land), it does suffer one disadvantage: it can be laborious to consume. The pulp which surrounds the seeds is encased in a honeycomb of interior membranes; and the seeds themselves, although edible, are intrusive and require a decision whether to swallow them down or spit them out. The problem is well illustrated by a classical legend. Persephone, daughter of Demeter, goddess of fruit, was carried off to the underworld by its god, Pluto. She vowed not to eat while in captivity, but eventually succumbed and ate a pomegranate, spitting out all the seeds except six, which she swallowed. When Pluto finally gave in to Demeter, he was allowed to keep Persephone for six months of every year on account of those seeds; and these six months became winter.

There are now some varieties of pomegranate which are almost free of seeds, or have soft seeds (for example, the cultivar Bedana in India). Had these been available in Pluto's orchard, Persephone would have swallowed far more than six seeds, and we would presumably be living in an eternal winter.

Spanish sailors took the pomegranate from the Mediterranean region to America. It was a useful fruit for sea voyagers since its hard skin helps it to keep well. It is now cultivated in parts of South America, and also in Mexico and California. It had already, in the early centuries AD, spread from India to China.

However, despite its wide dissemination, the pomegranate is still most popular in its region of origin. Indeed, for all who cherish the use of fruit in the kitchen, the pomegranate remains, first and foremost, a fruit of Persia. Here is what Olearius wrote in 1669, about Persian use of pomegranates:

> Pomegranate-trees grow there without any ordering or cultivation, especially in the Province of Kilan, where you have whole forests of them. The wild pomegranates, which you find almost everywhere, especially at Karabag, are sharp or sowrish. They take out of them the seed, which they call Nardan, wherewith they drive a great trade, and the Persians make use of it in their sawces, whereto it gives a color, and a picquant tast, having been steep'd in water, and strain'd through a cloath.

Pomegranates from wild trees contain a high proportion of seeds and membranes, and their scanty pulp is often sour and astringent. However, even these have their uses, for example in India, where their seeds are used as a sour condiment, "anardana".

Cultivated pomegranates, in contrast, have plenty of juicy pulp with a sweet, sharp flavor which is only slightly astringent. This can simply be eaten out of the half-skin with a spoon, or more delicately presented by separating it from the membranes around it and piling the glistening pulp and seeds into a dish.

Pomegranate juice makes a refreshing drink, and is also used in cooking, for example in some traditional Persian meat dishes, and in the southern republics of the Soviet Union. Grenadine is a concentrated syrup made from the juice.

Key to the Painting

Pomegranates

Elderberry, Barberry, Myrtle, Sea Buckthorn, Silverberry

Key to the Painting

top: elderberries and leaves;
the red scattered berries are Berberis
(*Berberis communis*);
the orange berries are sea buckthorn;
the blue berries are myrtle

ELDERBERRY and elderflower, borne by elder trees, of the genus *Sambucus*, are found almost everywhere in Europe, western Asia and North America. The trees bear white flower clusters and abundant black berries, both of which are edible when cooked. When raw, however, they contain small amounts of a poisonous alkaloid, and have a sickly smell and taste. Cooking destroys the alkaloid and transforms the taste.

Elderflowers are used to flavor cooked fruit and jam, by stirring the panful with a spray of flowers until the flavor is judged strong enough. Native-Americans are credited with the invention of elderflower fritters, which have since become popular in other countries, and of the practice of putting elderflowers in muffins and pancakes to lighten and flavor them.

In cooking, elderberries are often added to other fruits, especially apples. Combined with crab apples, they produce a pretty jelly; and they can be used in the same way with scarlet sumac berries. The elderberries need the additional pectin provided by these other fruits to produce a good gel.

Elderberry cordial, an unfermented and non-alcoholic concentrate, provided to me annually by a kind neighbour, makes a delicious summer drink and can also be used as a topping for ice cream.

The common elder of the Old World is *Sambucus nigra*. American species include *S canadensis* in the north and *S mexicana* in the south-western states. The berries of the latter have a fine flavor. The former has a less good reputation, which an issue of *The American Botanist* in 1905 sought to improve:

The trouble is not so much in the pie itself as the way it is put together. Pies made of fresh elderberries are scarcely likely to appeal to many palates. The fruit still retains some of the rank eldery flavor possessed by the entire plant and made evident when the stem is broken; but if one will collect the berries when fully ripe and dry them in flat trays in the sun or in a warm oven he will have a cheap and appetizing material from which to manufacture pies all winter . . .

The **BARBERRY** is the fruit of shrubs of the genera *Berberis* and *Mahonia*, of which many species grow wild in temperate regions. All bear berries which are edible but tart. *Berberis* berries are generally red, varying from coral to deep crimson. *B vulgaris*, the common barberry of Europe and Asia, has elongated, bright red berries which hang in clusters. *Mahonia* berries are usually blue, pale or dark. *M aquifolium*, the mountain grape or Oregon grape which is the floral emblem of the State of Oregon, has blue-grey ones.

Barberries make a fine jelly or jam, such as the French "confiture d'épine-vinette", made from a seedless variety of *B vulgaris*. In India some species are sun-dried to make "raisins" which are eaten as a dessert.

MYRTLE, *Myrtus communis*, a fragrant shrub which bears white flowers and blue-black berries, is native to southern Europe and the Near East. The ancient Greeks considered it sacred to Venus. However, this did not inhibit them from eating the berries, which are pleasantly acid and sweet with an aromatic quality slightly resembling that of juniper. They make a pleasant jelly. (Note: "bog myrtle" is something quite different.)

The berries of **SEA BUCKTHORN**, *Hippophae rhamnoides*, a plant which occurs in coastal areas of Scandinavia, are greatly appreciated in Finland, for example. They may be found further south in Europe, and also in Asia, including Siberia.

The **SILVERBERRY**, *Elaeagnus argentea*, is a shrub of northern North America, especially the Hudsons Bay region, which bears edible fruits. These are consumed locally, but are too dry and mealy to be of gastronomic interest.

Cranberry, Blueberry, Bilberry, Huckleberry, Bearberry, Arbutus

family ERICACEAE

Note: the popular names for fruits of the genus *Vaccinium* are highly confusing, and the lists of names which follow should be used with this caution in mind.

Other Names for *CRANBERRY*

for *V oxycoccus*
French: *canneberge*
German: *Moosbeere*
Italian: *mortella di palude*
Spanish: *arándano agrio*
Portuguese: *arando*
Danish / Norwegian: *tranebær*
Swedish: *tranbär*
Finnish: *isokarpalo*
Russian: *klyukva*
Polish: *żurawina*
Czech: *klikva, žoravina*
Slovak: *klukva močiarna*
Hungarian: *tözegáfonya*
Serbo-Croat: *brusnica*
Romanian: *răchitelele*

for *V vitis idaea*
French: *myrtille rouge*
German: *Preiselbeere*
Portuguese: *uva dos montes*
Danish / Norwegian: *tyttebær*
Swedish: *lingon*
Finnish: *puolukka*
Russian: *brusnika*
Polish: *brusznica, jagoda*
Czech: *borůwka*
Serbo-Croat: *borovnica*
Romanian: *merisoară*

Other Names for *BLUEBERRY / BILBERRY*

French: *myrtille, airelle*
German: *Blaubeere*
Italian: *mirtillo*
Spanish: *arándano*
Danish / Norwegian: *blåbær*
Swedish: *blåbär*
Finnish: *mustikka, pensasmustikka*
Russian: *chernika*
Polish: *czarnica, czarna jagoda*
Hungarian: *fekete áfonya*
Romanian: *afină*
Serbo-Croat: *borovnica*
Bulgarian: *borovinki*

Key to the Painting

top and bottom two rows: blueberries; 3rd and 4th rows: lingonberries and flowers; 5th and 6th rows: bilberries and flowers; 7th and 8th rows: large American cranberries

CRANBERRY is the most important of the edible berries borne by a group of low, scrubby, woody plants of the genus *Vaccinium*. These grow on moors and mountainsides, in bogs and other places with poor and acid soil in most parts of the world, but are best known in northern Europe and North America.

The generic name *Vaccinium* is the old Latin name for the cranberry, derived from "vacca" (cow) and given because cows like the plants. This accounts also for the old name cowberry. (Incidentally, the common names of these berries are highly confusing and often overlap with those of other berries, such as blueberry / bilberry, whortleberry and huckleberry.)

The plants to which the name cranberry was originally given are two species which occur in Europe as well as in other temperate parts of the world: *Vaccinium oxycoccus* and *V vitis idaea*. The former is sometimes called the small cranberry. The latter, which replaces it in the more northerly regions and at higher altitudes, is sometimes called mountain cranberry or foxberry in North America, but in Europe is better known as the lingonberry. Both plants bear red oval berries about ⅓ inch across with a piquant flavor. This fits them for making sharp sauces to go with game; and they also provide excellent jellies or preserves. The lingonberry (also called red whortleberry) enjoys great esteem in the Nordic countries. In Finland it is the most popular berry, because of its pleasant flavor and good keeping quality. Crushed with sugar or made into a sauce, it is often served with meat; indeed roast veal with cream sauce and lingonberry jam is one of the classic dishes of Finland. A compote / soup called "kiiseli" (also popular in Russia as "kisel") and a whipped oatmeal are also made from these and other berries.

When the Pilgrim Fathers arrived in North America they found a local cranberry, *V macrocarpon*, which had berries twice the size of those familiar to Europeans, and an equally good flavor. Native Americans were accustomed to eating these fresh or dried, and to adding the dried fruits as an ingredient in pemmican (a dried, preserved meat product). Cranberries contain large amounts of benzoic acid, which is a natural preservative and accounts for this practice. It was these large American cranberries which were made into sauce to accompany the settlers' other important discovery, the turkey, for Thanksgiving Day dinner.

For a long time now the American cranberry has been both cultivated and exported. Even in former times its remarkable keeping properties enabled it to withstand long sea voyages, stored in barrels full of plain water. Cranberries for storage were selected by tipping them down a flight of stairs: the sound berries bounced and fell to the bottom, while damaged ones stayed on the steps. This principle is still used in modern sorting machines.

Various *Vaccinium* species in other parts of the world produce fruits comparable to the cranberry but of less importance. One such is *V reticulata* of Hawaii, which bears the ohelo berry, red or yellow in color, sweet enough to eat raw, and suitable for jam if its low pectin content is strengthened.

BLUEBERRY is the small bluish fruit of various scrubby (lowbush) and bushy (highbush) plants of the genus *Vaccinium*. Wild blueberries are found wherever suitable conditions (acid soil and enough moisture at all seasons) exist, as far north as the limits of human habitation. In the past, the names blueberry and bilberry (see below) were applied to any of these, but the former name now belongs to the cultivated fruits.

The blueberry is the most recent example of a fruit plant taken from the wild and brought into commercial cultivation, a development which began in New Jersey in 1920. The cultivars then introduced by Dr F V Coville served as the basis of a new agricultural industry which put to good use acid, boggy soils which had previously been thought worthless for cultivation. The cultivated varieties of blueberry are mostly hybrids of three native American species, the highbush *V*

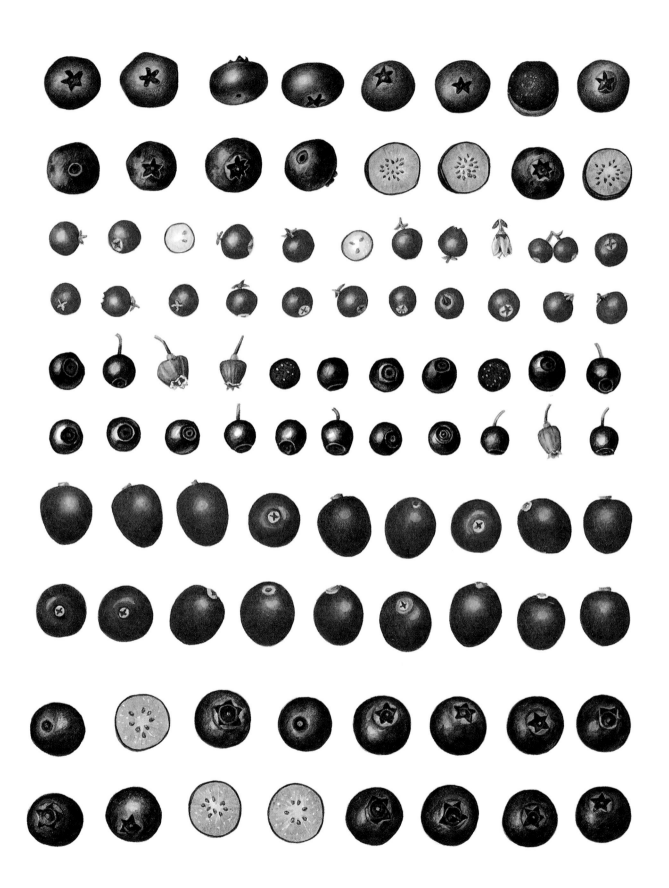

corymbosum, the "rabbit-eye" *V ashei* and the lowbush *V angustifolium*. The fruits of cultivated varieties are far removed from wild blueberries and may be four times as big. They have been bred not only for size but also to have a pleasing combination of acidity and sweetness.

Most commercially cultivated blueberries are grown in North America, but there is now some cultivation in Western Europe, and also in New Zealand.

The use of blueberries as fresh or stewed fruit, and in such dishes as blueberry pie and blueberry muffins, or with ice cream, is well known. Combined with other fruits which provide additional tartness and pectin, they make an excellent jelly. They are prized for this purpose in France, and also for jams, tarts and cakes.

BILBERRY is the fruit of a group of low scrubby plants in the genus *Vaccinium*, especially *V myrtillus*, which typically bear dark bluish purple berries with a characteristic bloom on their smooth skins.

In North America, bilberries (sometimes called whortleberries or huckleberries) are generally distributed in the far north, the mountainous parts of New England and the Lake Superior region.

The name comes from the Danish "bolle", meaning ball and referring to the round, smooth appearance of the berry. Other names in use in Britain are whinberry, because the plant grows among whins (a Scots term for gorse); and blaeberry, "blae" being a north-country and Scots word for blue.

Bilberries are good to eat raw, being less acid than cranberries, but are also often made into pies, tarts, jams, preserves and sauces. However, they are sparsely distributed on the plants, and picking a large quantity is tiring work, as we found when gathering them in Ireland. There, although we only learned this later, Lammas Sunday (the last of July) is also known as Bilberry Sunday, an occasion when these berries were gathered and festivities took place. In County Down there has been since prehistoric times a cairn where the "blaeberries" were picked and put into little rush baskets; a procedure which accompanied courting, ("many a lad met his wife on Blaeberry Sunday," they say).

WHORTLEBERRY is a puzzling name which bobs up here and there for various berries in this group. If it correctly applies to anything, it is probably to *V uliginosum*. The name also occurs in the form hurtleberry, supposedly because the purplish color of the berries is like that of bruises (hurts).

HUCKLEBERRY, *Gaylussacia baccata*, a name made familiar by Mark Twain's Huckleberry Finn, is as American as the hero of that book. The name is a corruption of hurtleberry, a version of whortleberry, applied to blueberries or bilberries; and the two sorts of plant grow in the same regions and are used in the same ways. However, the fruit of the huckleberry is different in structure. It is not a true berry, but a drupe, a fruit with a hard pit.

The black huckleberry, *G baccata*, is the most popular, but Fernald and Kinsey (1943) aver that the dangleberry, *G frondosa*, is just as good and will "make one of the most luscious of desserts, being remarkably juicy and with a rich, spicy and sweet flavor". The pits, however, make both species less attractive than the blueberry and they are not commercially gathered or cultivated.

Some blueberries are mistakenly called huckleberries: the red huckleberry, *Vaccinium parvifolium*, of the north-west; the squaw huckleberry, *V stamineum*, of the north; and the California huckleberry, *V ovatum*.

The **BEARBERRY**, *Arctostaphylos uva ursi* and other species of the same genus, is a low scrubby plant which grows wild in northern and Arctic regions of Europe, Asia and America. It provides dryish fruits which are eaten only in times of famine, or by bears. However, the berries of *A alpina*, the alpine bearberry, which are less dry and reasonably pleasant to eat, are consumed in Lapland and parts of Russia.

The **ARBUTUS**, or strawberry tree, *Arbutus unedo*, originated in the Mediterranean region. It grows up to 30 feet high, but is related to the lowly cranberry. It is cultivated chiefly for ornament, since it has attractive white flowers, shiny leaves and orange-red, strawberry-sized fruit. I picked and ate these in Apulia; quite refreshing, but somewhat acid and lacking in flavor.

48

Kaki,
American Persimmon, Date Plum

family EBENACEAE

Other Names for *KAKI / PERSIMMON*

French: *kaki, plaquemine*
German: *Kaki, Persimmon*
Spanish: *caqui*
Danish: *daddelblomme*
Swedish: *persimon(träd)*
Finnish: *kakiluumu, amerikanpersimoni*
Russian: *khurma*
Greek: *biospiros, trapexounia*
Turkish: *trabzon hurmasi*
Hebrew: *afarsemon*
Arabic: *kākī*
Persian: *kharmālū*
Chinese: *shi zi*
Japanese: *kaki*
Indonesian: *kesemak*

Minor Relations of the Persimmon

Oriental relatives of the kaki include *D blancoi*, a native of the Philippines or Malaysia which has been taken to other parts of South-East Asia and the West Indies. The fruit is known as "mabolo" or butter fruit. It is relatively large, hairy, brown or purplish red with a white pulp, and a pleasing flavor (do not be put off by the cheese-like smell from the skin).

Another persimmon native to America, *D texense*, known as the "chapote", or black or Mexican persimmon, has fruits which are small, hairy and black, sweet when ripe, but of little merit; and they leave an indelible black stain on everything they touch.

D digyna, native to Mexico, is another black persimmon, often called black sapote, but no relation of the true sapote. The fruit is round, about the size of an orange, ripens from a shiny green to a brownish green color and contains soft, dark brown flesh, mild and sweet.

Other Names for *DATE PLUM*

German: *Dattelpflaume*
Finnish: *taateliluumu*
Japanese: *shinanogaki*

Recipes

Persimmon Pudding: page 167
Persimmon and Rhubarb Jam: page 180

Key to the Painting

top and bottom: Kaki cultivars;
center: Sharon fruit and the small fruit of the date plum;
bottom: persimmon from South America

The **KAKI**, *Diospyros kaki*, belongs to China, Japan and Korea. Its introduction to the USA is credited to Commodore Perry in 1856. In Western countries it is often called the Chinese or Japanese or oriental persimmon.

The kaki fruit has many shapes (conical, round, flattened, or almost cubical), colors (yellow-orange to red, with a general resemblance to tomatoes) and sizes. The largest can weigh 1 pound. The thin skin encloses an orange-colored pulp within which there may or may not be seeds. A kaki, like other persimmons, may be sweet or highly astringent. The astringency is due to tannins which are normally present when the fruit is green and hard, but not in the flesh once it is ripe.

Americans regard the kaki as a fresh fruit to be eaten out of hand, or used in, for example, persimmon ice cream. In eastern Asia, however, the custom has been to dry them for storage and use during the winter and early spring. In this process the flesh turns blackish, and a fine coating of sugar develops on the surface. Dried and flattened fruits are known as pressed persimmons; these are packed in boxes in Japan, while in China they are often stored on cords. In China they are a particular favorite during the New Year celebration in February. The sugar is sometimes scraped from the surface of the dried kakis and compacted into molds to produce ornamental tablets, which couples engaged to be married present to friends from whom they have received wedding gifts; the tablets are also one of the eight comestibles offered with tea during the first course of Chinese banquets.

Cultivation of the kaki in the USA is confined to California. Seedless varieties are preferred. Whereas fruits with seeds ripen on the tree, often remaining there like lanterns long after the leaves have fallen, seedless ones can be picked while they are still hard, and then ripened by the use of ethylene gas (which can be done at home by placing unripe fruit in a lidded cardboard box with a ripening banana, which gives off the gas).

In Israel, an improved variety of kaki has been developed and is marketed under the name "sharon fruit". It is seedless, has no core and contains no tannin.

The **AMERICAN PERSIMMON**, *Diospyros virginiana*, is now little eaten, mainly because it has been eclipsed by the kaki. The name persimmon comes from "putchamin", a phonetic rendering of the name used by the Native Americans of the Algonquin tribe. They ate them when they were ripe and had fallen from the tree, and dried them to be eaten in the winter. Captain John Smith, in the 17th century, likened the fruit to the medlar, noting that: "if it be not ripe it will drawe a mans mouth awrie with much torment; but when it is ripe, it is as delicious as an Apricock."

A ripe American persimmon is usually yellowish pink or orange to red in color, but may be darker. In size it may be as small as a cherry or as large as a big plum. Its shape varies, and it may or may not contain seeds.

Artemas Ward (1923) having dismissed the old theory that a touch of frost is necessary if persimmons are to achieve perfection, observes that:

… the best types become veritable sugar-plums at maturity. Among commercial fruits they are exceeded in sugar content only by the date. Their sweetness has indeed earned for them the nickname of the American date-plum, and the oddly wrinkled lumps of richly concentrated sugar-flesh hanging among the varicolored leaves of autumn are as eagerly sought by possums and other wild creatures as by human beings.

The **DATE PLUM**, *Diospyros lotus,* a fruit which is related to neither the date nor the plum, but is closely akin to the American persimmon, grows from the Mediterranean as far east as Japan. The fruit is cherry-sized and yellowish brown to blue-black in color, simultaneously sweet and astringent, and of a pleasant flavor bearing some resemblance to that of dates.

Rhubarb/Pie-plant

family POLYGONACEAE

Other Names for *RHUBARB*

French: *rhubarbe*
German: *Rhabarber*
Italian: *rabarbaro*
Catalan: *ruibarbe*
Spanish / Portuguese: *ruibarbo*
Dutch: *rabarber*
Danish / Swedish: *rabarber*
Norwegian: *rabarbra*
Finnish: *raparperi*
Russian: *reven*
Polish: *rabarbar*
Hungarian: *rebarbarabor*
Romanian: *rubarbură*
Bulgarian: *reven*
Greek: *reon*
Serbo-Croat: *rabarbara*
Turkish: *ravent*
Hebrew: *ribas*
Arabic: *rawānd*
Persian: *rīwand*
Japanese: *daiō*

Recipes

Cumberland "Plate Cake": page 161
Rhubarb and Egg Tarts: page 162
Strawberry Rhubarb Crisp: page 164
Persimmon and Rhubarb Jam: page 180

Botanically, **RHUBARB** is not a fruit but a stem or leaf, so a vegetable; but the US Customs Court at Buffalo, NY, ruled in 1947 that it was a fruit, since that is how it is normally eaten. Very sensible, and that is why this "fruit" figures here. Rhubarb is mainly used for pies and similar dishes; hence it is also known as pie-plant. But it is also an ingredient for jams, usually mixed ones such as rhubarb and ginger jam. Orange and angelica are alternative companions.

Wild rhubarbs, *Rheum* species in the buckwheat family, flourish in regions such as the south of Siberia and the Himalayas. The rhizomes and crowns from which the leaf-bearing stalks grow survive readily in ground which is frozen during the winter.

Several species are inedible, or have only medical uses. The ones of interest in the kitchen are *R rhaponticum* and *R hybridum*, which belong to places like Mongolia and Siberia, and a species of the Near East, *R ribes*, which was probably the one known in classical times.

The Greek writer Dioscorides stated that the plant, "rha" in classical Greek, grew in the regions beyond the Bosphorus, inhabited by barbarians; for this reason it was subsequently styled "rha ponticum" or "rha barbarum" (the latter term being the origin of the word rhubarb).

It seems that the Chinese did not know rhubarb until relatively late in their history, since they call it by composite and descriptive names, such as "ta hwan" (the great yellow one); whereas all the plants they knew from ancient times have a root word of a single syllable. However, by about 200 BC, they certainly knew what is called Chinese rhubarb, *R officinale*, and valued it medicinally. It later became an important article of trade from China to western Asia, and to the Arab countries.

Rhubarb, with a reputation for medical rather than culinary use, seems to have reached England in the 16th century. Although the types introduced were edible, it was a long time before people thought of eating the stem. Ray, in his *Historia Plantarum* (1686), gave a lead when he compared rhubarb stalks favorably with those of the familiar sorrel. But the first recipe did not appear until 1783, when John Farley *(The London Art of Cookery)* advocated slicing the stalks and then cooking them like gooseberries. Recipes for sweet pies and tarts followed in the early 19th century; the first author to offer a whole range of rhubarb recipes was Mrs Beeton (1861), who had two rhubarb jams, rhubarb pudding, and rhubarb tart – plus rhubarb wine. The fact that rhubarb can be forced and will provide a "fruit" out of season helped to increase its popularity during Victorian times.

Rhubarb was hardly known in the USA until about 1820. Cultivation began in New England but has since shifted to the States of Washington, Oregon, Michigan, California and New York. Utica in Michigan has styled itself "rhubarb capital of the world", a bold declaration which raises eyebrows among the clan of rhubarb growers near Sheffield in England, whose boast it is that if you lurk at night in their black plastic tunnels, which hug the low Yorkshire hills, you can literally hear the rhubarb growing, as the leaves unfurl.

The forcing of rhubarb is done either by covering the plant with a pot to encourage early growth in the spring or by the modern method of hothouse cultivation. The practice has been observed in Afghanistan as well as in Western countries, where it was accidentally discovered at the Chelsea Physic Garden early in the 19th century. In Britain the best and sweetest variety, Hawkes Champagne, comes very early and has thin, tender stalks. By comparison, the unforced summer rhubarb is coarse and sour.

The purgative principle in rhubarb is a group of substances allied to chrysophanic acid and is present mainly in the root. The stalks contain oxalic acid, which is harmful if eaten to excess, but the amounts are no greater than those present in familiar vegetables such as spinach and chard. The central ribs of the leaves contain more, and should not be eaten.

Key to the Painting
the variety shown is Hawke's Champagne

Kiwi, Cornelian Cherry, Akebia

family ACTINIDIACEAE

Other Names for *KIWI*

French: *kiwi; souris végétale* (vegetable mouse)
German: *Kiwi*
Italian / Spanish: *kiwi*
Swedish: *kiwi(frukt)*
Finnish: *kiivi(hedelmä)*
Chinese: *qi wei guo*
Japanese: *kīwī furūtsu*

family CORNACEAE

Other Names for *CORNELIAN CHERRY*

French: *cornouille*
German: *Kornelkirsche*
Italian: *corniola*
Danish: *kornel*
Norwegian / Swedish: *kornell*
Finnish: *kanukka*
Turkish: *kizilcik*
Japanese: *seiyō sanshō*

family LARDIZABALACEAE

Other Names for *AKEBIA*

Japanese: *akebi*

Recipes

Exotic Crème Brûlée: page 165
Pistachio Ice Cream: page 172
Kiwi Fruit and Pineapple Jam: page 179

The **KIWI** fruit has an alternative name: Chinese gooseberry. This suggests a double origin. In fact, although it was first grown commercially on a large scale in New Zealand, it originated in eastern Asia, where several species of *Actinidia* grow wild.

Seeds of *Actinidia chinensis* from the Yangtze valley were taken to New Zealand early in the 20th century, and commercial cultivation began in the 1930s. The fruits ripen slowly after being picked, and keep well, so could be exported to Europe. The first shipment reached England in 1953. When nouvelle cuisine blossomed in France and elsewhere, the kiwi fruit quickly assumed a star role as an exotic, decorative ingredient in fruit salads and in many other dishes besides; the thin slices which can be cut from it to serve as a garnish had already become a cliché by the 1970s. Once kiwi fruits had become popular in Europe and North America, growers in the South of France and California began to cultivate them in competition with New Zealand. A mystery to which Jane Grigson drew attention is why the Chinese have never perceived the culinary potential of this fruit, but have treated it in the main as a tonic for growing children.

The fruit, which is the size of a large egg, has a thin skin, brown and hairy on the outside (although there is a kind, indeed a separate species according to some botanists, with a smooth skin). Inside is a firm, green pulp containing tiny, black, edible seeds. The taste is sweet and slightly acid.

Kiwi fruit are rich in vitamin C, ten times more than the equal weight of lemons would be. They also contain an enzyme similar to that in papaya or pineapple, which has a tenderizing effect on meat.

The **CORNELIAN CHERRY**, bright red and sometimes as large as a small plum, is the fruit borne by *Cornus mas*, one of the small trees or shrubs which are generally known as dogwoods. The flavor is acid and slightly bitter. The fruit was formerly used in Western Europe to make pies, sauces, and confectionery; or pickled.

It is in Turkey that the fruits (called "kizilcik") are most prominent. Evelyn Kalças (1974), after saying how much she likes their tartness and the flavor of jam or jelly made from them, tells the tale recorded below. She also observes, as evidence of the use of the tree in antiquity, that the famous and un-untieable Gordian knot was formed from a thong of its leathery bark. (Alexander the Great, acquainted with the problem, drew his sword and severed the knot, then went on to fulfil the prophecy that whoever could unfasten it would conquer the world.)

In the fascinating Turkish legend about this fruit, it seems that when Seytan – the Devil – first saw the kizilcik tree covered with blossoms when no other fruit showed even a bud, he said to himself: "Aha! This tree will produce fruit first of all. I must be first there to secure it." So he gathered up his scales and basket and took up his position under the tree. He waited and waited, but all other fruit trees came into bloom and fruit formed on them. Still the kizilcik fruit was not ready and ripe for eating. Seytan was patient, but he wondered what had happened. Then to his great surprise he discovered that this was one of the very last fruits to ripen at the end of summer, so his chagrin was great. Ever since then the Turks have called the tree "Şeytan alditan ağaci" – the tree that deceived Satan.

AKEBIA is the name of the fruit of either of two climbing shrubs in the genus *Akebia*. All belong to China, Korea and Japan. Although appreciated in their native region, the fruits are rarely cultivated. Each tree produces clusters of one, two or three greyish or bluish purple pendent fruits resembling small bananas in shape. Those of *A trifoliata* may reach a length of 5 inches. They burst open when ripe to reveal semi-transparent flesh and numerous black seeds. The flesh, which has only a faint flavor, and the skin, are both edible. The fruit is often mentioned in Japanese literature, where it is evocative of pastoral settings.

Key to the Painting

top and bottom: kiwi fruit;
center: akebia;
small red fruits: cornelian cherries

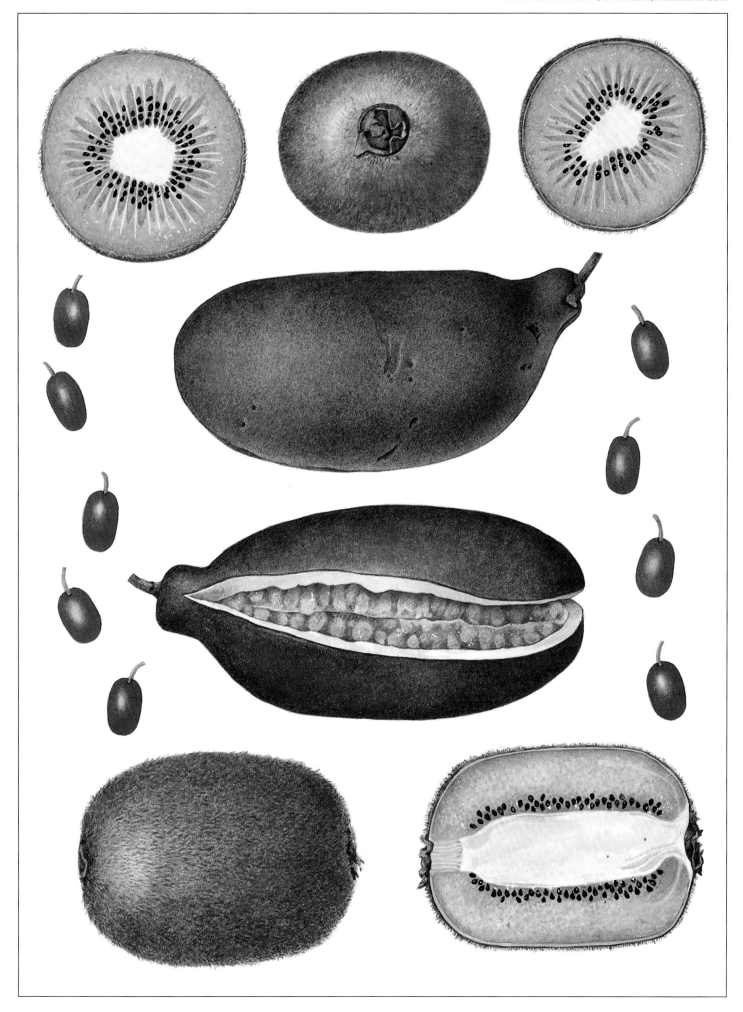

Fig

family MORACEAE

Other Names for *FIG*

French: *figue*
German: *Feige*
Italian: *fico*
Spanish: *higo*
Portuguese: *figo*
Danish: *figen*
Norwegian: *fiken*
Swedish: *fikon*
Finnish: *viikuna*
Russian: *inzhir*
Polish: *figa*
Serbo-Croat: *smokva*
Romanian: *smochină*
Bulgarian: *smokinya*
Greek: *sükon*
Turkish: *incir*
Hebrew: *te'ena*
Arabic: *tīn*
Persian: *anjir*
Hindi: *anjir*
Indonesian: *ara*
Chinese: *wu hua guo*
Japanese: *ichijiku*

Main Types of Fig

Smyrna (or **Calimyrna**) **Figs** are much like those cultivated in Asia Minor more than 2,000 years ago. The name derives from Izmir in Turkey. The Spanish variety Turon belongs to this group. Smyrna figs are large, amber in color both inside and out, and have the excellent nutty flavor which is characteristic of fertilized figs. They are among the best figs to eat fresh, but are often dried.

Common Figs are grown mainly for eating fresh or for canning. The Mission or Franciscana figs are a deep purple black outside and red inside. The texture is coarse but the flavor good. "Cadota" figs (Dottato in Italy) are usually eaten fresh, but may be canned: yellow-green outside, and amber or violet inside.

The **San Pedro** or **San Pietro Figs** now grown less than the Smyrna or common types, are intermediate in flavor.

Caprifigs or **Wild Figs** are cultivated for breeding purposes; but one variety, named for the French town Croisic, produces an unusually succulent fruit.

Recipes

Fresh Figs with Raspberry Cream: page 153
Koshaf (Iranian Dried Fruit Salad): page 155

Key to the Painting

above: White Ischia figs; below: a black fig from Turkey

For those of us who can sympathize with insects, the history of the **FIG** is one of the most pathetic chapters in natural history. Let me explain.

The original fig, called caprifig, came to the Mediterranean from western Asia. As Aristotle noticed in the 4th century BC, its structure is complex. The fig is botanically not a single fruit but almost 1,500 tiny fruits, which are normally what are thought of as the seeds. It belongs to the same family as the mulberry and the breadfruit, which are also multiple fruits, but differs from them in having its fruits fixed to the inside of a vase-shaped structure, termed syconium, which is the outer part of the fig. Earlier, at the flower stage, the syconium is the same shape but much smaller. It is closed except for a tiny hole at the opposite end from the stem.

The syconium contains both male and female flowers, but these are unable to fertilize each other because the female flowers mature some time before the male flowers produce pollen. However, nature has provided a solution to this impasse, in the form of the fig wasp, a tiny, gnat-sized insect, which inhabits the syconium. Only the female wasp has wings. She develops over the winter inside a female flower, and is impregnated by the male in the spring. She then crawls around the inside of the syconium, thus becoming covered with pollen from the male flowers which surround it, until she finds the way out through the little hole. She leaves and flies to another syconium which, with luck, will be at an earlier stage and contain fertile female flowers. Entering it through its little hole, she finds a female flower and lays her eggs down its style, ready to produce another generation of wasps. But the other female flowers nearby are pollinated as the wasp brushes against them, and will form fertile seeds.

The caprifig produces three crops of figs a year by this process. But it is usually a waste of time for the wasp, since even after she has forced her way through the hole, tearing off her wings in the process, she finds that the female flowers have styles too long for her to be able to push her eggs all the way into them. Wingless, frustrated, she perishes.

Early cultivated figs, which date back to Homeric times in Greece and even further in Egypt, were all of what is now called the Smyrna type. At the end of the BC period a new kind of fig appeared which formed its fruits parthenocarpically, that is, without the need for fertilization. The little internal true fruits are much the same to look at, but contain no true seeds. There is also an intermediate form, now called San Pietro in Italy and San Pedro in the USA, which produces its first crop by itself but needs to be caprified for the second.

A much more important variety, which also emerged in classical times, is what is now called the common fig, which produces two crops, neither of which needs to be caprified. Thus freed from the need to be accompanied by the fig wasp (which could not stand cooler climates), the fig began to spread northwards, reaching Britain in the first half of the 16th century. During the same period it arrived in North America, where it later found a real home from home in California. In 1769 the Franciscan mission at San Diego was founded and began to grow a Spanish black common fig which, under the names of Mission, Black Mission, or Franciscana, is still one of the leading varieties.

In the warm countries where the fig grows easily it is a cheap and staple food. Elsewhere fresh figs are a luxury and the fruit is better known in its dried form, whose characteristics are quite different.

Dried figs can be eaten as they are, or used in many other ways, for example in figgy pudding and for fig Newtons, which were first advertised in 1892 and named after the town of Newton in Massachusetts.

Mulberry

family MORACEAE

Other Names for *MULBERRY*

French: *mûre*
German: *Maulbeere*
Italian: *mora*
Spanish: *mora*
Portuguese: *amoreira*
Danish / Norwegian: *morbær*
Swedish: *mullbär*
Finnish: *mulperi*
Russian: *shelkovitsa, tutovaya yagoda*
Polish: *morwa*
Serbo-Croat: *dud, murva*
Romanian: *dudă*
Bulgarian: *chernitsa*
Greek: *moran, mouro*
Turkish: *dut*
Hebrew: *tut*
Arabic: *tūt aswad*
Persian: *tūt*
Indonesian: *bebesaran*
Chinese: *sang shen*
Japanese: *kuwa*

Recipes

Cranachan (Soft Fruit Browse): page 154
Summer Pudding: page 157
Raspberry Buckle: page 164
Marjapuuro (Whipped Berry Oatmeal): page 171
Berry Sherbet: page 174

If, in our egotistical way, we suppose that it was for human beings, plus perhaps some pretty birds and the fruit-eating bats, that God created fruits, we have to allow one exception: the **MULBERRY** was clearly His gift to the silkworm, which will eat nothing else. The one preferred by the worms, and cultivated in China for their benefit for at least 5,000 years, is *Morus alba*, the white mulberry.

The black mulberry, *M nigra*, probably originated in the mountains of Nepal or the Caucasus and is the species whose fruits are preferred by human beings. It came to Europe a long time ago, and it was probably the Romans who introduced it to Britain, as well as to France and Spain. Since a tree can live for over 600 years (the mulberry planted when the Drapers' Hall in London was built, in 1364, lived until 1969) and comes true from seed, Roman introductions would have survived until Anglo-Saxon times and beyond – although the first mentions by English authors seem to be of the 16th century.

The Romans showed themselves true connoisseurs of mulberries, preferring those from certain districts, such as Ostia, to others, and studying the behaviour of the trees. It was a Roman writer, Pliny the Elder, who first remarked on the curious combination of caution and impulsiveness which they exhibit: "of all the cultivated trees the mulberry is the last to bud, which it never does until the cold weather is past: but when it begins to put forth buds, it despatches the business in one night, and that with so much force that their breaking forth may be clearly heard." (The rhubarb, page 50, is the other audible grower.)

The mulberry tree is of medium size and attractively untidy in appearance. Although the fruit superficially resembles a blackberry, it is a different type of growth: a cluster of small berries, each with an individually lobed surface and each formed from one of a cluster of flowers. The fruit must be allowed to ripen fully before being gathered. Then, rather than being picked, it is allowed to fall off the tree, for which reason the tree is generally planted on grassy ground (and sometimes surrounded, when the season arrives, by a drop-cloth). A ripe mulberry is soft and easily damaged. Its purple juice readily stains the face and hands of the eater; hence Jane Grigson's advice that women who go mulberry gathering should wear purple dresses. (I never told her this, but I wear special purple trousers from California when I go annually to the Chelsea Physic Garden to crouch on the gravel path and collect the fruits which have fallen from their 300-year old tree.) Until comparatively recent times there were many trees in England which dated back to the 17th century, since that was when James I, in a fit of enthusiasm for rearing silkworms, sponsored plantations of mulberry trees. The yield was enough to make one dress for his Queen, whereupon anxious representations made by silk importers caused the king to desist from his experiments, while leaving the trees in place. A fine orchard of them covered the ground on which Buckingham Palace now stands; and Mulberry Garden, as it was known, was a fashionable rendezvous.

The white mulberry, the one whose leaves are for silkworms, bears fruits which are not always white (they may be white, pink, or purple). These are much less good than the black ones but are eaten in Asia.

Other mulberries native to Asia and the Americas have edible fruits, but only those of the red mulberry, *M rubra*, in the eastern USA, stand comparison with the black mulberry. The black mulberry itself is naturalized in the USA as a garden tree, but cannot withstand winter in the north.

For the cook, mulberries may be treated like the blackberries which they superficially resemble. The highest authorities all urge that they be eaten fresh with cream, and that is no doubt the best way; but it is worth knowing that they combine very well with other fruits, such as ripe pears; and that they can be made into a pudding or compote.

Key to the Painting

black mulberries with leaves and, bottom right, a white mulberry

Jujube, Indian Jujube

family RHAMNACEAE

Other Names for *JUJUBE*

French: *jujube*
German: *Jujube, indische Brustbeere*
Italian: *giuggiola*
Portuguese: *jujuba*
Danish: *jødetorn*
Swedish: *bröstbärsträd, jujub*
Finnish: *kiinanjujuba; intiaanijujuba*
Russian: *yuyuba*
Polish: *jujuba, chiński daktyl*
Serbo-Croat: *jujub, čičimak*
Romanian: *jujubă*
Bulgarian: *hinap*
Greek: *zhizhifon*
Turkish: *hünnap*
Hindi: *ber*
Malay: *medara*
Chinese: *zao*
Japanese: *natsume*

Here we have a fruit which is of real importance in Asia, yet little known in the West, although its juice was formerly used for making lozenges to alleviate chest complaints. Because of this the word jujube has acquired another meaning: "a confection, sweetmeat, or medicated lozenge, round, oblong, or square in shape", as Law's Grocers' Manual of *c* 1895 put it, explaining that such jujubes are made with gum Arabic or other gums, not with the true jujube fruits.

The **JUJUBE** or Chinese date, *Zizyphus jujuba*, is a small spiny tree which originated in China and which grows in mild-temperate, dry areas of both hemispheres and is cultivated in China, Japan, Afghanistan, Iran, and westwards to the Mediterranean region for its fruits.

Generally, the fruits are candied, but may also be eaten fresh. "Ripe jujubes, when eaten raw, are amusing rather than delicious, and have a crisp, sprightly flavor different from other fruits." Thus David Fairchild (1938) who recalled meeting them for the first time in candied form on a boat leaving Shanghai. The long, pointed seeds and caramel-like texture reminded him of the dried dates which he had eaten in the Persian Gulf region, but he knew they were not true dates and was puzzled by the scratches he saw on their surface. Later, the mystery was solved when he was sent one of the scoring knives with which the Chinese slash the tough skins of the fruit before stewing them in honey or sugar syrup. He recommended the honeyed kind.

Although Fairchild was impressed by the way in which the jujube stood up to adverse climatic conditions, and sought to popularize the fruit by having it served at a National Geographic Society dinner, it has not been introduced as a commercial fruit to North America. Its potential for successful commercial cultivation is limited by the fact that it does not ripen when picked green; nor do the fruits ripen simultaneously.

Popenoe (1932) emphasized the superiority of Chinese jujubes over those from other regions. Many fine specimens had been sent to him in the USA by Meyer. He quotes Meyer as his authority for a list of uses. "The fresh fruits of some varieties are excellent to eat out of hand. Dried, they resemble dates in character. Jujubes are sometimes boiled with millet and rice; they may be stewed or baked in the oven; they are used, raisin-fashion, to make jujube-bread; and they are turned into glacé fruits . . ." He could have added that they are featured, along with red bean paste, raisins and other ingredients, in the well known Chinese dish called Eight Treasure Rice Pudding.

The **INDIAN JUJUBE**, *Z mauritiana*, adapted to warmer climates, is grown commercially only in India, and is less good. The species *Z lotus* is less good again, and is only mentioned because it has sometimes been supposed to be what Homer's famed lotus-eaters ate on the Island of Djerba, the fruit which tasted of honey and wiped out memory, leaving the consumer in a state of perpetual languor. This is an implausible idea if ever there was one. As de Candolle (1886) remarks: "[The lotus-eaters] must have been very poor or very temperate, for a berry the size of a small cherry, tasteless, or slightly sweet, would not satisfy ordinary men." (The same author suggests, with some severity, that as we are dealing here with legend rather than history, it is probably impossible to establish the "facts" of the matter; but that the best, or anyway least feeble, theory is that the lotus fruits were those of the carob tree.)

Key to the Painting

various jujubes with Chinese jujube leaves (bottom right to top left) and the darker leaves of the Indian jujube

Pepino, Tree Tomato,
Naranjilla, Garden Huckleberry

family SOLANACEAE

Other Names for *PEPINO*

The name "pepino", which is Spanish for cucumber, seems to be universal, with slight variations of spelling or added epithets ("pepino dulce": sweet cucumber). But this name is also used in parts of South America for the cassabanana (page 80).

Other Names for *NARANJILLA*

Mexico: *lulun*
Ecuador: *naranjilla de Quito*
Colombia: *toronjo*

**Other Names for
*TREE-TOMATO***

French: *tomate d'arbre*
German: *Baum-Tomate*
Spanish: *tomate arbol*
Portuguese: *tomateiro-da-serra*
Finnish: *puutomaatti*
Central America and Mexico: *tomate*
Japanese: *kodachitomato*

Key to the Painting

top: garden huckleberry (left and right) with naranjilla (center);
center: pepino;
bottom: tree tomato;
the leaves and flowers are of the tree tomato

Here we have a miscellany of fruits of minor, but possibly increasing, importance. Each resembles, more or less, something more familiar: the cucumber or melon, the tomato, the orange. All belong to the nightshade family.

The **PEPINO** is the fruit of *Solanum muricatum*, a small bush which is native to temperate Andean areas of Peru and Chile and cultivated elsewhere in Central and South America. One variety, Rio Barba, is vine-like and its fruits resemble small cucumbers, thus justifying the name ("pepino" means "cucumber" in Spanish). However, since the pepino is usually more like a melon, it is often called pepino melon or melon pear.

Efforts to promote the pepino as a commercial crop in California during the 1920s were unsuccessful, but it has since been been brought into cultivation in Australia and New Zealand.

A typical fruit is about 3 inches in diameter near the stem end, and 5 inches long. The flavor is mild, but it makes an effective, albeit unassertive, partner for other fruits in fruit salads. Elizabeth Schneider (1986) describes it thus:

> It is as refreshing as a summer cucumber. Its sleek skin, which has a golden ground that is dappled or striated with mauve or violet, is as flawless and satiny as that of eggplant; its shape can also resemble an eggplant's – as can its sometimes bitter aftertaste. The yellow-to-gold pulp compares to the finest-textured and juiciest melon – although it is much less sweet, while its aroma suggests a perfumed Bartlett pear blended with vanilla and honey.

The **TREE TOMATO**, *Cyphomandra betacea*, resembles the tomato, but grows in bushes at high altitudes in tropical and subtropical zones. It was first cultivated by Peruvian Indians, but is now found elsewhere, in India, Sri Lanka, Malaysia, East Africa and California for example. It is also found in New Zealand, which is important because the New Zealanders, flushed by their success in bestowing the name kiwi on the Chinese gooseberry and making it stick, decided that the tree tomato should be called tamarillo, as it now widely is. In both instances the new name seems to me to be an improvement.

The fruits, 2 inches long, with their smooth reddish-yellow skin, are borne in clusters of three or more. The succulent red or yellow pulp surrounds black seeds. The flavor is rich and sweet, allayed by some acidity. The dark red strain called "black" is the most popular for fruit markets, but the yellow strain is considered best for preserving because of its superior flavor.

The **NARANJILLA**, *Solanum quitoense*, is another edible member of the nightshade family. Its name indicates its resemblance to a little orange.

The shrub is believed to be indigenous to Ecuador, Peru and Colombia, where it is grown commercially, chiefly for the production of juice, although the fruit is pleasant to eat. The brown hairy coat which covers it rubs off easily.

The fruit can grow up to $2\frac{1}{2}$ inches across, and splits into four sections divided by membranes. The pulp is yellowish green and has an acidly sweet taste, some say like that of a pineapple and a lemon. It has many tiny, flat seeds.

There are several wild relatives of the naranjilla; and there is one similar plant, *S sessiliflorum*, the cocona, also sometimes called tupiro or Orinoco apple. Its habit resembles that of the naranjilla, but it bears quite a different fruit. This has cream-colored flesh surrounding a jelly-like yellow pulp.

The so-called **GARDEN HUCKLEBERRY** is not a huckleberry, but *Solanum intrusum*, another nightshade plant. The smooth blue-black berries occur in bunches and may be used in place of blueberries; but the flavor is lacking, at least in those I tasted. Superior varieties may emerge.

Cape Gooseberry, Chinese Lantern, Tomatillo, Ground Cherry

family SOLANACEAE

Other Names for *CAPE GOOSEBERRY*

French: *coqueret du Péron*
German: *Kapstachelbeere, Goldbeere*
Spanish: *uvilla, membrillo*
Finnish: *karviaskirsikka, ananaskirsikka*
Indian languages: *rashari* (Hindi); *tepari* (Bengali)
Philippines: *lobolohoban*
Japanese: *shima hōzuki*
Hawaii: *poha*
Peru / Bolivia: *capuli*
Ecuador / Colombia: *uvilla*
Venezuela: *topotopo, chuchuva*
Chile: *capuli, bolsa de amor*
Mexico: *cereza del Peru*
South Africa: *golden berry, pompeloes, apelliefie*
Réunion: *poc-poc*

Other Names for *CHINESE LANTERN*

These are fewer, and most of them translate as winter cherry, while others are just translations of Chinese lantern.

Other Names for *TOMATILLO*

There are various names in Latin America: tomate verde / Mexicano / de fresadilla / de cáscara / de culebra; and miltomate.
  The fruit may also be known under variety names, such as Mayan husk tomato, Rendidora, and (a yellow-fruited variety) Golden Nugget Cape Gooseberry.

Physalis fruits all come gift-wrapped. The fruit is enclosed in an outer, papery thin calyx or husk, which has given rise to names like Chinese lantern.

The cape in the name **CAPE GOOSEBERRY**, *Physalis peruviana*, is the Cape of Good Hope. Although the fruit is thought to be a native of Peru and Chile, it enjoyed an early vogue in South Africa, whence it traveled to Australia and New Zealand. It has been introduced to many other countries, including India, Sri Lanka, China and Malaysia. It is now widely known by the Hawaiian name "poha", since it is cultivated and eaten with especial enthusiasm by the Hawaiians.
  The calyx is cream in color. The fruit is about the size of a cherry, yellow-green or orange, with a thin, waxy skin; and its juicy pulp contains many small seeds. The flavor is distinctive and pleasant, and the fruits may be eaten raw or used like strawberries in shortcake desserts. They make a good jam, but do not have enough pectin to make a jelly.

The **CHINESE LANTERN**, *Physalis alkekengi*, a plant commonly grown for decorative purposes, has edible berries. Like many of its relations, it has a whole string of other common names including strawberry tomato, bladder cherry, winter cherry, and sometimes ground cherry (but see below).
  The calyx does indeed look like a red Chinese paper lantern and is slightly toxic, but the berry within, which is also red, is perfectly edible. Its flavor is slightly acid, but pleasant when the fruit is fully ripe. It can be eaten fresh, but is usually cooked to make sauces and preserves.

The **TOMATILLO**, *Physalis ixocarpa*, is another plant of many names, most of which reflect the resemblance between its fruit and that of a true tomato in the green state. Tomatillo means little tomato, apt because its size is usually no more than 1 inch across.
  The tomatillo has the usual *Physalis* structure. As the fruit develops, the calyx enlarges and becomes straw colored and papery. This husk is so tight fitting that it often bursts. The fruit itself is thin-skinned, and when ripe may vary in color from green to yellow, or purple. The flesh is pale yellow, crisp or soft; acid, sweet or insipid; and contains many tiny seeds.
  Other names for the tomatillo include green tomato, since it remains green even when ripe; husk tomato; and sometimes Spanish tomato, not because it is known in Spain, but because it grows in Mexico. A better name is Mexican husk tomato; the plant was a prominent staple in the Aztec and Mayan economies.
  Elisabeth Lambert Ortiz (1979) writes: "The green tomato is very important in Mexican, and to a lesser extent Guatemalan, cooking, giving a distinctive flavor to the 'green' dishes and sauces. The flavor is delicate and slightly acid."
  The tomatillo fruits well in Queensland, Australia, and in South Africa. It was introduced into India in the 1950s and is used there to make a sweet chutney. The name jamberry, introduced in 1945 to promote sales in the USA, speaks for itself; but Cape gooseberry jam is considered to be better.

GROUND CHERRY is a name applied to various plants, especially *P pruinosa*, which all bear fruits about the size of a cherry in a papery husk. Of the many kinds in North America, the culinary writers Cora, Rose and Bob Brown (1938) observed:
  There's a lot of confusion about these homely little bundles of luscious flavor that grow about the size of cranberries, each enclosed in a tissue husk that looks like a Chinese lantern. Some say they taste like cherries, others like tomatoes. We've eaten them ever since we were kids and don't yet know which they resemble most. When preserved in syrup they taste like figs.

Key to the Painting

Among the scattered Cape gooseberries are:
top: four orange Chinese lanterns;
center: green tomatillos;
bottom: Cape gooseberries in their husks

Grapefruit, Pomelo, Ugli

family RUTACEAE

Other Names for *GRAPEFRUIT*

French: *pamplemousse*
German: *Pampelmuse*
Italian: *pompelmo*
Spanish: *pomelo*
Portuguese: *toranja*
Danish: *grapefrugt*
Norwegian: *grapefrukt*
Swedish: *grapefrukt*
Finnish: *greippi*
Russian / Polish: *grepfrut*
Serbo-Croat / Romanian: *grep(frut)*
Bulgarian: *grejpfrout*
Greek: *frapa*
Turkish: *altintap*
Hebrew: *eshkolit*
Persian: *tūsorkh*
Chinese: *pu tao you*

Etymological Note on Pomelo

The origin of the name can be traced back to the Malay word "pumpulmas". This became the Dutch "pompelmoes", which the English then blurred to pomelo (sometimes spelled pummelo). One charming old English name, closer to the Dutch, was pimplenose.

Other Names for *POMELO*

French: *pamplemousse*
German: *Pompelmuse*
Spanish: *toronja*
Portuguese: *toranja*
Danish: *pompelmus*
Finnish: *pummelo*
Arabic: *kabbād*
Indian languages: *chakotra* (Hindi);
Batabi lemu (Bengali); *bombilimas*
(Tamil)
Chinese: *you zi*
Japanese: *buntan, zabon*
Malay: *limau abong, limau Bali*
Indonesian: *jeruk Bali*
Philippines: *suha*

Tip for the Cook

An easy way, recommended by Jane Grigson, to remove the inner skin from a whole grapefruit: take off the peel, then leave the whole peeled fruit in the refrigerator for a day or two, after which the white skin will be stiff and easy to remove.

Recipe

Citrus Sherbet: page 174

Key to the Painting

top left and section below: ugli;
top right: section of Marsh White grapefruit;
bottom left: section of Ruby Red grapefruit;
right center and below: pomelo;
leaves are grapefruit leaves

The **GRAPEFRUIT**, *Citrus paradisi*, is the refined descendant of a bigger and rougher fruit, the pomelo or shaddock. It is something of a newcomer in the citrus family, having first been mentioned by Griffith Hughes (1750), as the "forbidden fruit" of Barbados. Around 1820 a French botanist wrote that he had observed in the botanical garden of Jamaica:

> ...a variety of shaddock whose fruits, which are not bigger than a fair orange, are disposed in clusters [French "grappes"]; the English in Jamaica call this the "forbidden fruit" or "smaller shaddock".

It may be the clustering habit which gave the new fruit the name grapefruit.

The grapefruit was introduced to Florida in 1823 by a French Count, Odette Phillippe, but was slow to achieve popularity. Towards the end of the 19th century, however, the industry had begun growing to its present large size. Cultivation spread to California, Arizona, Texas and then abroad. Israel, Argentina, and South Africa are now major producers.

There are two main varieties of grapefruit: Duncan, which has a lot of seeds but a good flavor, and Marsh, which is seedless but has less flavor. Duncan is a direct descendant from a seed planted by Phillippe, and is the variety used for canning. In 1907 a pink form of Duncan was found, and in 1913 a pink Marsh appeared. The latter is the ancestor of all the pink grapefruits grown today.

About half of the world grapefruit crop is made into juice. The flavor of grapefruit juice is less impaired by processing than those of other citrus fruits. The fruit itself is better used as an appetizer or fruit than in cooking, since its flavor is assertive. However, grapefruits make good marmalade.

The **POMELO** (or shaddock), *Citrus maxima*, the ancestor of the grapefruit, is still widely grown and eaten, and still grows wild in the region of Malaysia and Indonesia, where it probably originated.

A large pomelo is bigger than any other citrus fruit, measuring up to 1 foot in diameter. Much of its bulk is taken up by the thick and loose skin.

The pomelo spread westwards in the wake of other, more prized, citrus fruits. Arabs took it to Spain, where it is still cultivated on a small scale; but the European climate is generally too cool for it.

It was probably in the mid 17th century that it was introduced to the West Indies (where citrus cultivation was already well established) and acquired the alternative name shaddock. (Sir Hans Sloane asserted that the fruit had first been taken to Barbados by a Captain Shaddock, but the matter is doubtful.) It seems clear that it was in the West Indies that it developed into the thinner-skinned and juicier grapefruit. Whether this was the result of a mutation or of a hybridization between the pomelo and the sweet orange is not known.

The pomelo, whose flesh separates readily into segments, is usually eaten fresh.

The **UGLI**, unkindly named, is of Jamaican origin. It belongs to the category of citrus fruits called tangelos, which are mandarin × grapefruit hybrids, but is markedly different from either parent. It may weigh over 2 pounds, but much of it consists in a thick, baggy skin. The skin has a pulled up appearance at the top, like a kitten picked up by the scruff of the neck. Despite its thickness, it is easily peeled and has a fine fragrance of citron. The segments of flesh separate freely like those of the pomelo, but have a different flavor, more like that of a mandarin, with faint overtones of honey or pineapple.

Another large citrus fruit which is usually classified as a tangelo, the "New Zealand grapefruit" or "poorman orange", has the shape and size of a grapefruit, but is more orange in color and slightly less acid. It may really be a mandarin × pomelo hybrid. Whatever the truth about its origin, it is used like the grapefruit in New Zealand, where it is the leading citrus fruit on the market.

Oranges: Sweet, Bitter, Blood, Navel

family RUTACEAE

Other Names for *ORANGE*

French: *orange*
German: *Apfelsine, Orange*
Italian: *arancia*
Spanish: *naranja*
Portuguese: *laranja*
Danish / Norwegian: *appelsin*
Swedish: *apelsin*
Finnish: *appelsiini*
Russian: *apelsin*
Polish: *pomarańcza*
Serbo-Croat: *naranča*
Bulgarian: *portokal*
Greek: *portokáli*
Turkish: *portakal; turunç* (bitter *)*
Hebrew: *tapuz*
Arabic: *burtuqāl; naranj* (bitter *)*
Persian: *porteghal; nāranj* (bitter *)*
Indian languages: *narangi* (Hindi);
kamala lebu (Bengali); *sangtar*
(Kashmiri)
Indonesian: *jeruk*
Philippines: *dalanda*
Chinese: *tian cheng*
Japanese: *orenji; kan* (general term);
dai-dai (bitter)

Some Less Important Kinds of Orange

Acidless, or sugar, oranges are a freak variety which enjoys a small popularity in Brazil, North America and Italy.

Bergamot oranges are a special variety of bitter oranges grown in Calabria and Sicily for making fragrant bergamot oil, which is mainly used in perfumery. They are inedible, but the peel can be candied.

Tip for the Cook

The numerous delightful ways in which sweet oranges can be used for dessert dishes are well known. But remember that for most savory dishes the juice of bitter oranges is a better ingredient, and that, although their season is short, the juice can be frozen in cubes and kept for use throughout the year.

Recipes

Orange Medley: page 152
Strawberries with Orange: page 155
Orange and Almond Dessert Cake: page 168
Hot Orange Soufflé: page 169
Citrus Sherbet: page 174
My Marmalade: page 179
Canadian Peach Marmalade: page 178

Key to the Painting

top left and section: Moro, a blood orange;
top right: Seville orange with section behind;
center: Shamouti, the Jaffa orange, with section behind;
lower left: Valencia Late, with section below;
lower right: section of Washington Navel with whole fruit behind

The sweet **ORANGE**, most popular of the citrus fruits, originated in China, as its botanical name, *Citrus sinensis*, suggests. Indeed there were probably two kinds of wild orange in southern China, the other being *C aurantium*, predecessor of our bitter (Seville) oranges.

Oranges seem to have been first used for the fragrance of their peel; early Chinese documents mention them being held in the hand so that the warmth released their scent. Mandarin oranges were then the citrus fruits commonly eaten.

Meanwhile, during the first centuries AD, the orange began to spread beyond China, as the citron had done earlier: to Japan, India, the Near East and the classical world. In the 1st century AD the Romans became interested in the fruit, and the Arabs later spread it as far as Spain. But, except for Spain, where both orange and Arabs remained, the fall of the Roman empire obliterated orange cultivation in Europe. It was not until the time of the Crusaders that the bitter orange, along with the lemon and lime, was brought back to southern Italy by soldiers returning from Palestine. It was known then as the "bigarade". Its juice was used as a flavoring, and the whole fruit was made into preserves from which modern orange marmalade is descended.

The sweet orange reappeared later, in Italy in the 15th century. The "China" oranges which were an expensive delicacy in Britain from the late 16th century on were sweet ones, but from Portugal. The Portuguese orange spread through southern Europe, and the modern Greek for orange is still "portokáli".

The orange arrived in the New World remarkably early. Columbus himself took seeds of both kinds of orange, and of lemon, citron, and lime, to Haiti on his second voyage in 1493. The climate of the Caribbean proved ideal, as did that of the adjacent mainland. During the 16th century early settlers in Florida planted oranges and started what was to become that state's enormous citrus industry. The rival California industry began in 1739, when missionaries began to grow oranges in lower California (the part now in Mexico).

The first orange trees in southern Africa were planted in 1654. In Australia, orange seeds were planted in New South Wales by Captain Arthur in 1788. The remaining major orange industry, that of Israel, had a more gradual start.

There are now four main types of orange in cultivation.

Bitter oranges have declined greatly in importance since the general adoption of the sweet orange. They are grown mainly in Spain (hence their modern name Seville oranges), and the bulk of the crop is exported to Britain where it is made into marmalade. That, of course, is a cogent reason for its continued cultivation.

Common sweet oranges exist in numerous varieties, many of them of American origin. These have replaced older, less reliable European varieties. Examples are the Florida Midseason Pineapple and the Late Valencia, named for a supposed resemblance to an old Spanish variety. The well-known Jaffa orange of Israel (Hebrew "shamouti", Arabic "shamut", distaff, because the fruit is the same shape as the ball of thread on a distaff) is a mutation from earlier and inferior Palestine varieties, and dates back to about 1850. Blood oranges are grown mostly in Mediterranean countries, especially Italy, where there are several kinds including the round Moro and elongated Tarocco. The original mutation which produced the color probably happened in the 17th century in Sicily. The color is due to a pigment not usually present in citrus fruits but common in other red fruits and flowers: an anthocyanin. Blood oranges tend to be slightly less acid than normal oranges.

Navel oranges are an old variety. The Brazilian type, properly called Bahia, was introduced to the USA in 1870 to fill the need for a good early variety. This introduction was sponsored by the US Department of Agriculture in Washington DC, so the fruits came to be called Washington Navel. Navel oranges of this and other kinds are widely grown elsewhere.

Mandarin, Kumquat

Kumquat Hybrids

The kumquat can also form hybrids with true *Citrus* species. Growers have experimented with *Fortunella* × *Citrus* hybrids (orangequats, limequats) and *Fortunella* × *Poncirus* (trifoliate orange) hybrids (citrangequats). One citrangequat, Thomasville, has smallish golden fruits with a good flavor.

Tips for the Cook

Mandarins are almost always eaten fresh, since their delicate flavor is lost in cooking. In Chinese cuisine, the peel of selected, fragrant mandarins is dried and used as a flavoring.

Key to the Painting

center top: Clementine and section above;
below left: Ortanique with section behind;
right: Mapo, with section top right;
center: kumquats, Meiwa (round) and section of Nagami (oval) and seeds;
center right: Ponkan with section above;
below far left: Satsuma and section;
below: Minneola, with section

MANDARIN was originally no more than a nickname given to a small, loose-skinned orange-like fruit, *Citrus reticulata*, which was brought to England from China in 1805. The word also denotes a Chinese official or the form of Chinese spoken by such officials. However, it is not a Chinese word (their word for official is "kwan"), but came to English through the Portuguese form ("mandarin") of a Malay word for counsellor ("mantri").

Despite its strange origin, the nickname stuck, and has become the most useful general name for a wide range of similar fruits. Tangerine is less useful because it has more restricted, and different, meanings in the USA and Britain.

The simplest of rival botanical classifications puts all mandarins together in one species, *Citrus reticulata* (*reticulata* meaning netted, because of the fibrous strands of pith under the loose skin).

Mandarins are always smaller, sometimes much smaller, than oranges; of a flattened shape, except for some hybrids described below; loose-skinned; easily separable into segments; and less acid than oranges.

Mandarins were taken to the West later than the other citrus fruits, reaching Europe and the USA (as "Chinas") during the 19th century.

Common mandarins are the most widely grown kind in China and the USA. There are numerous varieties. The leading one in Florida is Dancy, a largeish, deep orange fruit. In California and the South-West it is the sweet Clementine.

Mediterranean mandarins are typically light in color, and of mild but good flavor; but tending to be seedy, and poor keepers. These are the fruits which the British (but not the Americans) call tangerines.

King oranges or King mandarins originated in Indochina and are large, with a thick, knobbly skin.

The ponkan, a large, pale fruit with a mild flavor, is cultivated in the far south of China, Indochina, and India.

Satsumas were developed in Japan in the 16th century. They are seedless, bright orange, less acid than other mandarins, and good keepers.

Tangors are hybrids between a mandarin and an orange, and tend to be intermediate in flavor, size, and shape between the two. The Clementine and King mandarin may be natural tangors, that is, hybrids that occurred spontaneously. Among tangors deliberately created are the large and richly flavored Temple orange, and the more acid Ortanique, which has a fine Seville orange fragrance.

Tangelos are hybrids between a mandarin and a pomelo or its descendant, grapefruit. They mostly resemble mandarins, though they do not have the typically flattened shape. Well known examples grown in the USA are Orlando, a mild-flavored, light-colored fruit; and Minneola, darker in color, with a rich, sharp flavor and a distinctive shape with a neck or knob on the stem end. The Mapo is an attractive newcomer, shaped like a small grapefruit and of a lovely green color until just before it is fully ripe. See also ugli (page 66).

KUMQUATS resemble miniature oranges, seldom more than $1\frac{1}{4}$ inches across, but are not true citrus fruits; they belong to the genus *Fortunella*. Their attractive golden skin is thin and soft, so they can be eaten whole, although they are usually too sour for the average palate unless cooked in syrup.

Kumquat trees are native to South-East China. The species most often cultivated is the oval-shaped *Fortunella margarita*; but the round *F japonica* has larger, sweeter fruits.

The most popular way of treating kumquats in China has been to preserve them in honey or, more recently, sugar. A 16th-century herbal, *Pen-ts'ao Kan Mu*, calls the kumquat "chi k'o ch'eng", meaning give-guest orange, because plants were often given as presents. In Western countries, kumquat plants used to be placed on the table at fashionable dinners so that guests could pick the fruits.

Citron

family RUTACEAE

Other Names for *CITRON*

French: *cédrat*
German: *Zitronat-Zitrone*
Italian : *cedro*
Spanish / Portuguese: *cidra*
Finnish: *sukaattisitruuna*
Russian: *tsitron, sladkiy limon*
Polish: *cedrat*
Hungarian: *citromsárga*
Romanian: *chitru, citră*
Greek: *kítron*
Turkish: *ağaçkavunu*
Arabic: *utrujj*
Hebrew: *etrog* (special type)
Chinese: *ju yuan*
Japanese: *bushukan* ("Buddha's hand" type)

Etymological Note

The citron gave its name to the whole group of citrus fruits, as they became known in Europe, simply because it had been the first of them to arrive. There was also a confusion with its smaller and juicier relative the lemon (French "citron", German "Zitrone").

Tips for the Cook

Look out for two interesting citron products. A sort of jellied citron paste called "pâte de cédrat" is a speciality of Bayonne in France. In India the raw flesh of the fruit is pickled, or cooked and preserved in mustard seed oil.

Recipe

Citrus Sherbet: page 174

Key to the Painting

left: citron Etrog and section; right: Buddha's hand and section above

The **CITRON**, *Citrus medica*, has two claims to distinction: it was the first of the citrus fruits to reach the Mediterranean region, and it has had great symbolic value for various religions. Perhaps because of its splendid size (some citrons measure up to 1 foot long) it came to represent wealth. Thus in India the god of wealth, Kuvera, is always represented as holding a citron in one hand and a mongoose spewing jewels in the other.

The fruit is like a huge, rough lemon. Most of the bulk is thick, dense skin; the flesh inside is dryish, either sour or sweet, with a weak lemon flavor. The peel, which has a unique and resinous fragrance, is the most useful part.

The citron is native to the north-east of India, where it was used from early times as a perfume and in medicine. After it had spread to Persia, and thence to Babylonia, it was discovered by the exiled Jews, who brought it back to Palestine. In 325 BC the army of Alexander the Great, returning from India to Macedonia, brought word of the citron to Europe; and soon afterwards the Greek writer Theophrastus described it as a plant "special to Asia", commenting correctly that "the Median or Persian apple is not eaten, but is very fragrant", and adding that it would protect clothes against moths.

Early attempts to grow the citron in Greece and Italy failed, but it seems that in the early centuries AD a slight warming in the Mediterranean climate allowed the fruit to be grown in the south of Europe, or further north in hothouses.

After the citron reached China, in the 4th century AD, a freak form (var *sarcodactyla*) developed in which the fruit was separated into five lobes looking like the fingers of a hand. This type, called Buddha's hand, was considered a symbol of happiness. For this reason and because of its especially fine scent, it was placed on household altars. Later it also became popular in Japan.

In modern Orthodox Jewish ritual a special type of citron (in Hebrew, "etrog") is used during the Feast of the Tabernacles as a symbol of God's bounty. It is ungrafted, non-edible, and must have its calyx intact. Trieste used to be the great market for distribution of such citrons to Jewish communities in Europe.

The original command for the Jewish practice is given in the Bible in the Book of Leviticus, composed at a time when the Jews could not yet have known the citron. Scholars believe that the cedar cone was meant, and that the Jews substituted the citron later because they were unhappy about the use of the cedar cone in the rituals of other religions.

There was indeed confusion between cedar and citron, and the confusion is not only Jewish. Both names are derived from the Greek word "kedros", meaning cedar. The earliest Greek word for citron was "mela medika" (Median apple), but this soon became "kedromela" (cedar apple) and later "kitrion" or "kitron". The reason for this may be no more than the resemblance in shape between citron and cedar cone.

Early uses of the citron were purely religious or medical. Even as late as the times of Pliny the Elder (about AD 75) it did not figure as an ordinary food. Soon afterwards, however, the practice of cutting the peel into strips for culinary use began. After the fall of the Roman Empire the citron remained important in Arab cuisine; and the introduction of sugar to the Arab world and later to Asia allowed citron peel to be candied.

Citrons are now used almost exclusively for the manufacture of candied peel. The main producers are Italy, Greece and Corsica, and, to a lesser extent, the USA. In China the Buddha's hand variety is also candied. Although the citron is not a juicy fruit, juice can be got from it, and this was used for making a refreshing soft drink which was the precursor of lemonade. In Italy it was called "acquacedrata" (one more example of the confusion between cedar and citron), and in the 17th and 18th centuries the vendors of this, with tanks on their backs, were a familiar sight in Italian cities.

Lemon, Lime, Calamansi, Kaffir Lime, Yuzu

family RUTACEAE

Other Names for *LEMON*

French: *citron*
German: *Zitrone*
Portuguese: *limão*
Spanish: *limón*
Italian: *limone*
Dutch: *citroen*
Danish / Swedish: *citron*
Norwegian: *sitron*
Finnish: *sitruuna*
Russian: *limon*
Polish: *cytryna*
Serbo-Croat: *limun*
Bulgarian: *limon*
Greek: *lemóni*
Turkish: *limon*
Hebrew: *limon*
Arabic: *laymūn*
Persian: *limoo*
Hindi: *bara nimbu*
Indonesian: *jeruk limon*
Chinese: *ning meng*

Other Names for *LIME*

French: *citron vert*
German: *Limone*
Italian / Spanish / Portuguese : *lima*
Russian: *laim*
Turkish: *misket limonou*
Hebrew: *limonit*
Arabic: *laimūn mālih*
Persian: *limoo*
Indian languages: *nimbu* (Hindi), *lebu*
(Bengali), *elumichai* (Tamil)
Chinese: *suan cheng*
Thai: *ma naao*
Malay: *limau nipis*
Indonesian: *jeruk nipis*
Philippines: *dayap*

Tip for the Cook

Dried or pickled lemons are common in
the Middle East and North Africa, and have
many uses. Dried limes are used in Iran,
Iraq and the Persian Gulf to flavor stews.

Recipes

Key to the Painting

top row: limequat, Kaffir lime leaves,
Kaffir lime and calamani;
2nd row: yuzus;
3rd row: Mexican or West Indian limes;
4th row: lemon Primofiori and Tahiti or
Persian lime

The **LEMON**, the fruit of *Citrus medica*, only reached the Mediterranean from northern India towards the end of the 1st century AD. Thus the fruit which can reasonably be regarded as the most important for European cookery was a comparatively late arrival. Nor was its use in cooking, as an acid element, appreciated at once. In classical Rome, it was a curiosity and decoration.

It was the Arabs who spread lemon cultivation in the Mediterranean region, especially Sicily and Spain and parts of North Africa, and it was in the Near East that the lemon's wide range of culinary uses was explored. However, the happy marriage between lemon and fish may have taken place in Italy, where Cristoforo di Messiburgo (1549) gave a recipe for marinated brill with lemon slices.

Once the lemon had reached the New World, in 1493, it spread rapidly. Since 1950 California has produced more lemons than all of Europe combined.

As an important acidifying and flavoring agent, the lemon has a primary role in the taste of many dishes. Certain tropical fruits, such as papaya, guava and avocado, need the sharpness which it or the lime imparts. The peel of the fruit contains the essential oil and thus acts not just to flavor but to perfume food.

The **LIME** is the tropical counterpart of the sub-tropical lemon. Like the lemon, it became abundant in the New World soon after its introduction there, particularly in the West Indies and Central America. This was the ordinary, small, acid lime, *C aurantifolia*, which is often known as the West Indian or Mexican lime despite its Old World origin. It is also the Key lime of Florida.

Another species, *C latifolia*, bears larger fruits, the size of a small lemon, and probably originated as a hybrid between the common lime and the citron. It is called Persian lime (though not known in Iran) or Tahiti lime (because it reached the USA from Tahiti).

The sweet lemon or limetta, *C limetta*, is a non-acid lemon grown on a small scale in India and around the Mediterranean. *C limettioides* is the Indian sweet lime; probably a hybrid between a Mexican lime and a sweet lemon or citron.

CALAMANSI (or kalamansi or calamondin / kalamondin), *Citrofortunella mitis*, is a small citrus fruit of the Philippines which plays an important role in Filipino cooking. The fruits, which look like small mandarins, are very acid. The juice can be used like lemon juice. It is exceptionally good to squeeze over papaya.

The **KAFFIR LIME**, *Citrus hystrix*, a member of the citrus family which is important in South-East Asian cookery, is also called papeda. The fruit itself, which is knobbly and bitter, is used for its acrid juice, but the leaves are a more common ingredient and appear in South-East Asian dishes with a frequency bordering on automaticity, rather like bay leaves in European cookery.

The **YUZU** is a distinctive citrus fruit which was formerly recognized as a species, *Citrus junos*, but is now described as either a variety of *C aurantium* (the bitter orange) or a hybrid. It is one of the most cold-resistant of the citrus fruits and grows wild in Tibet and the interior of China. It is cultivated sparingly in parts of China, and more commonly in Japan.

The yuzu tree bears fruit from late autumn; and the sight of ripe, golden yuzu suggests to the Japanese mind the approach of winter. The fruit is the size of a mandarin orange, with a thick uneven skin and paler flesh containing many seeds. It smells something like a lime, yet its fragrance is unique.

There is a tradition in Japan to take a "yuzu-yu", that is, a yuzu bath, on the evening of the winter solstice. This is a hot bath in which several whole fruit of yuzu, usually wrapped in cheesecloth, are floated. One sits in it, enjoying the rising scent and occasionally rubbing oneself with the softened fruit.

White Sapote,
Bael, Wampee, Wood Apple

family RUTACEAE

Other Names for *WHITE SAPOTE*

Central America (various places): *matasano*
South Africa: *Mexican apple*

Other Names for *BAEL*

Hindi: *bil*
Thai: *ma toom*
Vietnamese: *bau nau*
Malay: *bilak, maja pahit*
Indonesian: *kawista, maja*

Other Names for *WAMPEE*

Thai: *mafai cheen*
Malay: *wampi, wampoi*
Philippines: *uampi, huampi*

Other Names for *WOOD APPLE*

French: *pomme de bois, pomme d'éléphant*
Persian: *kabit*
Indian languages: *kaith* (Hindi); *vilam pazham* (Tamil)
Burmese: *bman*
Thai: *mak khwit*
Malay: *belinggai*

Of all fruit names sapote, or sapota (the anglicized form of the Latin American "zapote", from the Mexican name "tzapotl"), are just about the most confusing. They are applied to numerous American tropical fruits, of which many but not all are related to each other within the family Sapotaceae (see page 116).

However, the names **WHITE SAPOTE** (or sapota) and "zapota blanco" are applied to *Casimiroa edulis*, not a member of the family Sapotaceae but a relation of the citrus fruits in the family Rutaceae. It is a sub-tropical fruit which grows wild in Central Mexico and is cultivated in some Latin American countries. The small, pale yellow fruit has the flavor of a ripe pear.

Studying what experts such as Dr Julia Morton have recorded about the white sapote, one feels that a certain pathos invests it. It was given its generic name in honor of an 18th-century Spanish cardinal, who was also a botanist; so it sounds like an aristocrat. And it is very eager to please, growing vigorously and bearing masses of fruit. But in many places where it has been cultivated experimentally it has failed, or not been liked. There is some commercial growing in New Zealand and South Africa; but the verdict in Israel, the Philippines, California, Florida and some other areas has for one reason or another been that it is not worth cultivating. Even where it is grown and consumed, its reputation may be shadowed by names such as "matasano" (kill health), which suggest that it should be eaten with caution. Chemists, verifying comments on the fruit made as long ago as the 16th century, have found soporific substances in it; and these also have been named after the Spanish cardinal.

BAEL, *Aegle marmelos*, a tree which grows wild in much of northern India and Southeast Asia, also belongs to the citrus family. It is not related to the quince, although sometimes called Bengal or Indian quince. The fruits, which look something like grayish-yellow oranges, may have a thin hard shell or a less hard but thick skin. Inside, the ripe pulp is yellow, gummy and full of seeds. However, it has an aromatic, refreshing flavor. It can be eaten as it is or served with jaggery (palm sugar), or made into a marmalade, a jelly, or a drink.

Hindus hold the tree sacred to Shiva and use its leaves in his worship. It is sacrilegious to cut down a bael tree, but to die under one assures immediate salvation.

The **WAMPEE** is a small yellow-green fruit which grows in clusters on *Clausenia lansium*, a Chinese fruit tree which is also cultivated in Southeast Asia and in the West Indies. The ripe fruit contain an aromatic, mildly acid pulp which is pleasant to eat.

Other trees of the same genus have medicinal rather than edible properties. *C excavata* has interesting Malay names: "pokok kemantu" (ghostly tree) and "pokok cerek" (diarrhoea tree).

The **WOOD APPLE** is the fruit of a small tree, *Feronia limonia*, found in most parts of the Indian sub-continent and eastwards to the China Sea. It is also called elephant apple, and formerly had the botanical name *F elephantum*, because elephants like to eat it.

The round gray fruits, the size of apples, have hard shells and contain a brown pulp which is used to make sherbets, jellies, and chutneys in India. The pulp is also eaten raw with sugar, or seasoning; but it is inconveniently full of small seeds.

Key to the Painting

top and bottom: Indian bael;
center: sapote and seed;
small scattered fruit and seeds: wampees

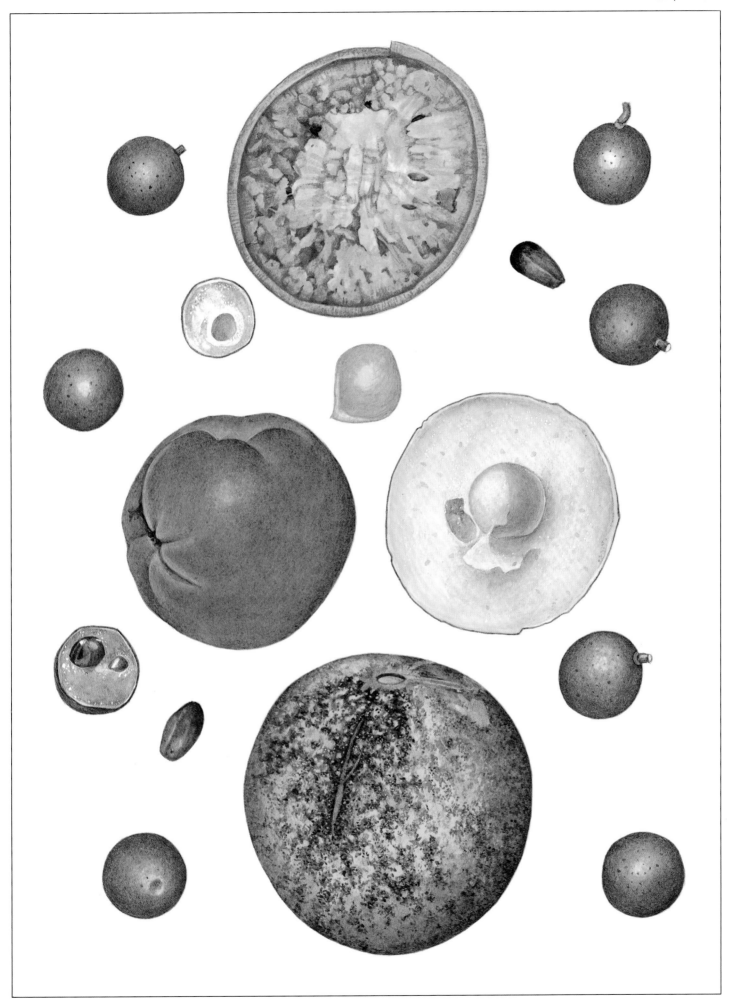

Melon

family CUCURBITACEAE

Other Names for *MELON*

French: *melon*
German: *Melone*
Italian: *melone, popone*
Spanish: *melón*
Catalan: *meló*
Portuguese: *melão*
Dutch: *meloen*
Danish / Norwegian / Swedish: *melon*
Finnish: *meloni*
Russian: *dynya*
Polish: *melon*
Serbo-Croat: *dinja*
Romanian: *pepene-galben*
Bulgarian: *pupesh*
Greek: *pépon, pepóni*
Turkish: *kavun (casaba)*
Hebrew: *melon*
Arabic: *shammām*
Persian / Afghanistan: *kharbouza*
Hindi: *kharbuja*
Chinese: *tian gua*
Thai: *taeng thai*
Philippines: *milon*
Japanese: *meron*
Indonesian: *semangka*

Tips for the Cook

Many people have remarked on the difficulty of knowing in advance whether a melon will be good or not. A French writer declared pessimistically that it was necessary to try 50 to be sure of finding one really good specimen. Ripeness may, however, be gauged by pressing the end opposite the stem; if the melon is ripe, it will yield quite noticeably. Cantaloupes and netted melons do not ripen much after being picked, so should not be bought if they are definitely hard. Ripening is best accomplished at room temperature; it is retarded by refrigeration.

Recipes

An Italian Fruit Salad: page 151
Swimming Melon: page 153

Key to the Painting

top left: Earl's melon from Japan;
top right: Honeydew;
center: Ogen;
bottom left: Galia;
bottom right: Charentais

When the library of the town of Cavaillon in the South of France asked the great and prolific French author Alexandre Dumas père for a complete set of his works, he told them that they were asking for over 400 books, but that he would do his best to comply if they would send him every year a consignment of Cavaillon melons. They did, and he did, and it was a highly satisfactory exchange for him.

Dumas knew that these were good melons, and they still are, but neither he nor anyone else has ever been capable of relating the whole story of the varieties and nomenclature of the **MELON**, *Cucumis melo*, partly because all forms of this species hybridize readily with each other (or with other family members; it is recorded that in the 19th century the French took care to cultivate melons well apart from other gourds, to avoid "incestuous intercourse" with cucumbers!).

The wild ancestors of *C melo* seem to have been native to the Near East and perhaps the north-west of India. After the fall of the Roman Empire the rising Arab civilizations began to cultivate them. Ibn Al Awam (d 1145), the agricultural writer of Andalusia, followed his chapter on cucumbers with one on melons, and gave dietary advice applying to both (for example neither should be eaten at the same meal as eggs or fish).

In 1493 Columbus took melon seeds to Haiti, where they throve and whence they spread. The new fruit was adopted with such enthusiasm by the Native Americans that settlers, as they penetrated further into the country, were apt to find melons already growing, and formed the mistaken conclusion that they were native to America as well as to the Old World.

Melons certainly reached England by the 16th century, although some say that they had arrived earlier and then been lost in the commotion caused by the Wars of the Roses. They had to be grown under glass bells or in glasshouses, or in steam-pits.

Dessert melons fall into three main categories, but there are also hybrids of an intermediate kind.

Cantaloupe melons are named for the town of Cantalupo near Rome, where they are supposed to have been first grown in Europe. They are the most fragrant and delicious of melons, small and round, and usually with a rough surface fissured into segments. The French variety, Charentais, has a yellow skin and orange flesh. The Ogen, named for the Israeli kibbutz where it was bred, has a yellow skin with green stripes, and green flesh. Sweetheart has bright scarlet flesh.

However, the name cantaloupe is used in North America for a type of melon in the next category: the netted, musk or nutmeg melons. These vary greatly but have one feature in common: a light network pattern which overlays and stands out from the surface. The flesh is usually orange. Size varies from small to quite large. The skin may be whitish, yellow or green; and it may or may not be segmented.

In North America the two most important types of netted melon are known as Cantaloupe and Persian. The American Cantaloupe has a prominently raised net, and is round to slightly oblong. The Persian has a less prominently raised net, with larger spaces between the net lines, and a distinctive aromatic flavor.

Winter melons are so called because they ripen slowly and are not ready until late autumn. They are elongated, like footballs, and their skins are ribbed lengthways. The finest are the melons of Cavaillon, otherwise known as "melons d'hiver de Provence". However, the best known of the winter melons is the Honeydew (properly Honey Dew), which has a yellowish skin and pale green flesh. Casaba melons, often miscalled Honeydew, are similar but variable in color, usually with green or green and yellow skins and pale yellow flesh.

A common practice is to chill melons before eating them. This makes them more refreshing, but diminishes the flavor. A good melon should not need sugar. Some add a sprinkling of pepper or ginger, or salt. Italians serve melon with paper-thin slices of smoked ham, a good combination.

Watermelon, Kiwano, Cassabanana

family CUCURBITACEAE

Other Names for
WATERMELON

French: *pastèque*
German: *Wassermelone*
Italian: *cocomero*
Spanish: *sandia*
Portuguese: *melancia*
Danish: *vandmelon*
Norwegian: *vannmelon*
Swedish: *vattenmelon*
Finnish: *vesimeloni, arbuusi*
Russian / Polish: *arbuz*
Serbo-Croat: *lubenica*
Romanian: *pepene-verde*
Bulgarian: *dinya*
Greek: *karpouxzi, ibropepon*
Turkish: *karpuz*
Hebrew: *avaṭiaḥ*
Arabic: *baṭṭikh*
Persian: *hinduwana*
Indian languages: *tarbuza* (Hindi),
palam (Tamil)
Thai: *taeng mo*
Malay / Indonesian: *semangka*
Philippines: *pakwan*
Chinese: *xi gua*
Japanese: *suika*

Other Names for
CASSABANANA

Mexico: *melocotonero, calabaza mélon*
Brazil: *cura, melao caboclo, melao maca*
Guatemala: *melo-cotón*
Nicaragua: *cojombro*

Tips for the Cook

On the whole, it is best to buy ready-cut slices of watermelon; a whole one is probably too big anyway, and you need to see that the flesh is good and red and fresh-looking. Slices or whole fruits keep well under refrigeration.

The **WATERMELON**, *Colocynthis citrullus*, is a fruit quite distinct from the ordinary sweet melons and with a longer history of cultivation. The plant is a native of Africa, and watermelons were eaten and cultivated in Egypt well before 2000 BC. The large green fruits are refreshing, so it is not surprising that the children of Israel, wandering in the desert after their flight from Egypt and regretting the fruits they had left behind, thought wistfully of watermelons (wrongly translated in the Authorized Version of the Bible as melons).

The watermelon has one great advantage which encouraged its spread to lands around the Mediterranean and eastwards into Asia. It is especially useful as a source of potable liquid where water supplies are polluted. However, in some places, if watermelons are being sold by weight, one must beware of the practice of injecting additional water into them; or so our cook in Cairo told us. (He used to carve up slices artistically for us, freeing the black seeds, and would always assure us that the slices came from a fruit with no tell-tale pinpricks in it. We welcomed the assurance, as the thought that we might be imbibing Nile water was indeed horrifying; but we never really established whether the malpractice took place.)

Watermelons can be grown in the hotter parts of southern Europe, but have never been as important there as ordinary melons. In America, however, it was another matter: great interest and potential for cultivation. Modern improved varieties have been bred mainly in the New World. By 1822 there were reports of watermelons weighing 20 pounds; but nowadays 55 pounds is common and 99 pounds is not unknown.

Numerous cultivars exist, of various shapes, colors, and sizes. Small ones are generally round, one of the best known being Sugar Baby, a dark green, early variety. "Baby" is a comparative term, for the fruits average 7–9 pounds in weight, whereas wild watermelons may be only the size of an orange. "Sugar" and "sweet", names which are wished onto many varieties, are also exaggerations: no watermelon has more than a faintly sweet, insipid but refreshing flavor. One of the largest and most common is Charleston Gray, an elongated fruit with a pale green, marbled skin. Striped varieties are also widespread. Most have pink or red flesh, although there are also yellow-fleshed kinds, such as Yellow Baby.

In North America, pickled watermelon peel has long been a favorite relish. When "an American Orphan" (Amelia Simmons) brought out her *American Cookbook* in 1796, the inclusion of a recipe for Spiced Watermelon Pickles was one telltale sign that this really was an American book. Americans in the southern states also like to fry cubes of the peel, cut from under the skin. In some European countries, in contrast, pieces of peel have been candied.

An emigrant to Australasia and elsewhere from Africa, the **KIWANO**, *Cucumis metuliferus*, also known as the horned melon or horned cucumber, wins prizes for appearance, with rich green flesh inside a golden skin whose shape and protuberances suggest some sort of space craft. But the flavor is unremarkable.

The cucurbit family also includes the **CASSABANANA**, *Sicana odorifera*, also known as sikana or musk cucumber. This is probably native to Brazil, where it is grown as an ornamental vine, but is popular as a fruit in the Central American region, especially Puerto Rico.

The fruit resembles a large thick cucumber, wearing a smooth, shiny shell, which can be red, purple or black in color. The orange or yellow flesh is melon-like in texture and smell, and juicy. It surrounds a large central cavity of soft pulp and rows of tightly packed, flat, oval seeds. The fruit is usually 12–24 inches long, and 3–5 inches thick.

Unripe fruits can be used in soups and stews. Ripe ones are refreshing if eaten raw, but more often end up as jam.

Key to the Painting

the watermelon is Galaxy from Cyprus;
top left: part of a kiwano

Prickly Pear, Pitaya, Barbados Gooseberry

family CACTACEAE

Other Names for *PRICKLY PEAR*

French: *figue de Barbarie*
German: *indische Feige*
Italian: *fico d'India*
Portuguese: *figo do inferno*
Spanish: (European) *higo chumbo*, (Latin America) *nopalito, tuna*
Greek: *frangósika*
Turkish: *hintinciri* (Indian fig),
frenkinciri (European fig)
Hebrew: *tsabar*
Arabic: *ṣubbār*
Persian: *anjir hindi*
Hindi: *nag-phana*
Finnish: *kaktusviikuna*
Japanese: *uchiwa saboten*

Recipe

Prickly Pear Jelly: page 180

The **PRICKLY PEAR**, also called Barbary pear, cactus pear, Indian pear, Indian fig or tuna fig, is not a kind of pear or fig, but comes from any of numerous cacti of the genus *Opuntia*. These are native to the drier regions between Central America and the great deserts of the USA, and have become firmly established in the Old World, especially around the Mediterranean and in India; and also in Australia.

Their fleshy, spiked leaves take the form of flattish discs or pads stacked one on another, inspiring the American name beavertail for the plants.

As for the fruits, the best are said to be those of *O megacantha*, presently found in Mexico and the southern USA. The common Mediterranean species is *O ficus-indica*, of which there are several varieties.

The insects, called scale insects, which produce cochineal, feed on these cacti. In both India and Australia attempts have been made to take advantage of this for the production of cochineal, for purposes such as dyeing soldiers' uniforms red. But chaos resulted. Either the insects fed so heartily that they wiped out the cacti; or the cacti multiplied so excessively that they became a real plague.

The prickly pear fruit resembles a small, soft cucumber, but with little seeds distributed evenly through its flesh and with rosettes of little spines on the outside. Size varies from tiny to 5 inches long. Color may be cream, yellowish green, pink, red, or purple shading almost to black. The best types in the USA are the large purplish red Cardona and yellow Amarilla, which have relatively few spikes. Around the Mediterranean the best are usually pale yellow, though there are also good red ones. In Sicily several large, sweet, almost seedless types are cultivated, the finest being called "surfarina" and "bastarduni".

Prickly pear fruits are generally eaten fresh and raw. Good ones are tender and pleasantly sweet, though lacking in acidity, so a squeeze of lime or lemon juice helps. They need to be peeled and it is advisable to remove the spines from the peel first. The original Native American way of doing this is to pick the fruits in the early morning, while the spines are still wet with dew and soft, and rub them in sand until the spines have all come off. Otherwise, the fruit is best attacked with a knife and fork. The peel comes away easily. The seeds are no more troublesome than grape pips.

In Tunisia the fruits are often made into a jam, which is acceptable; and in the USA into a jelly, which I bought in Arizona and found exceptionally good.

Native Americans sometimes dried the fruit for winter use. They also boiled it to make a pulp resembling apple sauce. Spanish settlers boiled it down further to make a syrupy paste, "queso de tuna" (prickly pear cheese).

PITAYA, the Spanish name for the fruit of *Hylocereus undatus* and some other closely related cacti, is spelled in various ways and sometimes acccompanied by an epithet (such as "pitahaya roja" or "blanca" in Mexico and "pitahaya de cardón" in Guatemala). In English the fruit may be called strawberry pear.

The cacti bearing these fruits are indigenous to Central America, but are now cultivated also in the West Indies, Florida, and other tropical regions.

The fruit is oval to oblong, up to 4 inches long, and may be bright red, peach-colored or yellow. The pulp inside is sweet, white, and juicy. It contains numerous tiny black seeds.

The juice makes a refreshing beverage. The fruit can be cut in half and chilled, then eaten with a spoon.

Key to the Painting

top: yellow pitayas from Columbia;
center: red pitayas from Nicaragua;
bottom left and right: prickly pears;
bottom center: Barbados gooseberries

The **BARBADOS GOOSEBERRY** is the edible fruit of a cactus, *Pereskia aculeata*, grown in the West Indies. It is not at all a typical cactus, seeming rather to be a leafy, climbing shrub. The yellowish or reddish fruits are tart and of minor importance.

Papaya, Babaco

family CARICACEAE

Other Names for *PAPAYA*

French: *papaye, papayer*
German: *Papaya, Baummelone*
Italian: *papaia*
Spanish: *papaya, fruta bomba*
Portuguese: *papaia, mamão*
Danish: *melontræ*
Swedish: *papaya(frukt)*
Norwegian: *pawpaw*
Finnish: *papaija*
Russian: *papaya, plod dynnovo dereva*
Indian languages: *papita* (Hindi); *pepe paka* (Bengali); *pappali* (Tamil)
Thai: *malako*
Malay: *betik*
Indonesian: *papaja, katés*
Philippines: *papaya*
Chinese: *mu gua*
Japanese: *papaya*

Spanish-American names include lechosa (a term of abuse in Cuba), melón zapote and mamón, besides papaya

Other Names for *BABACO*

Ecuador: *chamburo*

Tip for the Cook

After blending a dressing for a green salad, add papaya seeds and blend further until the seeds are like coarsely ground pepper.

Recipes

Tropical Fruit Salad: page 152
Papaya Fritters: page 168

The **PAPAYA**, *Carica papaya*, one of the best tropical fruits, looks rather like a pear-shaped melon. It is native to the lowlands of eastern Central America, but even before the arrival of Europeans it was already being cultivated well beyond this area. The Spanish and the Portuguese invaders took to it and quickly spread it to their other settlements in the West and East Indies, taking with it its Carib name "ababai", altered to "papaya". It was also taken to the Pacific islands as Europeans discovered them, and by 1800 was being grown in all tropical regions. Hawaii and South Africa are now the main exporters.

The papaya plant is large, shaped like a palm tree but with big fingered leaves. The fruits hang from the top down the central stem in large clusters. It bears fruit within a year, continues to fruit well for another two years, and is then cut down.

Its sexual habits are peculiar. Some strains, such as Hortus Gold of South Africa, have separate male and female trees. Seedlings are planted in threes and the males, which bear no fruit and are useful only for pollination, are thinned out when they flower and their sex becomes apparent. Others, such as the Hawaiian Solo, have fruiting hermaphrodites and females, of which the former are preferred and the latter thinned out. These two strains produce the majority of papayas in the West.

The preferred type of commercial papaya is generally just over 1 pound, occasionally twice as large. It is pear-shaped, pale green when unripe and becoming blotchy yellow or orange when ripe. A fruit is ripe when it is mostly yellow and just beginning to soften to the touch. The pulp inside is of a creamy orange color, soft, delicately scented, and sweet. The taste is slightly lacking in acidity, and is usually complemented by a squeeze of lime juice. Living in Southeast Asia, I came to feel a definite need for a fix of papaya, thus dressed, at breakfast-time.

At the center of the fruit is a mass of black seeds encased in a gelatinous coating. These are edible, although often discarded. They are crunchy, have a slightly peppery taste, like mustard and cress, and can be used, crushed, as a mildly spicy condiment.

Papaya fruits, especially unripe ones, and also the leaves of the plant contain an enzyme of a digestive character, papain, which has a powerful tenderizing effect on meat. Wherever papayas are grown, tough meat is cooked in a wrapping of papaya leaves; or left under a papaya tree whose unripe fruits have been cut, so that they drip a milky latex on to the meat; or is mixed with papaya in some other way. Commercial meat tenderizer, available in powder form, is made from papayas.

At least eight other species of the genus *Carica* bear edible fruits, including the babaco. *C candamarcensis* is the mountain papaya of the Andes, best eaten cooked, because of its high papain content. (The papain content of the different species varies considerably.)

Papaya is not to be confused with the quite different fruit papaw (page 122); but it is not uncommon to find papayas labeled "papaws".

The **BABACO**, *Carica pentagona*, a large fruit of Ecuador, has now been introduced for cultivation elsewhere, for example in New Zealand and Europe as far north as the Channel Islands (where a special babaco cookbook has been produced), and is also available in North America. The plant is not known in the wild, and botanists suggest that it may be a hybrid, perhaps of the mountain papaya mentioned above and another fruit of Ecuador.

The fruit may reach a length of 1 foot, is star-shaped in section, and has tender juicy flesh of a pale apricot color with a mild and faintly acid taste and a delicate fragrance. Since it is normally seedless and the skin (green, turning to yellow when ripe) is soft, the entire fruit can be eaten; or it can be liquidized to make a refreshing drink, or be used as a flavoring in ice creams. A little sugar or honey is often added.

Key to the Painting

left: papaya;
right: babaco;
both against a papaya leaf

Pineapple

Main Varieties

These are really groups of varieties, mostly including various cultivars. The name Sugarloaf is correctly applied to one cultivar, but is used quite loosely.
Cayenne: moderately large, yellow flesh, plenty of both acid and sugar;
Queen: smaller, rich yellow flesh, less acid, mild flavor;
Red Spanish: mostly eaten fresh, from the Caribbean, with a spicy, acid flavor;
Sugarloaf: large, sweet, with a mild flavor and yellow-white flesh.

Tips for the Cook

The lower part of a pineapple is usually the sweeter part.
Many Asians, as a matter of course, sprinkle a little salt on fresh pineapple. I learned to do this in Laos.
If some Kirsch, the cherry-based liqueur, is poured over fresh pineapple pieces some time before they are served, the effect is excellent: this partnership is common in France.

Recipes

Key to the Painting

left and right: Smooth Cayenne;
center: Cayenne Liffe from Honduras

The **PINEAPPLE**, *Ananas comosus*, the most popular of all tropical fruits, is grown in hot regions all round the world. But, although easily propagated, it is a complex growth: a composite fruit, formed of one to two hundred berry-like fruitlets fused together, giving its outside a tessellated appearance. It grows on a short stem springing from a low plant with large pointed leaves, small versions of which form the crown of the fruit.

The original home of the pineapple was the lowlands of Brazil, where several *Ananas* species grow wild. The plant is easily propagated by cuttings, and cultivation had spread to the West Indies before Europeans arrived there. The sailors of Columbus' expedition of 1493 discovered the pineapple on Guadeloupe, and were astonished and delighted by its qualities.

By the 1520s European gardeners had managed to grow the fruit. One of the first was presented to the Spanish King Charles V. He refused, with characteristic hesitancy, to touch it. Others were more enthusiastic in their response, and pineapple cultivation spread quickly throughout the tropics. The Portuguese sailors who traded to and from Brazil played a large part in this. That is why in most languages the word for the fruit is descended from the Brazilian Tupi Indian word "nana" or "anana" (excellent fruit), and not from the name "piña" (pine cone) which its first Spanish discoverers gave it because of its appearance.

Europeans tried to grow pineapples in hothouses. The first English pineapple was grown in 1661 by John Rose, one of Charles II's gardeners. A celebrated and mysterious painting of Rose presenting the fruit to the king includes pots containing young pineapple plants. Charles is said to have consumed it with relish, showing better judgement than his Spanish namesake. Fashionable enthusiasm for pineapples is reflected in the frequency with which they appear as a decorative motif in the buildings and furniture of the next hundred years.

Hothouse cultivation of pineapples was developed into a fine art by the great Victorian gardeners of the 19th century in England. But when the varieties which they developed (Cayenne and Queen) were introduced to the Azores, which were just near enough for the perishable cargo to survive the voyage to Europe, the reason for hothouse cultivation disappeared.

The main varieties grown are listed in the left-hand column. There are also excellent dwarf varieties whose core is conveniently edible. These I first met in the island of Phuket in Thailand in the 1970s, but now they come from South Africa and elsewhere. At the other extreme is Abacaxi, weighing up to 11 pounds.

The main producers include Hawaii, Puerto Rico, Malaysia and Brazil; and the bulk of the crop goes for canning. The huge pineapple canning industry began in Hawaii in 1892 and in Singapore at about the same time. When pineapple is canned, the fruit is trimmed severely to make the rings fit the can. The offcuts are used for juice. The harder core is also removed, and may be candied.

A pineapple, unlike most other fruits, does not continue to ripen or sweeten after picking, since it has no reserve of starch to be converted into sugar. On the contrary, it will start a gradual deterioration. Holding the fruits at a low temperature slows down this process.

In its natural state pineapple contains bromelin, an enzyme which breaks down protein; it is similar to the enzyme papain (that comes from papaya), which is used as a meat tenderizer. The enzyme in the pineapple is so abundant and powerful that plantation and cannery workers have to wear rubber gloves to avoid having their hands eaten away. Meat marinated in fresh pineapple juice is not merely tenderized but likely to fall apart. Bromelin is also responsible for the fact that a gelatin dessert, made with fresh pineapple juice and gelatin, will not set unless a gelling agent such as agar-agar is added. Bromelin is, however, quickly destroyed by heating, so cooked or canned pineapple and juice no longer have these properties.

Durian, Baobab, Chupa-Chupa

family BOMBACACEAE

Other Names for *DURIAN*

French: *durione, durian*
German: *Durian, Stinkfrucht*
Dutch: *doerian*
Greek: *doureos karpos*
Burmese: *duyin*
Thai / Malay: *durian*
Indonesian: *duren*
Philippines: *durian*
Chinese: *liu lian guo*
Japanese: *dorian*

Other Names for *BAOBAB*

Chinese: *bou mian bao*

Recipe
Sherbet: page 174

The **DURIAN**, *Durio zibethinus*, has been giving off its notorious smell for millions of years; it is one of the longest-established inhabitants of the rain forests of South-East Asia.

"Duri" is the Malay word for spike, and the tree takes its name from the hard, spiky shell of the fruit. A full-grown fruit may weigh 5 pounds or more. Since the tree may be as high as 100 feet and the fruit drops off when ripe, it is wise to take care when walking near such trees in the durian season. Death by durian is not uncommon. (Another hazard is the appeal the fallen, split fruit has for tigers.)

As the fruit ripens the flesh becomes yellowish white. Dark yellow durians are esteemed most highly. In Thailand the variety called "Mon tong" is the best and most expensive; and there is a new variety with white flesh, "Kratoey".

There is even a cultivar which has no smell, but almost all durians have it, and it has been the subject of striking comparisons: the civet cat, sewage, stale vomit, or (more mildly) onions, and over-ripe cheese. Even Indonesians acknowledge that prolonged exposure to the smell may have negative effects, and the carriage of durians on public transport is forbidden.

However, others have expressed enthusiasm with equal vigour. Alfred Russell Wallace in his *Malay Archipelago* (1869) declared that, if he had to choose, he would name the durian and the orange as "the king and queen of fruits". Here is his description of the flesh:

> A rich butter-like custard highly flavoured with almonds gives the best general idea of it, but intermingled with it come wafts of flavour that call to mind cream-cheese, onion-sauce, brown-sherry, and other incongruities. Then there is a rich glutinous smoothness in the pulp which nothing else possesses, but which adds to its delicacy. It is neither acid, nor sweet, nor juicy, yet one feels the want of none of these qualities, for it is perfect as it is.

Most people find that, while the smell repels them, they are no longer aware of it when they start eating; it somehow combines with non-smelly but tasty substances to produce a characteristic rich, aromatic flavor. This can be further enriched; some people bury durians in order to ferment them prior to consumption.

To eat the fruit, the procedure is to split open the shell, revealing the large seeds, each with a generous coating of sticky pulp surrounding it. This is gnawed or sucked off. Durian is sometimes cooked and made into a sausage-shaped cake which retains some of its proper flavor but very little smell. Malaysians make both sugared and salted preserves from it. The large seeds can be roasted and eaten as nuts.

Wallace cited many other ways of preparing durian, for example mixed with rice and sugar as "lempog". But his enthusiasm exposed him to a counter-attack in a quasi-limerick published in the journal *Horticulture* (1973):

> The durian neither Wallace nor Darwin agreed on it.
> Darwin said: "may your worst enemies be forced to feed on it."
> Wallace cried "It's delicious".
> Darwin replied "I'm suspicious,
> For the flavor is scented
> Like papaya fermented,
> After a fruit-eating bat has pee'd on it."

The **BAOBAB**, *Adansonia digitata*, a broad, spreading tree with a thick, spongy trunk, belongs to tropical Africa and bears fruits whose pulp is a popular food and seasoning, often called monkey bread. Another name, cream of tartar tree, refers to the tartaric acid which is in the whitish yellow pulp.

Key to the Painting

durian with sections showing flesh and seeds;
in each corner: chupa-chupa

The **CHUPA-CHUPA**, *Quararibea cordata*, is grown in Peru and Colombia. It is oval, about 5 inches long, with a flavor between that of an apricot and a mango.

Jackfruit

family MORACEAE

Other Names for *JACKFRUIT*

French: *rimier*
German: *Nangka*
Indian languages: *kathal* (Hindi); *pala pazham* (Tamil)
Thai: *khanun*
Malay / Indonesian: *nangka*
Philippines: *langka*
Chinese: *mu bo luo*
Japanese: *paramitsu*

Here is the largest of all tree-borne fruits: the **JACKFRUIT**, *Artocarpus heterophyllus*, also known as jak. It and its close relation *A integer*, the champedak (or chempedak) are thought to be native to southern India, whence they spread to Sri Lanka and over the mainland of Southeast Asia, keeping to a more northerly habitat than the tropical areas favored by their relation, the breadfruit (which is used as a vegetable, so is not in this book).

The name jack or jak goes back to a Sanskrit word; and the jackfruit has been cultivated in India since ancient times. It is cultivated in many Southeast Asian countries, including Laos, where I had a venerable specimen in my garden; and also in Africa and tropical regions of America and Australia.

The fruit itself is enormous, occasionally reaching 90 pounds. It grows directly from the trunk of the tree on a short stem. It is a composite fruit with a structure like that of the pineapple, but less tidy; the sections are clustered in irregular clumps. The fruit is elongated, its green skin fissured by the hexagonal boundaries of the sections and covered with spikes. Each fruit contains up to 500 large, starchy, edible seeds which are sometimes known as breadnuts, although the true breadnut belongs to a different species. These seeds are "med kha-nun" in Thailand, where they are usually boiled and eaten rather like chestnuts.

The champedak, a slightly smaller but similar fruit, is popular in Indonesia, but elsewhere in Southeast Asia is grown mainly as a source of these "breadnuts".

A general distinction is made between those jackfruits which are classed as soft (with some names meaning "break open with the hands") and those which are considered to be hard ("cut open with a knife"). The latter are preferred. There are special terms used for the two types such as "koozha chakka" and "koozha pazam" in southern India. There are, however, many varieties and they do not all fall neatly into this twofold classification. Some hold that the "peniwaraka" (honey jak) of Sri Lanka is the best of all.

The interior of the jackfruit is complex. It consists of large bulbs of yellow flesh, massed among narrow ribbons of tougher tissue and surrounding a central, pithy core. Each bulb encloses a smooth, oval seed.

The flesh of the unripe fruit may be used as a starchy vegetable, or dried, or pickled.

As the fruit ripens, it may be covered with a bag, not to keep away birds or insects directly, but to encourage ants to swarm around it and thus repel other creatures. It is ready for consumption as a fresh fruit when its skin is stretched out, with the spikes standing clear of each other, and as soon as it starts to give off an aroma. When the smell of a fresh jackfruit fills a room, it is already overripe. The smell of a ripe fruit, before it is opened, is disagreeable, at least to those not used to it; but the aroma of the pulp inside is akin to those of the pineapple and banana. The pulp is banana-flavored, firm, thick and sweet. It will continue to ripen even after being peeled.

Dr Julia Morton (1986) observes that if the "bulbs" are boiled in milk, "the latter when drained off and cooled will congeal and form a pleasant, orange-colored custard".

The flesh of the ripe jackfruit is sometimes candied by Chinese and Malaysians. The seeds, after being boiled to remove a slight bitterness, can be made into a flour, or candied.

All this applies to the champedak also, except that its odor before it is opened is even richer. The word is not a euphemism, since people such as Malaysians actually like the smell; but it should not be taken as a recommendation.

Key to the Painting

jackfruit, section and leaves

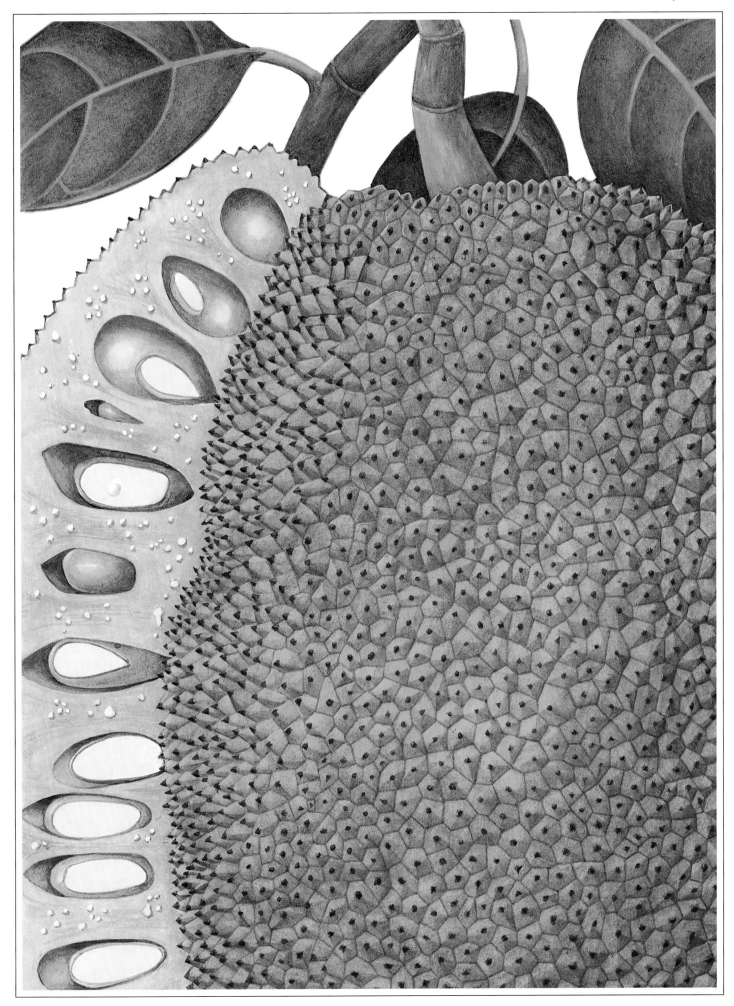

Monstera

This item, the **MONSTERA** or ceriman, is definitely one for those who have a bent for the exotic. Here is a fruit with multiple claims to be unusual, including the surprising fact that it takes just over a year to ripen on the tree.

More people know the plant better than the fruit. The plant, a creeping vine of the arum lily family, is the familiar Swiss cheese plant, *Monstera deliciosa*, grown as a houseplant for the sake of its unusual leaves, which have holes in them. The reason for the holes in the leaf tissue, a phenomenon known as fenestration which affects many aroid plants, has been explained in various ways; some supposed that the holes were to let rain through to reach the roots, others that they were meant to reduce resistance to the wind in gales. It is now thought that they are cooling devices which operate by creating turbulence in the air round the leaves.

In her admirable and thoughtful book *Aroids*, Deni Bown refers to the monstera plant as "the archetypical indoor plant of the 20th century", and comments that this is quite surprising in view of the lack of interest shown in it when it was first taken to Europe in the 1830s. It was only when plants reached Copenhagen and Berlin around the middle of the 19th century that "the exponential growth of *M deliciosa* as one of the greatest horticultural successes of all time" began.

The monstera is a native of Mexico and Guatemala; and in its natural habitat the plant grows to a great size and bears fruit which somewhat resemble green corn cobs.

The fruit, like that of any arum lily, for example the poisonous "lords and ladies" common in the English countryside, is composed of a mass of berries on a spadix, the fleshy central spike first seen in the flower. In the case of the ceriman the spadix itself, which reaches a length of 8–12 inches, is eaten. Provided that the fruit is fully ripe, and carefully peeled, the flavor and texture are delicious; somewhere between banana and pineapple or "pineapple, mango and banana", as Elizabeth Schneider puts it, (or "like fruit salad", as another author succinctly says), but with a special aromatic quality.

Dr Julia Morton gives a very precise account, quoted below, of how one should deal with the fruit. She adds that oxalic acid in the unripe fruit, and what are called the "floral remnants" on the spadix, besides other parts of the plant including, for some people, the ripe fruit itself, can cause irritation. So it is well to eat sparingly on the first occasion and check that there are no undesirable results.

> The fruit, with at least an inch of stem, should be cut from the plant when the tile-like sections of rind separate slightly at the base, making it appear somewhat bulged. . . . If kept at room temperature, the ceriman will ripen progressively towards the apex over a period of 5 or 6 days.

Left to itself, a monstera is likely to ripen unevenly. One can tell which parts of the fruit are ripe by seeing where the rind segments have become loose. The flesh underneath these loose segments can then be eaten. Wrapping the fruit in plastic or aluminium foil will often help it to ripen in a more uniform way. Once the rind is loose for the whole length of the fruit, the flesh will also come away from the core. At this stage the ripe fruit can be kept for up to a week in the refrigerator.

The monstera is still an uncommon fruit outside its native region. However, it has been available in London, for example, since the 1930s at least. I was surprised when browsing through *The Practical Fruiterer and Florist* (of around 1935) to come across a little essay about the "monsteria", explaining that it was imported from Madeira during the winter, although in limited quantities, and claiming that it ranked in importance with the mango and avocado. There was even a color plate showing off its remarkable appearance.

The ripe pulp can be incorporated in fruit salads or served with ice cream. In the unlikely event of anyone having a glut of the fruit, it can be preserved by stewing segments with sugar and lime juice, then putting it up in jars.

Guava, Feijoa

family MYRTACEAE

Other Names for *GUAVA*

French: *goyave*
German: *Guave*
Italian: *guaiva*
Spanish: *guayaba*
Portuguese: *goiaba*
Hebrew: *guyava*
Arabic: *gawāfa*
Indian languages: *amrud* (Hindi); *koya* (Tamil)
Burmese: *malaka*
Thai: *farang, ma kuai*
Malay: *jambu batu*
Indonesian: *jambu biji, jambu klutuk*
Philippines: *bayabas*
Chinese: *fan shi liu*
Japanese: *banjirō, guaba*
Hawaii: *kuawa*
Réunion: *guave de Chine*

Tips for the Cook

Canned guavas are available but their flavor bears only a faint resemblance to that of the fresh fruit.

Feijoa fruits should be dipped in lemon juice after peeling to prevent them from going brown.

Recipes

Key to the Painting

top: pear-shaped guavas;
center: pink-fleshed guavas;
the small purple fruits are Strawberry guavas;
bottom: white-fleshed guava with feijoa fruits and flower left and right

The oldest known traces of the **GUAVA** being eaten date from about 800 BC, from archaeological sites in Peru. The tree, *Psidium guajava*, was probably first cultivated there, but had spread as far north as Mexico by 200 BC. Europeans first met and enjoyed the fruit when they arrived in Haiti, where the local name for it was "guayavu"; Spanish and Portuguese mariners soon spread the tree and its name to other regions. In the 17th century it was well established in India and Southeast Asia, and has remained popular there ever since. It is also grown in Hawaii and in southern Florida and southern California.

Guava fruits vary in size, shape, and color, even within the principal species, *P guajava*. They range from the size of an apple to that of a plum, and may be round or pear-shaped, rough- or smooth-skinned, and greenish white, yellow, or red in color. Large, pear-shaped, white ones are considered the best. The fruit has an outer and inner zone, the last with many small gritty seeds; but there are seedless varieties.

The taste is acid but sweet, with an unusual aromatic quality partly due to eugenol, an essential oil found also in cloves. Unripe guavas are astringent, but if picked when nearly ripe they are soon ready to eat. Because of this rapid ripening, fresh guavas cannot be sent over long distances.

Apart from being eaten fresh, guavas can be used like many other fruits in the confection of custards, ices and cool drinks. They can also be made into a particularly good jelly, for which small, sour fruits are best used. This jelly, which has a musky flavor, was declared by the illustrious American author Wilson Popenoe (1920) to be generally accepted as easily the best jelly in the world. Another preserve sometimes made is a stiff paste of "guava cheese", similar to the thick Brazilian jam called "goiabada".

In the West Indies the fruit shells are stewed to make "cascos de guayaba", often served with cream cheese.

Of the various other closely related species, *P cattleianum*, the strawberry or Cattley guava, is the best. It is a native of Brazil, produces round reddish-green fruits, and is now widely cultivated. The variety *lucida*, known as the Chinese strawberry guava, bears yellow fruits which are particularly good. These fruits are called strawberry guava because their sweet and aromatic (but not musky) flavor recalls that of the strawberry.

The **FEIJOA**, *Feijoa sellowiana*, a small evergreen tree with gray-green leaves, is a native of South America where it is found at high altitudes in parts of Argentina, Uruguay, southern Brazil, and Paraguay. It can be grown in many warm temperate zones of the world, and was probably brought to southern Europe by the Spaniards. Some very old trees in Seville survive. The feijoa is often treated as an ornamental tree, but it bears edible fruit and is grown commercially, for example in New Zealand, where the flavor and keeping qualities of the fruit have made it popular.

It is oval in shape, not more than 3 inches in length, with a green, bloom-covered skin which may be blushed with red. The granular whitish flesh surrounding a pulp containing many tiny seeds has a flavor somewhere between pineapple and strawberry. The aromatic appeal of the fruit increases as it ripens.

The traditional method of harvesting was to gather the fruits when they fell to the ground. This is awkward for commercial growers, whose system is to have the few fruits which ripen daily on each tree picked immediately, at just the right stage, before they drop off. Subtle changes in color enable the expert picker to select the right fruits.

The earlier part of the feijoa crop is best marketed as fresh fruit. The fruits which ripen later are mostly used to produce canned juice, but can also be stewed, or made into jams and jellies.

Jaboticaba, Grumichama, Jambolan, Rose Apple, Pitanga

Here we come to a group of tropical fruits of which several have names which sound as though they come from Edward Lear's *Book of Nonsense*. A convenient collective name for them is Eugenia fruits, after the genus *Eugenia*, to which all of them used to be assigned.

The **JABOTICABA**, *Myciaria* (formerly *Eugenia*) *cauliflora*, is a Brazilian species, much cultivated in the region of Rio de Janeiro. The large tree bears its fruits directly on the trunk, main limbs and branches. The fruits are round and about 1 inch in diameter, maroon or purple in color and not unlike a grape, but with a thicker skin. The white or pinkish pulp is translucent, and Brazilians enjoy it fresh.

The **GRUMICHAMA** of Brazil, sometimes called Brazil cherry, *Eugenia brasiliensis*, is a tree of southern Brazil and Peru, also grown in Hawaii, which bears a crimson fruit with soft flesh of a mild flavor. Popenoe (1923) compared it with a Bigarreau cherry. The grumichama exists in several varieties, distinguished by the color of the flesh (dark red, vermilion or white) but of equal merit. Among various close relations is *E luschnathiana*, the pitomba. Its small fruits, orange in color and reminiscent of apricots, are little known outside Brazil.

The **JAMBOLAN**, *Syzygium cumini* (formerly *Eugenia jambolana*), grows wild in India and much of Southeast Asia and is cultivated in some countries of the region and in Hawaii. It may also be called Java plum and black plum. The flesh is either white or purple, depending on the variety. The white-fleshed kind is sweeter than the other, but the taste is always astringent, which is why Asians rub the fruit with salt before eating it. The juice is a good basis for cool drinks.

ROSE APPLE is the unsatisfactory English name most commonly applied to any of a group of fruits of the genus *Syzygium* (formerly *Eugenia*), which it might be better to call by the Indian / Malay name jambu, the meaning of which is explained on the left. Rose apples are all indigenous to Southeast Asia or the Indian subcontinent. They do bear a superficial resemblance to apples, but are quite different to eat. The four principal species in the group are:
Syzygium jambos, the true rose apple or Malabar plum, is cultivated in the West Indies as well as in Asia. The fruit may reach the size of a small apple and is yellow, often tinged with pink, or greenish in color, with a waxy surface and a delicate aroma of rose. The flesh within is also rose-scented, whitish, crisp and juicy but rather tasteless, so best mixed with other fruits which have more flavor.
S malaccense, the Malay (rose) apple, is the fruit of a tall and striking tree which is cultivated from India to Hawaii (where it had arrived before the Europeans). The fruits, which are roundish but slightly oblong and narrowed at the stalk end, measure about $2\frac{1}{2}$ inches and have waxy skins, rosy when ripe, with faint white markings. The flesh is scented, juicy, and slightly sweet.
S samarangense, the Java (rose) apple or Semarang rose apple, has fruits which are nearly round, or bell-shaped, and measure about 2 inches. They are commonly pale green or whitish, but sometimes pink, and have little flavor.
S aqueum, the watery rose apple or water apple, has an uneven shape, wider at the apex than at the base. Color varies from white to bright pink. The flesh is crisp and watery (so a good thirst-quencher) and scented.

The **PITANGA**, or Surinam cherry, is the fruit of *Eugenia uniflora*, native to a region extending from Central America to Brazil. The ribbed fruits, up to $1\frac{1}{2}$ inches wide, are red to dark purple when fully ripe. These are edible, after suitable preparation. It is best to slit them open, rid them of their resinous seeds, chill them for a while to dispel the resinous aroma, and then sprinkle them with sugar.

Carambola, Belimbing Asam, Goraka

family OXALIDACEAE

Other Names for *CARAMBOLA*

French: *carambole*
German: *Carambola*
Spanish: *carambola*
Portuguese: *carambola*
Hindi: *kamrakh*
Sri Lanka: *karamanga, yeongtoh* (foreign peach)
Malay / Indonesian: *belimbing manis*
Thai: *ma fueang*
Japanese: *gorenshi*

Other Names for *BELIMBING ASAM*

French: *carambole bilimbi, cornichon des Indes*
Bengali: *kamranga*
Thai: *taling pling*
Malay: *belimbing asam, belimbing buloh*
Indonesian: *belimbing wuluh*
Philippines: *kamias*
Japanese: *birinbin*
Jamaica: *bimbling plum*
Haiti: *blimblin*
Cuba: *grosella China*
El Salvador / Nicaragua: *mimbro*

We come now to a pair of fruits which have a distinct resemblance to each other, but play different roles in Southeast Asia, the region where they are mainly grown and most popular. One can be sweet enough to eat raw with pleasure; but the other is too acid for this, and is mainly used in chutneys and curries, although it can also be used for making a good drink of the lemonade type.

CARAMBOLA, *Averrhoa carambola*, is a small tree or shrub native to parts of Indonesia, and perhaps also Sri Lanka. It is cultivated not only in Southeast Asia, India and Sri Lanka, but also, to a lesser extent, in other tropical countries. The fruit may be up to 5 inches long and has five prominent ridges running down it, so that a cross section is star-shaped. Hence the alternative name starfruit, and others such as "five corner" and "five fingers".

The fruit has a waxy, orange-yellow skin, with crisp, yellow, juicy flesh when ripe. Of the two principal sorts of carambola, one is small and acid (and makes a good metal polish), while the other is larger, with a bland but sweeter flavor. However, there are numerous varieties, and these exhibit different degrees of sourness and sweetness. The best seem to be those which have a relatively high content of ascorbic acid and only a little oxalic acid.

The Javanese sometimes propagate the trees vegetatively by air layering, a technique which involves making a parcel of soil around a branch so that it strikes root and can be cut off and planted. (Growing fruit from seed may produce a sour-fruited tree, which would not suit the Javanese, who eat the fruit as dessert and like it to be as sweet as possible.)

The ridges are trimmed off before the fruit is eaten fresh, but slices still retain their star shape and look well in fruit salads. The ripe carambola is also cooked, in both sweet and savory dishes. The juice is drunk or used as a seasoning.

BELIMBING ASAM, *Averrhoa bilimbi*, is a fruit-bearing tree, native to Malaysia, which has no English name. "Asam" refers to the sourness of the fruit. The fruit is also distinguishable by its smooth, unridged, yellowish-green skin, looking a little like a pickle.

Juicy and acid, the fruit is used in Malaysia, Indonesia and the Philippines for making pickles, such as the Malay "sunti"; in curries; and to stew as a vegetable. In Indonesia, however, it is caramelized with sugar to make a sweetmeat known as "manisan" (something sweet). Dried slices of the fruit are available in the markets.

The bilimbi reached the West Indies towards the end of the 18th century, and has since been planted throughout Central America. It is also grown extensively in Zanzibar.

The **GORAKA** deserves mention as another relation of the carambola. It is the fruit of a small tree, *Garcinia cambogia*, and is used as a flavoring, thickening and souring agent in Sri Lanka. The fruits are about the size of an orange, yellow or orange in color, and fluted on the outside. The interior is divided into segments, and it is these which are sun-dried and stored. They turn black as they dry.

Key to the Painting

top: bilimbis;
below: carambolas

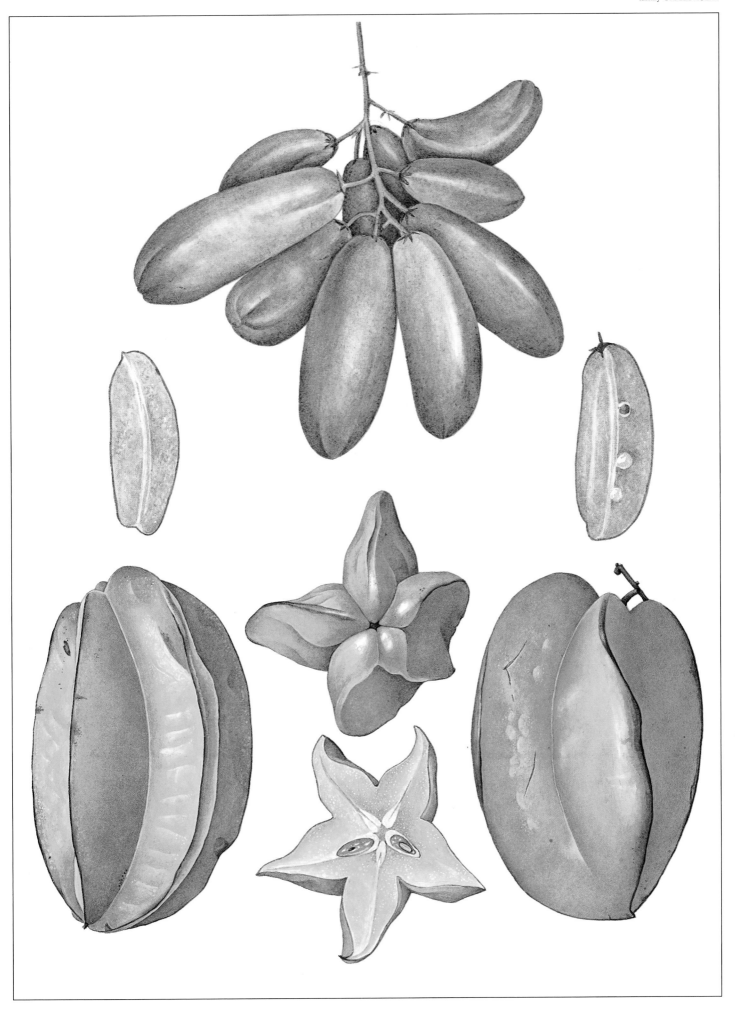

Banana

family MUSACEAE

Other Names for *BANANA*

French: *banane*
German: *Banane*
Italian: *banana*
Spanish: *plátano, banana*
Portuguese: *banana*
Dutch: *banaan*
Danish / Norwegian / Swedish: *banan*
Finnish: *banaani*
Russian: *banan*
Polish: *banan*
Hungarian: *banbán*
Serbo-Croat: *banana*
Romanian / Bulgarian: *banan*
Greek: *banana, mpanána*
Turkish: *muz*
Hebrew: *banana*
Arabic: *mūz*
Persian: *mūz*
Indian languages: *kela* (Hindi); *vazha
pazham* (Tamil)
Burmese: *hnget-pyaw*
Thai: *kluey* / *kluay*
Malay / Indonesian: *pisang*
Philippines: *saging*
Chinese: *jiao*
Japanese: *banana*
African languages: *maso, ndizi* (Swahili):
ikindu, kitoke (East Africa); *banema*
(Guinea)
Pacific languages: *usi* (New Guinea); *uch,
ut* (Micronesia); *vudi* (Fiji); *futo* (New
Caledonia); *futi* (West Polynesia)

Etymological Note

The whole story of the botanical names for the banana is interesting. *Musa* goes back to the Sanskrit "moca", but does not seem to have attained its latinized form until the Middle Ages, via the Arabic "mouz", first used in the 13th century. The old specific name *sapientium* (meaning "of the wise men") had its origin in a pleasing legend recounted by the classical writer Theophrastus: that wise men sat in the shade of the banana tree and ate its fruit. This old name was reserved for sweet, eating bananas. Plantains or cooking bananas were assigned to *M paradisiaca*, another name with a story behind it. In an Islamic myth, probably of Indian origin, the banana was the fruit of the Tree of Knowledge of Good and Evil, in the Garden of Eden (which was fittingly situated in Sri Lanka). Furthermore, after the Fall, Adam and Eve covered their nakedness with banana leaves rather than those of the fig. This may account for the common West Indian practice of calling a banana a fig. It is certainly true that large pieces of banana leaf would have been much more effective for Adam and Eve than small fig leaves.

Key to the Painting

top right: lady's finger bananas;
bottom left: rice bananas

The **BANANA** is remarkable in many ways. According to Ochse (1961) "more bananas are consumed daily than perhaps any other fruit in the world". Those which are imported and eaten by inhabitants of the temperate countries are almost uniform in appearance. A banana is a banana, and the buyer's choice is normally limited to size and degree of ripeness. But in the tropical regions where bananas grow there are countless varieties, and purchasers can exercize the same sort of discrimination that Europeans and Americans apply, or used to apply, to apples and pears.

There are, moreover, both eating bananas and cooking bananas. The latter are usually called plantains, and are edible only when cooked. But they are not a separate species.

The banana plant, of the genus *Musa*, is a strange growth, which looks like a palm tree, but is not a tree at all. It is a perennial herb which grows a complete new "trunk" every year, and dies back to its roots after it has flowered and fruited. This is all the more remarkable in that some kinds grow to a height of 40 feet. The "trunk" is in fact composed of overlapping bases of leaves wrapped tightly to make a fairly rigid column. New leaves constantly emerge at the top, forming a crown of leaves which are blown into tattered strips by the wind (a neat evolutionary adaptation to lower their wind resistance, for the "trunk" is not as strong as a real tree trunk and risks being blown down).

Eventually the flowering stem emerges at the top, bearing a large flower surrounded by red bracts, the whole growth having a strikingly phallic appearance. The bananas develop some way back from the flowering tip of the stem. The increasing weight causes the stem to bend over, so that the fruits point upwards. They are arranged in "hands" of 10 to 20 bananas set in a double row in a half spiral around the stem. There may be up to 15 hands in a complete bunch, which can weigh 99 pounds or more.

The flowers of the wild banana of the Malaysian / Indonesian region, *Musa acuminata*, often fail to be fertilized, and then produce reasonable fruits. This wild plant, sometimes known as the monkey banana, must have been used for food from the earliest times. At some time in the prehistoric era cultivation began, and growers would have encouraged varieties with the least tendency to produce seeds. However, before the plant had been driven into complete insterility, it crossed with an inedible wild species, *M balbisiana*. The resulting hybrid bore fruits which were of superior quality and almost invariably seedless. Improved descendants of both *M acuminata* and the hybrid form the majority of cultivated bananas; and botanists classify bananas of this group in the series of *Eumusa* (good banana) cultivars. The earliest written record of their cultivation is Indian, of the 6th century BC. The banana was certainly known to the Greeks in the 4th century BC, when the army of Alexander the Great encountered it on the tree in India.

The banana reached China about AD 200, when it is mentioned in the works of Yang Fu. By the T'ang dynasty (618 to 907) it was already well established, but it was grown only in the south, and was considered a rare, exotic fruit in the north. This attitude lasted into the 20th century, as the following story of the nationalist wars of the 1930s shows. The northern Manchurian warlord, Wu Chünsheng, had been invited to Peking, and was attending a banquet. At the end of the meal, a bowl of fresh fruit was set in front of him. He selected a banana and ate it, peel and all. His host, wishing to offer a tactful hint, also took a banana and conspicuously peeled it before eating it. Wu, now well aware of his error but not wanting to lose face, took a second banana and said, "I always eat these things with the peel on". Then he did it again.

During the first millennium AD the banana reached Africa, probably taken directly from the Malay region to Madagascar. By the end of the 14th century the

The main commercial varieties of the banana are Gros Michel and Cavendish. Gros Michel is the familiar, big, yellow eating banana which has for decades been the main export variety. It is thick-skinned, robust in shipment, reliable in quality and of adequate flavor. It has long been grown in Southeast Asia and Sri Lanka. In Malaysia and Indonesia it is called "pisang Ambon" (Amboyna banana) and in Thailand "kluay hom". Introduced to the West Indies in 1835, it soon became the dominant variety, and is often called the Jamaican banana.

Cavendish bananas are of southern Chinese origin. The most popular cultivar is Dwarf Cavendish, named not for the size of the fruit but because the plant has a short stem. This variety can stand a cooler climate than most bananas. The Canary banana is a subvariety of Dwarf Cavendish. Cavendish bananas are shorter, blunter, duller colored and thinner skinned than Gros Michel. The flavor of most kinds is better, and they are preferred in Asia.

Lacatan is another export variety very similar to export types of Dwarf Cavendish. It is the Lakatan of the Philippines, where it is regarded as the best banana in the world. It is highly aromatic and its pulp is sweet, firm, and light orange-yellow when ripe.

Other varieties, including some particularly good ones, are usually eaten only in the regions where they are grown, because their skins are too thin or their lives too short to permit export except by air, as a luxury item.

Among these less familiar varieties is the silk banana, grown in tropical regions worldwide. In the French West Indies alternative names are used, meaning plum, apple, or pineapple fig. It has very white flesh and a sweet but sharp taste.

A similar variety, also widely grown, is the lady's finger or apple banana.

A small, thin-skinned, deep yellow banana of bulbous shape is called "sucrier" or bird's fig in the West Indies and "pisang mas" (golden banana) in Malaysia and Indonesia. It is a major variety in New Guinea and is known in the Philippines. The flavor is sweet and pleasing.

The Mysore banana grows well in poor soil and is often cultivated in the more barren parts of Asia. It is quite a good eating variety. The Thai name for it means milk of heaven.

Both in Asia and the West Indies there are several kinds of red banana, sometimes green striped, with pink flesh. They are delicious, but frail and shortlived. Nevertheless a few are exported to the USA.

Recipes

Key to the Painting

red bananas

fruit was being cultivated right across the continent to the west coast. During the same period it was taken eastward through the Pacific islands. And the Arabs spread cultivation through their lands south of the Mediterranean before AD 650, but no farther north than Egypt. It was, incidentally, an Egyptian banana which prompted Disraeli, writing to his sister in England from Cairo in 1831, to exclaim: "the most delicious thing in the world is a banana."

Since the climate in southern Europe is too cool for the plant, the banana remained unknown to most Europeans. The first serious European contact with the fruit came not long after 1402, when Portuguese sailors found it in West Africa and took it to the Canary Islands. That is why the European name banana comes from a West African word, the Guinean "banema" or "banana". The Canaries have remained an important banana-growing area ever since.

In 1516, the Spanish missionary Friar Tomas de Berlanga took banana roots from the Canaries to the West Indies. Later, when he was made Bishop of Panama, the fruit reached the American mainland with him. Other missionaries followed his example, and the new plant spread quickly through Central America and the northern parts of South America. For some reason the Spaniards saw a likeness between the banana tree and the totally different plane tree ("plateno"), which is how the plantain got its confusing name.

During the 19th century occasional small consignments of bananas were sent by fast ships from the Canaries to Europe and from Cuba to the USA. Early varieties had not been bred for keeping qualities, so the fruit had to arrive in little more than two weeks and was an expensive luxury.

The international banana trade was started by two American entrepreneurs, Captain Lorenzo D Baker and Minor C Keith, who independently in 1870 and 1872 began to ship bananas from the Caribbean to New Orleans, Boston, and New York. They also set up plantations on virgin soil in producing areas. In 1899 they merged their interests to form the United Fruit Company. This organization had and still has great influence in Central America and the islands, for most of the trade of these lands depended on it. Thus the producing countries acquired the derogatory name "banana republics", while liberal politicians castigated the company for its allegedly repressive influence.

Whatever view is taken of this influence, the company must be given credit for making the banana a familiar and inexpensive fruit in temperate lands. Other companies followed its lead. West Indian bananas began to appear in Europe as well. Once Europeans had seen the handsome, big, yellow Caribbean bananas they lost interest in the small, brown Canary ones, although these had a finer flavor.

Ripening of eating bananas has aroused some argument. Bananas grown for export are picked when only two thirds ripe, and continue to ripen during shipment. Some say that bananas ripened off the tree are inferior in flavor, and that they should be left attached to ripen in the sun until the last possible moment. This principle is undoubtedly correct for some fruits, such as apricots; but the United Fruit Company questions its applicability to bananas:

> The truth is that no resident of the tropics eats bananas directly from the tree. He gathers the bunch at the same stage of ripeness as the fruit which is harvested for export (fully developed but green), then he hangs it in a shady spot and waits for it to ripen. He does this because experience has taught him that the majority of bananas, if left upon the tree until they ripen, split open and are attacked by insects which render the pulp unfit for eating, and that those which reach full ripeness without splitting have a pulp which has little flavor, is dry and unpleasantly mealy in character.

The ripening process involves a chemical change in which starch is converted to sugar, made up of sucrose 66%, fructose 14%, and glucose 20%. Protopectin is also converted to soluble pectin. As bananas ripen they give off ethylene gas. Most fruits do this during ripening, but bananas produce an exceptionally large amount. Ethylene causes ripening and development of color, as well as being produced by it, so one fruit can help another to ripen. A ripening banana put in a closed box with green tomatoes turns them red. It also helps a hard avocado to ripen overnight.

Apart from being eaten fresh, bananas may be made into interesting desserts, such as banana fritters and Caribbean sweet dishes in which bananas are flavored with rum. In India, bananas are made into various confections, spiced and sweetened with honey.

Date, Salak

Soft and Hard Dates

Soft dates have a high moisture content, relatively little sugar, and a mild flavor. They are grown in the Middle East mainly for eating fresh, though they are also dried, and compressed into blocks. Soft dates, especially those from Iraq, are mostly traded within the Middle East; but sometimes further afield, such as during the fasting month of Ramadan in Indonesia.

Hard dates, also called camel dates, are dry and fibrous even when fresh, and when further dried become extremely hard and sweet. They may be left whole or ground into flour. Either way, they keep for years. These are staple food dates of the Arab world, particularly for nomads.

Stages of Ripening and Drying

Date growers, including those in the USA, describe the stages of ripening and drying of the fruit with Arabic terms. When the fruit has reached full size and taken on its characteristic color (red or orange in Deglet Noor, dull yellow in Halawi, greenish in Khadrawi, yellow in Zahidi, and rich brown in Medjul) it is said to be at the "khalal" stage. After picking comes the "rutab" stage, when it softens, darkens, and begins to shrink. The final, "tamar", stage is when the fruit is fully cured and ready for packing.

Recipes

Koshaf (Iranian Dried Fruit Salad): page 155
Pears in Syrup: page 156

Key to the Painting

center: salak;
each corner: fresh dates at different stages of ripeness against date leaves

I t is said that the **DATE PALM**, *Phoenix dactylifera*, has 800 uses; and in gratitude to this universal provider the Arabs have a tradition that, in creating the world, Allah formed the date palm not from common clay but out of material left over from the making of Adam.

The date palm is a splendidly large tree which may exceed 100 feet in height. It is long-lived and never stops growing; but usually, after 100 years or so, it is so tall that it falls over.

The tree grows a new section every year, with fresh leaves emerging above the previous year's section; and the leaves live for an average of five years. Thus the tree consists of about five leafy sections on top of a stack of sections whose leaves have died, and this stack rises higher and higher from the ground.

The fruits are produced in large bunches of over 20 pounds in weight and containing as many as 1,000 dates. An average yield is about 100 pounds of fruit from each tree every year.

The place of origin must have been somewhere in the hot, dry region stretching from northern Africa through the Middle East to India; but somewhere with water, such as desert oases. As the Arabs say, "the date palm needs its feet in water and its head in the fire of the sky".

Date cultivation is of prehistoric origin, and dates were already a staple food in the earliest period of the Egyptian and Mesopotamian civilizations. The Romans were certainly fond of them. Since sugar was then almost unknown, the fruit was used as a sweetener, or else stuffed to make a sweetmeat.

Most dates are still grown in their region of origin, the biggest producers being Iraq, Iran, and Saudi Arabia. However, large quantities are also grown in North African countries, India, and Pakistan, in the drier parts of the American tropics, and in the hotter parts of the USA, especially California and Arizona.

The chief food value of the date lies in its very high sugar content, which can be 70% by weight in a fully dried date. It contains some protein, and some vitamins. Although it is not a perfectly balanced staple food, desert Arabs can exist in good health for long periods on almost nothing but dried dates and a little milk, which makes up most of the deficiencies.

There are three main types of date: "soft", "hard", and "semi-dry". There is a note on the left about the first two. The dates most popular in the West, and nearly all those grown in the USA, are of the third, "semi-dry", type. It is these which are sold packed in the familiar long boxes with a stem, or plastic imitation thereof, between the rows. They are less sweet than the other types, but more aromatic and distinctive.

The principal variety is Deglet Noor, a large date of fine flavor. Two varieties of Iraqi origin now also grown in the USA are Halawi (meaning sweet) and Khadrawi (green); but in Iraq itself the principal semi-dry variety is the less succulent Zahidi. The main Moroccan variety, Medjul (meaning "unknown"), is also cultivated in California.

Dried dates, but not those of the finest varieties, are sometimes sold "pitted". Whether they come this way or not, dates are fine material for stuffing, for example with cream cheese, thick cream, and the like, additionally flavored as you please. When I was living in Tunisia I kept a large earthenware pot on my desk, full of dates treated in the contrary manner: they were the stuffing inside a coat of pistachio marzipan.

SALAK is the Malay name for the fruit of some small, stemless palms which grow in parts of Southeast Asia. The best is *Zalaccia edulis*. The fruit is pear-shaped but smaller than a pear, and has a distinctive, shiny brown, scaly skin which peels off crisply to reveal a few white segments, tightly packed and containing seeds. The flesh is slightly dry and waxy, with a pleasant and slightly acid flavor.

Duku, Langsat, Santol

family MELIACEAE

Other Names for *DUKU* and
LANGSAT

French: *doukou* / *lansiam*
German: *Duku*
Spanish: *lanza*
Thai: *du-ku* / *lang-sat*
Malay / Indonesian : *duku* / *langsat*
Philippines: *lanzone(s)*

Other Names for *SANTOL*

Burmese: *thit-to*
Thai: *kra thon*
Malay: *sentul, kecapi*
Philippines: *santol*

The trees which bear the fruits described on this page are among the most attractive of Malaysia's native trees. The duku is not very tall, but has a broad and shapely crown, with dark leaves which make it a fine shade tree. The santol is large and tall, a stately sight. It is not only in Malaysia that one sees them, but I think of them as being typical of that country.

DUKU and **LANGSAT**, two Southeast Asian fruits of a Tweedledum and Tweedledee character, are both classified as *Lansium domesticum*, although one can readily be distinguished from the other and the two of them are recognized as separate botanical varieties. *L domesticum* var *domesticum* corresponds to the name duku and is the more widely cultivated. *L domesticum* var *pubescens*, which is the langsat, is often called "wild langsat" but it too is cultivated. Each variety has some desirable characteristics.

Cultivation takes place mainly in Malaysia, Indonesia (especially Java), and Thailand. Although the trees are native to West Malaysia, they have become common all over the region. It takes about 15 years for them to reach maturity, but the long wait is worthwhile since they then bear clusters of fruit twice a year.

Langsat has about 20 fruits in a cluster, each oval and just under $1\frac{1}{2}$ inches long, with a thin, pale fawn skin. Duku has only about 10 fruits to a cluster. They are round and larger, about 2 inches in diameter, with thicker skins. The flesh of both fruits is usually white, but in some cultivated varieties of duku it is pink. It is juicy and refreshing, with a taste ranging from sour to sweet. Each fruit is composed of five segments, some of which may contain bitter, inedible seeds. There are, however, seedless forms.

The fruits have excellent thirst-quenching properties. They may be eaten raw or preserved with sugar; and the seedless ones can be bottled in syrup.

According to folklore in the Philippines, where the fruits are known as lanzones, they used to be so sour as to be quite inedible, and indeed toxic. But it happened one day that a beautiful woman with a child, traveling through the countryside, could find nothing else to eat but lanzones. She accordingly picked one and gave it to the child. From then on the fruit acquired its present desirable characteristics, for the woman was none other than the Virgin Mary. However, the transformation which she wrought was not complete, since some lanzones still turn out to be very sour.

The **SANTOL**, *Sandoricum koetjape* (formerly *S indicum*), a fruit tree of Malaysia and parts of Indochina, was introduced long ago to Indonesia and the Philippines, and grows also in Mauritius. This is another case of twins, for it occurs in two main forms, one with sweet fruit and leaves which wither yellow, the other with sour fruit and leaves which turn to red. The latter is often called "kechapi".

This tree grows fast and produces an abundance of round fruits which have a tough, yellowish-brown skin enclosing five segments of white pulp. These fruits sometimes have an attractive aroma of peach. They are eaten fresh, dried or candied; or pickled, as in Thailand. Filipinos seem to be the greatest enthusiasts for the santol, and are busily breeding trees of superior quality.

Key to the Painting

langsats and seeds

Barbados Cherry, Carissa, Karanda, Roselle

The **BARBADOS CHERRY**, *Malpighia punicifolia* (formerly *glabra*) is the most important member of a group of small fruiting trees and shrubs of which most are native to tropical and subtropical America. It is also known as "acerola", and as the West Indian / Puerto Rican / native / garden cherry, and is much cultivated in the West Indies, where the fruit is eaten fresh or made into pies and preserves; and has been introduced elsewhere, for example Hawaii.

The fruit, bright red and the size of a cherry, has shallow furrows running down the outside, indicative of the three pits which fit closely together inside. The flesh is juicy and moderately acid, more like a raspberry than a cherry in flavor. When cooked it tastes like a tart apple. It is remarkably rich in vitamin C, outdoing even rosehips in this respect.

CARISSA and **KARANDA** are two closely related fruits of which the former is indigenous to South Africa and the latter to South Asia. *Carissa* is a botanical as well as a common name, referring to the genus of thorny, fruiting shrubs to which both fruits belong.

The more popular of the two species, *Carissa macrocarpa*, is also known as Natal plum, because it belongs to southern Africa, and "amantungula". In many places the tree is valued mainly as a thorny hedge and for its fragrant white flowers. However, it is sometimes cultivated for its edible fruits, which look like small scarlet plums, with dark red streaks on the skin. The flesh is red, flecked with white, and contains about a dozen thin brown seeds. The whole fruit can be eaten out of hand, without peeling or deseeding; the texture is slightly granular, the flavor mildly sharp. In the semi-ripe stage the fruits are used for making jellies and jams. Ripe fruits make a filling for pies.

The karanda, *C congesta*, is cultivated in India, where it was popular with British residents because it reminded them of the gooseberry, and some parts of Southeast Asia and East Africa. Its fruits resemble the carissa and are used in similar ways.

The **ROSELLE** (sometimes rozelle), *Hibiscus sabdariffa*, is also called red sorrel or Jamaica sorrel, although it did not reach Jamaica until the beginning of the 18th century and is not a close relation of sorrel. It probably originated in Africa, but is now cultivated in many tropical regions, including Southeast Asia. A woody annual, it bears green leaves on stems which are usually red. Of the two main varieties, *H sabdariffa* var *sabdariffa* is the one which includes all the cultivars grown for food.

The plant is unusual in that its main edible part is not the fruit but the calyx of the fruit. The calyx is what is familiar as the little green star on top of a tomato or strawberry. In this instance it is red, large and fleshy, and enwraps a small, useless fruit. It is made into a refreshing, sour "sorrel" drink in the West Indies and elsewhere, and is also used to produce jellies and jams. Gladys Graham (1947), writing from Panama, says of it:

> Sorrel is such an important beverage and jam-jelly ingredient that highway crews widening Central American roads will cut down every other shrub and tree in their way, leaving the sorrel to blossom on the road shoulders. It comes at the end of wet season, or the beginning of dry, and the sorrel drinks of Christmas times are almost as important as the attendant ceremonies and fetes. The product will taste a little more like cranberries than cherries.

The calyces are marketed dried as well as fresh, and are the source of a red food colorant. The Filipino author Maria del Oroso, whose collected essays on food were published in 1970, recommended a remarkable range of uses for them embodied in 60 recipes; these included sauces and omelets and cakes, as well as beverages. The roselle was introduced to the Philippines in 1905, shortly after it arrived in Australia and the USA.

Mangosteen, Mamey

family GUTTIFERACEAE

Other Names for *MANGOSTEEN*

French: *mangoustan, mangouste*
German: *Mangostane*
Italian: *mangostana*
Spanish: *mangostán*
Portuguese: *mangostão*
Tamil: *manggis*
Burmese: *mingut*
Thai: *mang khut*
Malay / Indonesian: *manggis*
Philippines: *manggostan*
Chinese: *shan zhu*

Minor *Garcinia* species

These are only some of them. . .

G atroviridis is "asam gelugur" in Malay and Indonesian and "som khaek" or "som mawon" in Thai. The fruit is as big as a large apple, vertically ribbed, and yellow to orange in color. It is sour, best stewed with sugar.

G cochinchinensis, found in Vietnam and South China as well as Indonesia, has plum-sized, reddish or reddish-yellow fruits of agreeable flavor.

G dulcis, wild in the Philippines but cultivated in Malaysia, has yellow fruits the size of a small orange. They are eaten raw, although sour, or cooked with sugar, or made into jam.

G globulosa is common in Malaysia and Indonesia, where it is called "asam kandis". It bears grape-sized fruits whose sweet pulp is eaten raw. It is sometimes cultivated.

G nigrolineata has orange fruits like the above, but larger and sweeter, so called "kandis jantan" (big kandis).

G hombroniana, an Indonesian and Malaysian species called "manggis hutan" (jungle mangosteen) has a fruit with the flavor of a slightly sour peach, which is eaten raw.

G prainiana, sometimes cultivated in West Malaysia as "cepu", has fruits the size of a plum, acid but edible.

Other Names for *MAMEY*

French: *abricot de St Domingue*
German: *Mameyapfel*
Spanish: *mamey de Santo Domingo*
Portuguese: *abricozeiro*
Brazil: *abricó do Pará*

Key to the Painting

top and bottom: mangosteen;
center: mamey

The **MANGOSTEEN** is the fruit of a small tropical tree, *Garcinia mangostana*, which is native to Malaysia and Indonesia. This is a pernickety tree: slow-growing, difficult to propagate, and exacting about climate and soil. However, it has been successfully cultivated in parts of Vietnam (which had the largest mangosteen orchard in the world), Thailand, Cambodia, Burma, Sri Lanka, and the Philippines. The reward is great; witness the following eulogy from Fairchild (1930):

The fruit is about the size of a mandarin orange, round and slightly flattened at each end, with a smooth, thick rind, rich red-purple in colour, with here and there a bright, hardened drop of the yellow juice which marks some injury to the rind when it was young. . . . they are strikingly handsome . . . but it is only when the fruit is opened that its real beauty is seen. The rind is thick and tough, and in order to get at the pulp inside, it requires a circular cut with a sharp knife to lift the top half off like a cap, exposing the white segments, five, six, or seven in number, lying loose in the cup. The cut surface of the rind is of a moist delicate pink colour and is studded with small yellow points formed by the drops of exuding juice. As one lifts out of this cup, one by one, the delicate segments, which are the size and shape of those of a mandarin orange, the light pink sides of the cup and the veins of white and yellow embedded in it are visible. The separate segments are between snow white and ivory in colour, and are covered with a delicate network of fibres, and the side of each segment where it presses against its neighbour is translucent and slightly tinged with pale green. The texture of the mangosteen pulp much resembles that of a well-ripened plum, only it is so delicate that it melts in the mouth like a bit of ice-cream. The flavour is quite indescribably delicious.

Some other minor *Garcinia* species which provide food are listed in the left-hand column. Two more important ones are:

G indica, the kokam or kokan, an Asian tree which produces round, purple fruits the size of a small orange. These have various uses, the best known being the production of "kokam butter", extracted from the kernels, in south-western India. The description of this by Watt (1890) is not enticing. "Kokam butter, as found in the bazaars of India, consists of egg-shaped or concavo-convex cakes of a dirty white or yellowish colour, friable, crystalline, and with a greasy feel like spermaceti." He adds, however, that the product, when fresh, has a smell which is "not unpleasant", and melts in the mouth like butter, leaving a sensation of cold on the tongue.

G xanthocymus, the gamboge tree of Malaysia and South India, has been introduced to the New World tropics. It bears large crops of yellow peach-shaped fruits, the size of an apple, with yellow pulp. Some are sweet enough to eat raw. The flavor is mysteriously described by Uphof (1968) as: "between that of a good strawberry and a sour apple"; fine for breakfast, he says, with sugar and cream.

The **MAMEY** (or mammee), *Mammea americana*, a fruit native to the West Indies, is now cultivated throughout tropical America, and to some extent in Southeast Asia. Its other names include mammee apple, and San Domingo or South American apricot; but it belongs to the same family as the mangosteen, and is related neither to apples nor to apricots.

A mamey fruit is the size of an orange or larger, round but with slight points at the top and bottom. The tough skin, yellowish russet in color, is bitter, as is the covering of the three seeds. The pulp between is firm, has something of the flavor of an apricot, and is of the same golden color. This is usually stewed, often in wine, or made into jam.

Ramontchi, Lovi-Lovi, Rukam, Paniala, Ketembilla, Abyssinian Gooseberry

family FLACOURTIACEAE

Other Names for *RAMONTCHI*

French: *prune de Madagascar, grosse prune de café*
German: *echte Flacourtie*
Spanish: *ramontchi, ciruela governadora*
Sri Lanka: *uguressa*
Burma: *na-yu-wai*
Thai: *ta khop paa*
Malay / Indonesian: *kerkup kechil*

Other Names for *LOVI-LOVI*

French: *prune de la Martinique*
German: *Lovi-Lovi*
Spanish: *louvi malayo*
Thai: *ta khop thai*
Malay: *tomi-tomi*
Indonesian: *lobi-lobi*
Philippines: *louvi; governor's plum, ratiles*

Other Names for *RUKAM*

French: *prune malgache, prunier café, prune de Chine*
German: *Batoko, Madagaskarpflaume*
Spanish: *ciruela de Madagascar*
Thai: *ta khop thai*
Malay: *rukam*
Indonesian: *rukem*

It must be said that the family Flacourtiaceae, to which this page is devoted, does not include any fruits of outstanding merit, although it is possible that greatly improved varieties of some of them may be developed. All are cultivated, and may be met here or there in the markets of tropical countries.

The **RAMONTCHI**, *Flacourtia ramontchi*, also known as Governor's plum, is a shrubby tree, a native of India, but introduced in the distant past to islands of the southern Indian Ocean and now planted throughout the tropics. Like other *Flacourtia* species, it often becomes naturalized after having escaped cultivation.

The fruit is like a red plum in shape, size, and color. The pulp is yellowish white, juicy and usually acid; but some cultivated varieties are sweet enough to be eaten raw. Unripe fruits are good for making jellies, jams, preserves, syrups and similar products.

The pleasantly named **LOVI-LOVI**, *F inermis*, is of unknown origin; it is now found in the Far East and other tropical areas, where it is cultivated both for its fruit and for its decorative foliage. The fruits are round, the size of large cherries, and dark red when ripe. Some are sweet; but most are sour and astringent, and are normally used for making jams, jellies, preserves and syrups. They are the best of the *Flacourtia* fruits for these purposes.

The **RUKAM**, *F rukam*, perhaps native to Madagascar and South Asia, is often found naturalized throughout the Asian tropics, and has been introduced to the American tropics and subtropics.

The roundish fruits are about 1 inch in diameter, nearly black in color when ripe, and have a juicy, acid, yellowish-white pulp. They vary in sweetness but there is at least one variety which is fine to eat raw when ripe. Like the ramontchi, the rukam can also be made into jams and so forth when slightly unripe.

F cataphracta, the **PANIALA**, a native of India and Malaysia, is cultivated in the Far East and has also been introduced to the New World. It resembles the rukam except that its fruits are maroon-purple in color.

The **KETEMBILLA**, the fruit of *Dovyalis hebecarpa*, a small shrub native to Sri Lanka, resembles a deep purple cherry but is covered with fine hairs. It is sometimes called Ceylon gooseberry. The flavor is very acid, and the fruit is generally used to make jams and jellies. It is now cultivated in a few other tropical countries including the Philippines, and is known in Hawaii, California and Florida.

A related African species, *D caffra*, is commonly called "kei apple" or "umkokolo". It occurs in both wild and cultivated forms in south-west Africa, near the Kei River. It has been introduced to the Mediterranean region, and is grown in the Philippines with the abbreviated name "umkolo". The fruit is soft and golden yellow when ripe, and is used to make jam.

The **ABYSSINIAN GOOSEBERRY**, *D abyssinica*, a native of the forests of East Africa, bears fruits which have the color and something of the flavor of the apricot; but there is not much flesh in them. A promising hybrid of it and the ketembilla may eventually prove to be a viable crop in Florida.

Key to the Painting
top: ketembillas and seeds;
center: Kei apples and leaves above;
bottom: ramontchis and leaves

Litchi, Longan, Rambutan, Pulasan, Mamoncillo

L ITCHI or lychee, *Litchi chinensis* (or *Nephelium litchi*), is the best known of a group of tropical fruits native to China and Southeast Asia. Indeed this fruit, canned, has achieved a sort of notoriety as the sole dessert which Chinese restaurants outside China are apt to offer. But it deserves to be treated on its merits, which are considerable.

Litchis are borne by a large, evergreen tree which has been cultivated in southern China since antiquity. During the 1st century AD it was considered the finest of southern delicacies and a special courier service with swift horses was set up to bring fresh litchis from Canton north to the Imperial Court.

Cultivation now spreads along a narrow belt of suitable climate through Thailand to Bangladesh and northern India. The Bengal region is especially productive and its crop has become larger than that of China. South Africa is a major producer, and litchis are also grown in Hawaii and in New Caledonia.

The round fruit is about $1\frac{1}{4}$ inches in diameter with a tough, knobbly skin which is red in the ripe fruit but turns brown during shipment abroad. Inside is a delicate, whitish pulp surrounding a single, large, shiny, dark brown seed. Only the pulp is eaten. It has a flavor reminiscent of the muscat grape.

The fruit travels well if picked just before it is fully ripe, so fresh litchis are available in Western countries, as well as canned pulps. Litchis are also dried whole; the skin becomes distorted, the inside rattles when the fruit is shaken, and the pulp takes on the character of a raisin.

The **LONGAN**, *Dimocarpus longan*, is a smaller fruit. It ripens later than the litchi, and withstands lower temperatures. Thus it thrives more than the litchi in certain areas, for example southern Florida. However, it is generally less esteemed, having what has been tactfully described as "a less sprightly flavor than the litchi" (or, a quite undeserved insult, as "not really worth eating if you can find anything else like an old car tire").

The **RAMBUTAN**, *Nephelium lappaceum*, native to the western lowlands of Malaysia, is now cultivated in many parts of Southeast Asia; in Sri Lanka; in Zanzibar, where it was introduced at an early date by Arab traders; and elsewhere. It is closely related to the litchi.

The fruits vary in quality and type. There are crimson, greenish and yellow or orange varieties. The inner part of the fruit is smaller than a litchi, but the outside looks larger because of the long "hairs" which give it its name: "rambut" is Malay for hair. It looks slightly like a sweet chestnut. The flavor is usually more acid than a litchi, but highly aromatic, and the seed has an almond-like flavor.

The **PULASAN**, *Nephelium mutabile*, is a fruit which resembles the rambutan, but differs in having much shorter hairs on the skin, and is usually dark red. In most kinds the seed is large and there is little pulp, but what there is is delicate and sweeter than that of the rambutan. In addition, the seed is more easily removed. Indeed a seedless variety is grown in Thailand.

MAMONCILLO or genip are just two of numerous names for a fruit which is widely available in the markets of tropical America. It is borne on a large tree, *Melicocca bijuga*, and is also known as honeyberry (echoing the generic name, in which "meli" means honey and "kokkos" means berry). In Barbados it may bear the name "akee", the unusual "vegetable fruit" to which it is related.

Since the cherry-sized green fruit looks like a small lime, it is sometimes called Spanish lime or "limoncillo". It has a single seed, or two seeds flattened together. The sweet, gummy pulp is orange-pink in color and has a refreshing flavor, reminiscent of grapes.

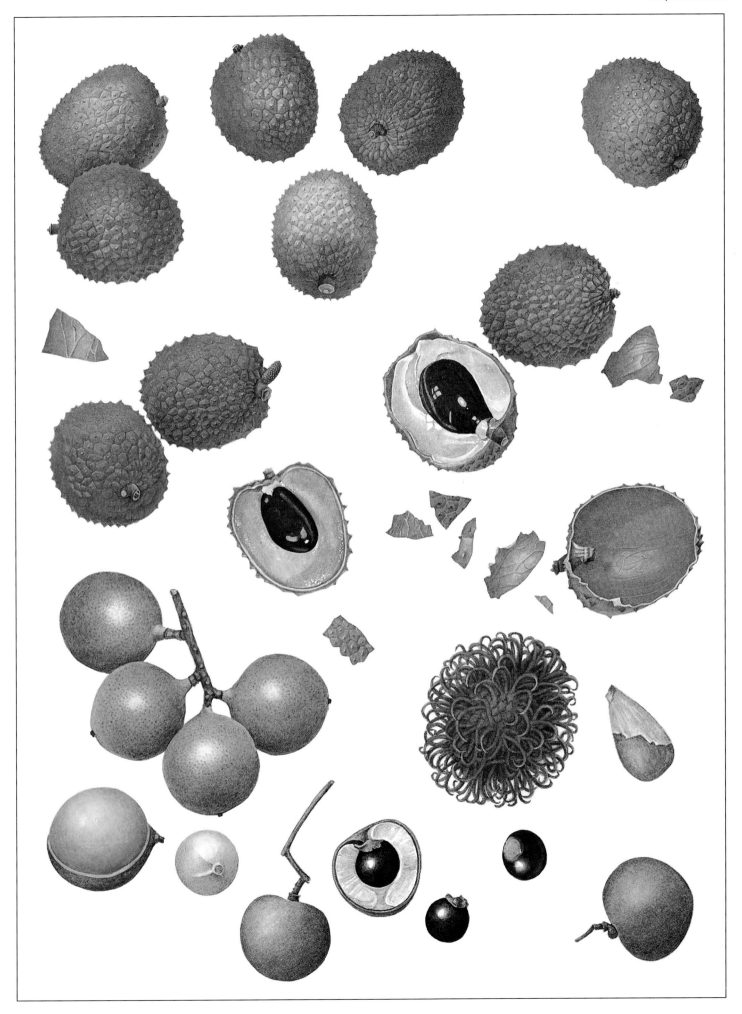

Sapodilla, Sapote, Canistel, Star Apple

Key to the Painting

top left: star apple with section, leaves
and seeds;
right: sapodillas, leaves and seeds; oval
variety from Indonesia above, round
from West Indies below;
bottom: canistel and section

The **SAPODILLA** is the fruit of *Manilkara zapota* (or *achras*), an evergreen tree native to Mexico and Central America, which also produces the gum chicle, from which chewing gum is made. The name is a diminutive of "sapota", on which see below. The tree was cultivated in the region long before the arrival of the Spaniards. The Spaniards liked the fruit and introduced it to the Philippines, whence it spread through Southeast Asia and to India.

The fruit is a round or oval berry between 2–4 inches in diameter, with a brown fuzz over its yellow skin. The flesh is yellow-brown, sometimes pinkish, with a soft, translucent juicy pulp containing flat black seeds. The aspect of the interior resembles that of a pear, except that the seeds are larger. The French botanist Descourtilz described it as having "the sweet perfumes of honey, jasmine, and lily of the valley". Another comparison is with brown sugar.

The sapodilla is usually eaten raw from the half-shell, though in the West Indies it may be boiled down to make a syrup. Some prefer to eat it when thoroughly overripe, like a medlar. This is reflected in the name naseberry from the Spanish "níspola" (medlar) and in the French "nèfle d'Amérique".

SAPOTE, or sapota, anglicized forms of the Latin American "zapote", are names applied to numerous American tropical fruits (see also left-hand column). The word was taken up by the Spanish in Mexico from the native "tzapotl", which apparently just means "soft".

Pouteria (formerly *Lucuma*) *sapota* is the species with the best claim to the name sapote. It is found in the wild from southern Mexico to Nicaragua, but is now cultivated in other areas, including parts of Southeast Asia. It bears large fruits: generally oval in shape, from 3–8 inches long, with a rough, russet-colored skin, and a soft, sweet, salmon-colored pulp which is often made into jam.

The **CANISTEL**, *Pouteria campechiana* (formerly *Lucuma rivicoa*), is sometimes called egg-fruit, or yellow sapote because of its orange flesh. It occurs wild in parts of Central America, and is cultivated there and in some Caribbean islands, especially Cuba, for its fruits. These may reach a size of 5 inches long. The skin of the ripe fruit is lemon-yellow or orange-yellow and shiny. Inside, the flesh is relatively firm but becomes softer towards the center. Dr J Morton (1987) writes: "It has been often likened in texture to the yolk of a hard-boiled egg. The flavor is sweet, more or less musky, and somewhat like that of a baked sweet potato."

The former generic name of the sapota, *Lucuma*, is derived from a Peruvian fruit, *P obvata*, called "rucma" by the original inhabitants, and adapted to "lucuma" by the invading Spaniards. It is still popular in western Peru. The fruit is round, the size of an orange, with firm, sweet flesh. The flavor is rich but cloying.

Long before Europeans arrived in the West Indies and Central America, the **STAR APPLE**, *Chrysophyllum cainito*, was being cultivated there. It has always been prized for its ornamental value as well as for its fruits. The Victorian writer Charles Kingsley described it as being "like an evergreen peach, shedding from the underside of every leaf a golden light".

The tree is cultivated in tropical America, but attempts to introduce it into Asia have had limited success. The fruit is the size of a small apple, white ("cainito blanco") or purple ("cainito morado"), with a soft pulp containing a central "star" of flat, brown seeds set in translucent jelly. To be good, the fruit must be ripened on the tree. It is usually eaten fresh, but can be made into preserves. In Jamaica, the pulp is mixed with bitter orange juice to make a drink called "matrimony".

Several other *Chrysophyllum* species have edible fruits. Those of *C africanun*, the African star apple, are sometimes called Odara pears. *C monopyrenum*, the damson plum of Jamaica, is used mainly for its juices.

Mango

family ANACARDIACEAE

Other Names for *MANGO*

French: *mangue*
German: *Mango*
Italian: *mango*
Spanish: *mango, manguey*
Portuguese: *manga*
Greek: *mango*
Turkish: *mango, hint kirazi*
Hebrew: *mango*
Arabic: *māngū*
Persian: *amba*
Indian languages: *aam paka* (Hindi, Bengali); *mam pazham* (Tamil)
Burmese: *tha-yet*
Malay / Indonesian: *manga*
Thai: *ma muang*
Philippines: *mangga*
Chinese: *mang guo*
Japanese: *mangō*

Minor Edible Species

Most of the edible species of mango are found in South-East Asia. In Malaysia and Indonesia *M caesia* (binjai) and *M lagenifera* (lanjut) are both wild and cultivated. The pungent-smelling white flesh may be sweet enough, in some varieties, to be eaten raw.

M foetida, the "horse mango", is also pungent. The ripe sweet fruits are cooked, made into pickles, or sweetmeats. (It is "bacang" in Malay, "bawang" in Indonesian, "ma mut" in Thai.)

Other species used in cooking include *M kemanga* ("kemang" in Malay) and *M odorata* (Malay / Indonesian "kuwini").

Tip for the Cook

In Mexico one can buy special mango forks, designed to pierce the end of the pit, from which the remaining flesh can be nibbled.

Recipes

Tropical Fruit Salad: page 152
Mango and Almond Tart: page 162
Mango Ice Cream: page 173
Lime Bombe with Mango Sauce: page 173
Sherbet: page 174

Key to the Painting

mango

The **MANGO**, one of the finest tropical fruits, has been cultivated in India for several thousand years. The Indian mango, *Mangifera indica*, is only one of about 50 species of *Mangifera*, which grow naturally in the region from India east to the Philippines and Papua New Guinea, and of which nearly half have edible fruits. But of all these it is indisputably supreme.

The mango was first made known to the outside world, it is said, by the Chinese traveler Hwen T'sang who visited India in the 1st century AD. In succeeding centuries, cultivation of the fruit spread eastwards and also westwards, for it arrived in Persia by the 10th century.

On its home ground in India the mango became a status symbol. The Moghul ruler Akbar (1556–1605) planted an orchard of mango trees at Darbhanga in Bihar, called "Lakj Bagh" because the number of the trees was supposedly one lakh (one hundred thousand). And it was in Moghul India, during the same period, that the technique of vegetative reproduction was worked out, to avoid the problem caused by the fact that the trees often do not grow true from seed.

Meanwhile, still in the 16th century, the Portuguese took the mango from India to Africa. It reached Brazil and the West Indies in the 18th century, and Hawaii, Florida, and Mexico in the 19th century. However, although mangoes are now grown in all these areas, India remains the world's largest producer.

Fruits vary in length from 2 inches to over 10 inches and in weight from under 4 ounces to over $4\frac{1}{2}$ pounds. Some kinds are almost round, others long and narrow, but they generally have a slight ridge on one side and a more or less pronounced "beak" at one end. The skin may be yellow or orange with a red flush, or else greenish yellow (in the "white" varieties) through to a rich golden yellow. The large pit has fibers attached to it: very small and short in good varieties but thick and extending through the pulp in inferior ones.

The fruit is highly aromatic. At its best the scent has a pleasant resinous quality; at worst it smells strongly of kerosene which it actually contains, giving rise to a description of it being like "a ball of tow soaked in turpentine and molasses".

There are scores, indeed hundreds, of varieties of mango being grown. In her survey of them, Morton (1987) makes the interesting point that in India most of the preferred varieties have yellow skins, while Europeans prefer yellow turning to red, and Americans (in Florida, at least) go for red skins. Alphonso, an Indian cultivar, is the variety most often exported. The Haden variety is exceptionally large, and is suitable for use in cooking as well as for eating fresh. In the Philippines, pride of place goes to the "carabaou" mango (known as Manila Super in international trade), which is yellow outside and inside and has a fine spicy aroma, besides having only short fibers attached to the pit. And others are highly prized in other countries. (Which are the best of all? I both know and don't know. A friend in Laos told me of a princess in Thailand who had "the absolute best". When he visited the princess and brought me some back, my scepticism was completely dispelled. But, alas, I lost the notes which might have led me to the princess and her orchard.)

Mangoes ripen satisfactorily if picked before they are fully ripe, so they can be exported fresh. But mangoes should not be thought of only in terms of dessert. Some sorts of mango are considered to be most desirable when they are in the unripe, green, tart stage. Patricia Arroyo Staub (1982) remarks that Filipinos, especially women, like to eat green mangoes between meals, mitigating the tartness of these fruits by the application of salt or soy sauce or some other salty condiment. And vast numbers of mangoes are fated to become mango chutney, or amchur, the spice which is made by reducing dried mango to a powder.

The green mango from Thailand, shown in the painting on page 121, is sweet and ripe when green. After painting it, Charlotte Knox ate it and found it the best mango she had ever had.

Ambarella, Mombin, Imra, Imbu, Gandaria

family ANACARDIACEAE

Other Names for *AMBARELLA*

(Other "English" names include Brazil plum, hog plum, and Tahitian quince.)
French: *pomme cythère* (also in some former French territories); *évi*
German: *Cytherea, Tahiti-Apfel*
Spanish: *cirnela dulce* (Cuba)
Hindi: *amara*
Malay / Indonesian: *kedongdong*
Thai: *ma kok farang*
Tahiti: *vi*
Brazil: *caja-manga*
Venezuela: *jobo de la India*

Other Names for *IMRA*

hog plum (see text)
Thai: *ma kok*
Malay: *buah amara*
Indonesian: *kedongdong*

Other Names for *MOMBIN*
(names with asterisks are for *S lutea*)

French / French colonial: *mombin rouge; mombin jaune**
Spanish: *ciruela* (plum); *jobo**
Portuguese: *cajá mirim**
Mexico / Guatemala: *jocote (xocotl)*
Cuba: *ciruela roja; ciruela amarilla**
Brazil / Costa Rica: *caja, jobo*
Philippines: *siniguelas*

Other Names for *GANDARIA*

Thai: *ma prang*
Malay: *kundang*

Key to the Painting

center: green mango from Thailand with leaves;
above right: red mombin, yellow variety;
below left: gandarias and leaves;
below right: ambarella and leaves

The fruit called **AMBARELLA** is borne by *Spondias dulcis* (or *S cytherea*), a tree native to islands in the South Pacific, but now widely distributed in tropical and subtropical regions. It is cultivated, but not on a large scale.

The greyish-orange plum-like fruits are produced in pendent clusters of two to ten. Each fruit is about the size of an egg, and contains several seeds surrounded by a yellowish pulp. The taste of the pulp is pleasantly sour; the flavor midway between apple and pineapple; and the aroma sometimes resinous and pungent. The unripe fruits are often made into relishes. The ripe fruits are used for sauces, preserves, jams and marmalades.

The ambarella (a Sinhalese name) is widely known as Otaheite (Tahiti) apple in former British colonies, and as Jew plum in Jamaica. I found it very much in evidence in the markets of Trinidad, where it is known either by the French name "pomme cythère" or as golden apple.

MOMBIN is a name applied to some other fruits of the genus *Spondias*. The red mombin, or Spanish plum, *S purpurea*, is a native fruit of tropical America, and was long ago introduced to the Philippines by Spanish colonists. The fruits vary greatly in size, form and palatability. They are commonly oval or roundish, from 1–2 inches long and range from deep red to yellow in color. Good fruits have juicy flesh with a fairly acid, spicy flavor, not unlike that of the cashew fruit but less pronounced. They may be eaten fresh, preferably ice-cold, or boiled and dried. The large, hard core at the center may be cracked and eaten like a nut.

The yellow mombin, *S lutea* (or *S mombin*) is native to Brazil and Costa Rica. Its yellow fruits are mildly acid, and juicy, and generally inferior to those of the red mombin.

The name hog plum, vexing because it is applied in various places to a host of different fruits, is sometimes applied to both mombins, especially the yellow one, and also to imras (below). It simply refers to the food preferences of hogs.

IMRA is the fruit of a tropical tree, *Spondias* (or *Mangifera*) *pinnata* which grows in the American tropics and Southeast Asia. As mentioned above, it is also called hog plum. The fruits are sour and have a disagreeable smell, but can be used for pickling. The tree is cultivated for this purpose in Malaysia. In Indonesia the fruits are occasionally cooked in "Rujak" (a spicy fruit salad); but the ambarella would always be preferred.

IMBU (or umbu) is the fruit of the tree *Spondias tuberosa*. This grows wild in the north-east of Brazil, and is occasionally cultivated. It is described by Popenoe (1923) as the best of the genus.

Some trees are so productive that the fruit, when allowed to fall, forms a carpet of yellow upon the ground. In general appearance the imbu may be likened to a Green Gage plum. It is oval, about $1\frac{1}{2}$ inches in length, and greenish yellow in color. The skin is thicker than that of a plum, and quite tough. The flavor of the soft, melting, almost liquid flesh is suggestive of a sweet orange. If eaten before it is fully ripe, the fruit is slightly acid. . . . In its native home the imbu is eaten as a fresh fruit, and also furnishes a popular jelly. It is used besides to make imbuzada, a famous dessert of northern Brazil. This is prepared by adding the juice of the fruit to boiled sweet milk. The mixture is greenish white in color and when sweetened to taste is relished by nearly every one.

GANDARIA is the common name of the best known of the small mango-like fruits borne by trees of the genus *Bouea*. These "miniature mangoes" vary greatly in edibility, but the best are well worth eating. The thin skin, yellow or apricot-colored when the fruit is ripe, is edible as well as the yellow or orange pulp within.

Soursop, Cherimoya, Bullock's Heart, Papaw, Sugar Apple, Ilama, Biriba

family ANNONACEAE

Other Names for SOURSOP

French: *corossol, cachiman épineux*
German: *Sauerapfel*
Spanish: *guanabana, zapote agrio*
Dutch: *zuurzak*
Thai: *thurian thet*
Malay: *durian Belanda*
Indonesian: *sirsak*
Philippines: *guayabano*
Chinese: *ci guo fan li zhi*
Japanese: *togehanreishi*
Fiji: *seremaia*

Note on the Name Soursop

The name may originate from the Dutch "zuurzak", which is also used in the Netherlands Antilles and Indonesia; but the derivation is uncertain. The Malay name is interesting. "The word Belanda (meaning Hollander) was used to indicate something which was foreign and made known by the Dutch, and the spiny fruit of this plant must have suggested that of the native Durian. This interpretation, indicating that the object is foreign but resembles something already known, has resulted in some interesting etymology: thus halwa Belanda is chocolate, and kuching Belanda (foreign cat) is the rabbit, which has been introduced into Malaya." (Betty Molesworth Allen, 1965)

A Minor Relation

A montana, the mountain soursop of the West Indies, is a larger tree than the ordinary soursop, but bears smaller and less good fruits. It is rarely cultivated.

Other Names for CHERIMOYA

French: *cherimoyer*
German: *Cherimoyer-Frucht*
Spanish: *cherimoya, chirimoya*
Portuguese (Brazil): *cherimolia, graveola*
Other: *anona, anona blanca* (various places); *cachiman la Chine* (Haiti); *chirimorriñon* (Venezuela); *pox, poox* (Mexico); *guanaba* (El Salvador); *huanaba* (Guatemala); *zapote de viejas, cabeza de negro* (Mexico); *catoche, catuche* (Venezuela); *anona de puntitas* (Argentina); *sinini* (Bolivia); *graviola, jaca do Pará* (Brazil)

Recipe

Soursop Mousse: page 170

Key to the Painting

soursop and section

The **SOURSOP**, *Annona muricata*, a tropical fruit native to the West Indies and northern South America, is now cultivated also in Mexico, India, Southeast Asia and Polynesia. This, the largest-fruiting member of the family of annonaceous fruits, was one of the first fruit trees taken from America to the tropical regions of the Old World, where it became widely distributed from Southeast China to Australia and the lowlands of East and West Africa. It seems to thrive especially well on tropical islands.

The small tree bears its fruits indiscriminately on twigs, branches, or trunk. The fruits, which range from 4–12 inches in length and up to a maximum of nearly 11 pounds in weight, are ellipsoid or irregularly ovoid, one side growing faster than the other. The skin, which has a leathery appearance, is thin and surprisingly tender; dark green to begin with, later yellowish green and yellow when over-ripe. Because of the soft spines on the skin, the soursop is sometimes called the prickly custard apple.

The white flesh of the fruit consists of numerous segments, mostly seedless (just as well, since the seeds contain toxins and are to be avoided). The quality of this flesh varies from poor (one unkind writer likened it to wet cotton) to very good. At its best, it is soft and juicy with a rich, almost fermented quality; pleasantly aromatic with an aroma reminiscent of pineapple. The soursop is more acid than its relations, but the acidity varies and some fruits are suitable for being cut open like a melon and eaten raw. Others have to be dressed with sugar to make them palatable. The fruits are often so juicy that it would be appropriate to speak of drinking them rather than eating them; so they are obviously good candidates for use in beverages (such as the Brazilian champola) or sherbets.

"Deliciousness itself," declared Mark Twain on sampling the **CHERIMOYA**. This is the fruit of *Annona cherimola*, a tree native to the mountains of Peru and Ecuador. It has since been introduced to sub-tropical regions around the world and is cultivated in many of them. Its name comes from the Peruvian "chirimuya", meaning cold seeds; presumably an allusion to the wet freshness of the fruit and the large seeds which it contains.

Its particular excellence is often obscured by the undiscriminating application of the name custard apple to some of its close relations as well as to itself. The development of hybrids has added to the confusion.

The fruit looks something like a globe artichoke, although the "scales" on its thin green skin are not separate like the leaves of an artichoke but mere protuberances (and are anyway not present in all varieties). "The flesh is white, melting in texture, and moderately juicy. Numerous brown seeds, the size and shape of a bean, are embedded in it. The flavor is subacid, delicate, suggestive of the pineapple and banana." (Popenoe, 1923)

Size and shape vary greatly. A fruit may weigh anything from about 3½ ounces to 5 pounds or even more. The different shapes are indicated in a list of the principal forms, given in the left-hand column. However, the development of new varieties and of hybrids such as the atemoya (a cross between the cherimoya and the sugar apple), is obscuring the traditional classification of forms. The atemoya has now become a fruit in its own right.

BULLOCK'S HEART and custard apple (see note in left-hand column) are two names commonly applied to the fruit of *Annona reticulata*, a tree native to the West Indies, which thrives in coastal and lowland regions. It spread to Central America and southern Mexico in very early times, and had Aztec and Mayan names. The Portuguese were largely responsible for disseminating it, via Africa, to other tropical areas.

The coloration of the fruit (reddish or brownish on the sunny side, dull yellow

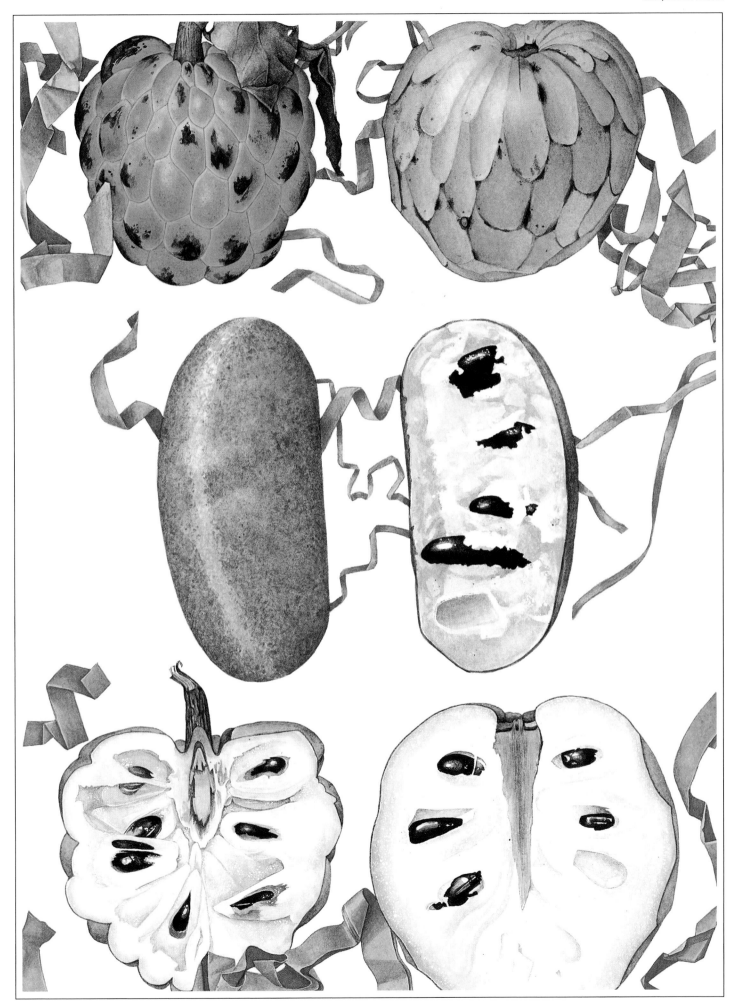

Note on the Name Custard Apple

This is a name widely applied to various annonaceous fruits, referring to their creamy and often yellowish pulp.

No custard apple is related to the true apple; indeed use of the term "apple" is only explicable on the assumption that the use of a single word in ancient times to mean both "fruit" and "apple" lingered on until recent times.

The fruits most likely to be intended by the term are cherimoya, sugar apple (alias sweetsop), and bullock's heart; for all of which see the main text. In the USA the name is sometimes used for the pond apple (see note below).

Note on the Pond Apple

The pond apple is the fruit of a small tree, *Annona glabra*, which grows wild in the American tropics, especially the West Indies and southern Florida. It bears small yellow fruits which smell like oranges but have little flavor. The names custard apple and alligator apple are sometimes used in the USA and the West Indies respectively. The fruit may be found in West Africa and, for example, the Philippines, and is capable of being made into jelly, but it is relatively unimportant as food for humans.

Notes on the Name Ilama

This name is derived, via Spanish, from the native Mexican name "illamatzapotl" (which translates as "zapote de las viejas", or "old woman's sapote").

The name ilama is also applied, in Mexico, to a related Central American fruit, *A purpurea*, generally known as the "soncoya" or "cabeza de negro". This is common in the region, and is cultivated on a small scale. It may grow to a large size, but is commonly about 6 inches long, and gray-brown in color, with hard protuberances on the skin. The orange flesh within tastes something like that of the papaw or mango.

Recipes

Soursop Mousse: page 170
Sherbet: page 174

Key to the Painting

top left and bottom left: sugar apple; top right and bottom right: cherimoya; center: papaw

on the other) and its shape show enough resemblance to the heart of a bullock or other large mammal to justify the West Indian name; but other names are often used, for example sweetsop (in contrast to soursop).

The size of the fruit varies from 3–6 inches in diameter, and it may weigh over 2 pounds. The skin may be faintly or distinctly "netted" (hence the term netted custard apple). The flesh, which is yellowish white, has the typical custard-like and somewhat granular texture. It is used as a dessert fruit, possibly with a sprinkling of sugar; or strained and added to confections such as ice cream and milk shakes. Appreciation of it is notably higher in Latin America than in India.

The **PAPAW**, the fruit of a small North American tree, *Asimina triloba*, is found as far north as New York State. It has for long been cultivated by Native Americans and whites alike. Its name is sometimes spelled "pawpaw", a corrupted name which is, confusingly, often also given to the completely different papaya (page 84). And it is yet another of the fruits which are referred to by the general name custard apple.

The papaw has a smooth, yellowish skin without the knobs or reticulations which are characteristic of its tropical relatives. The shape is slightly elongated and curved, and the average fruit is 4 inches long. The pulp, like that of other annonaceous fruits, is yellow, soft, and smooth. It has a rich, sweet, creamy flavor evocative of both the banana and the pear. All this is overlaid with a heavy fragrance, and some find the whole effect cloying. "Edible for boys" is one verdict. Papaw is usually eaten raw, but can be baked or made into various desserts.

SUGAR APPLE is the English name used in the West Indies and America for the fruit of *Annona squamosa*, a small tree native to tropical America but now distributed in tropical regions around the world. It is also called sweetsop (in contrast to the soursop). The British in India, where it is extensively cultivated, called it custard apple, and it is also known more precisely as the "scaly custard apple" because of the scales which cover the greenish-yellow skin, under a whitish bloom.

The sugar apple is grown in Southeast Asia and in Queensland, among other places, but enjoys greatest popularity in Latin America, the West Indies and India. Representations of what appeared to be sugar apples in ancient Indian sculptures led some authorities to suppose that the tree was indigenous there. This idea has been discarded, but some still hold that the sugar apples grown in India surpass those of the West Indies.

The range of the sugar apple in America extends from Mexico and the West Indies down to parts of Brazil. At Bahia in Brazil, where it is said to have been first introduced by the Conde de Miranda, it has a name meaning "the Count's fruit". In Cuba its popularity rivals that of the mango. A Spanish 17th-century author wrote of the fruit: "The pulp is very white, tender, delicate, and so delicious that it unites to agreeable sweetness a most delightful fragrance like rose water, and if presented to one unacquainted with it he would certainly take it for a blanc-mange." The pulp may indeed be white, but is commonly yellow, like custard.

The fruit is of delicate construction and liable to come apart when ripe, unless carefully handled. It is eaten as a dessert fruit, and also used to make sherbets and to flavor ice creams. A purée can be made by passing the pulp through a strainer to separate the black seeds.

The **ILAMA**, the fruit of the tree *Annona diversifolia*, is native to Mexico but found elsewhere in Latin America, in regions of low elevation. The shape of the fruits is elongated. The skin is commonly rough, but sometimes smooth; the color may be anything from green to magenta pink, with a white bloom. When the skin is pink, the flesh may also have a pink tinge. The flavor of the pink varieties has a pleasant acidity like that of the cherimoya. That of the green varieties is sweeter and closer to the sugar apple.

Finally, the fruit which many people think the best of all in this group. It is the **BIRIBA**, fruit of the tree *Rollinia mucosa*, which is native to Brazil. It is now cultivated there and in other parts of tropical America. The fruit is 3–4 inches long and has a creamy-yellow skin. The white or cream-colored flesh is sweet, juicy and of a good flavor. I mentioned above that some Brazilians call the sugar apple "the Count's fruit". Well, the biriba is known in Rio de Janeiro as "the Countess' fruit".

Otaheite Gooseberry, Emblic, Bignay, Rambai

The **OTAHEITE GOOSEBERRY**, *Phyllanthus acidus* (or *P distichus*), is one of the few useful fruits in a large genus whose botanical name means "leaf-flower". This refers to the curious manner in which flowers grow along the edges of the leaf-like branches; and, since the flowers develop into fruits, the fruits too occupy this odd position.

The tree has been cultivated for centuries in southern India and parts of Southeast Asia, and has since spread throughout the Caribbean islands and the mainland of Central America.

"Otaheite" seems to indicate a connection, real or supposed, with Tahiti; I don't recall coming across the fruit there, but Pétard (1986) confirms that it has been introduced and says that Tahitian children enjoy eating it in the form of sweets called "seurettes".

The tree is an astonishingly abundant bearer. It usually provides two crops a year, when its branches are festooned with clusters of fruit. The fruits are ribbed; grape-sized and green at first, light yellow when ripe. Their tart flavor recalls that of the gooseberry, but there is no other connection. They can be made into pickles and preserves, as in India, or cooked with sugar to provide a compote or a filling for fruit pies.

EMBLIC, or emblic myrobalan, *Phyllanthus emblica*, is a prized fruit in tropical Asia. Commercial growing takes place mainly in the Indian sub-continent, but the tree is also cultivated in South China and Southeast Asia. It is regarded as sacred by Hindus, whose religion prescribes that the fruits be included in the diet for 40 days after a fast, in order to restore vitality.

The fruit is ridged, round, hard to the touch, and almost stemless: light green when under-ripe, and ripening to a whitish or dull yellowish green, or occasionally red. The skin is thin, translucent, the flesh crisp and juicy.

This is a very sour fruit, so much so that anything drunk after it will seem sweet. However, it can be stewed with sugar, made into jams and relishes, or candied. It has a very high vitamin C content; during World War II Indian troops were issued with emblic tablets and candies.

The **BIGNAY**, *Antidesma bunius*, a tree native to Southeast Asia and Western Australia, is also known as Chinese laurel, salamander tree or currant tree. It bears long clusters containing up to 30 or 40 purple berries, each of which is up to $\frac{3}{4}$ inch in diameter. These are too acid for eating raw, but their high pectin content fits them for making jam and so forth.

RAMBAI is the Malay name, also used in English, for the fruits of several trees of the genus *Baccaurea*, most of which are native to Malaysia and Indonesia. Two or three, which have sweeter and better fruits than others, are cultivated.

B motleyana, the principal Malaysian and Indonesian species, is a moderately large evergreen tree, of which the female produces abundant clusters of fruit hanging in long strings. Each fruit is oval, about $1\frac{1}{2}$ inches long, with a thin, velvety, pale brown skin. When ripe this skin becomes soft and wrinkled, which is one way of distinguishing rambai from the duku and langsat fruits (see page 106) which it closely resembles. A soft, translucent, whitish flesh surrounds a few flat, brown seeds. Cultivated varieties have a sweet, mild flavor and are refreshing when eaten raw.

B dulcis, with similar fruits, is grown in the south of Sumatra, where it is known as "tjoepa", and has large sweet fruits.

B sapida, sometimes known as the Burmese grape, is "mai fai" in Thailand. And there are many other wild *Baccaurea* species of the jungle whose fruits are eaten locally in Malaysia and Indonesia, or made into alcoholic drinks.

Passion Fruit,
Sweet Calabash, Sweet Granadilla

Recipes

Pavlova: page 154
Exotic Crème Brûlée: page 165
Passion Fruit Sauce: page 169

The **PASSION FRUIT** is the best known of the fruits of various species of the genus *Passiflora*. This is a large group of climbing herbs and shrubs native to tropical America, Southeast Asia and Australia. The names granadilla (or grenadilla) and water lemon (see page 130) are also used for fruits in this group, and overlap with the name passion fruit in a way which is sometimes confusing.

In South America, the passion flower became known as "flor de las cinco lagas" (flower of the five wounds) because Jesuit missionaries used it in their teachings to illustrate the crucifixion of Christ. Each part corresponds to a particular emblem of The Passion. Thus the three styles represent the three nails; the five stamens the five wounds (hands, feet and side); the ovary, which is oval and set on a stalk, is taken to be either the sponge soaked in vinegar and offered on a stick, or the hammer used to drive in the nails; the spiky corona, prominently visible above the petals, is the crown of thorns; and the equal petals and sepals signify the 12 apostles.

The name passion fruit is most usually, and correctly, applied to *Passiflora edulis*, a plant native to Brazil. Since the 19th century it has been grown in Australia, New Zealand, South Africa, and Hawaii; and it is now being grown in other countries, such as Israel. An alternative name is purple granadilla, referring to the deep purple skin of the main variety.

There is also a yellow type, var *flavicarpa*, which is the basis of the passion fruit industry in Hawaii and Fiji. The yellow passion fruit, which likes a hotter climate than the purple kind, is catching up on the latter in terms of cultivation.

A passion fruit, which is about the size of a small hen's egg, has a brittle outer shell which becomes slightly wrinkled when it is ripe. The soft, orange pulp is full of tiny seeds. These are edible, and liked by many, but others avoid them and prefer their passion fruit in the form of jelly or juice. (Over 100 fruits are needed to make 4 cups of juice, so it is a costly delicacy; but the juice has exceptional viscosity, because of its high starch content, and calls for considerable dilution.) Passion fruit is also used in sherbets and confectionery, and in ice cream and yogurt. The flavor is of subtle composition and delicious.

The flavor is also outstandingly strong. The American writer Elizabeth Schneider (1986) has good advice to offer on how to take advantage of this.

Most recipes that I have read come from places where the fruit is grown on a large scale. They begin: "Take a cup of pure, strained passion-fruit pulp." Today, in the United States, that would cost $25. Fortunately, however, passion fruit works best as a flavoring. There is so much perfume and so little pulp that you can think of it as you would vanilla, or Cognac, or a spoon of dense raspberry purée – something to aromatize a dish.

A minor species in this family is the **SWEET CALABASH**, *P maliformis*, which grows in Central America (notably Ecuador and Brazil) and the West Indies, and enjoys local popularity. The fruit is apple-shaped, with a thin yellowish-brown skin, which can be either leathery and flexible or hard and brittle, but is always difficult to open. The pulp, grayish or orange-yellow, is juicy and has a pleasantly aromatic taste.

The **SWEET GRANADILLA**, *P ligularis*, is cultivated in mountainous areas of Mexico and also in Hawaii. It has an orange shell, speckled with tiny white dots, when ripe; and its flavor is more interesting than that of its larger relation, the giant granadilla described on page 130. It is also very juicy.

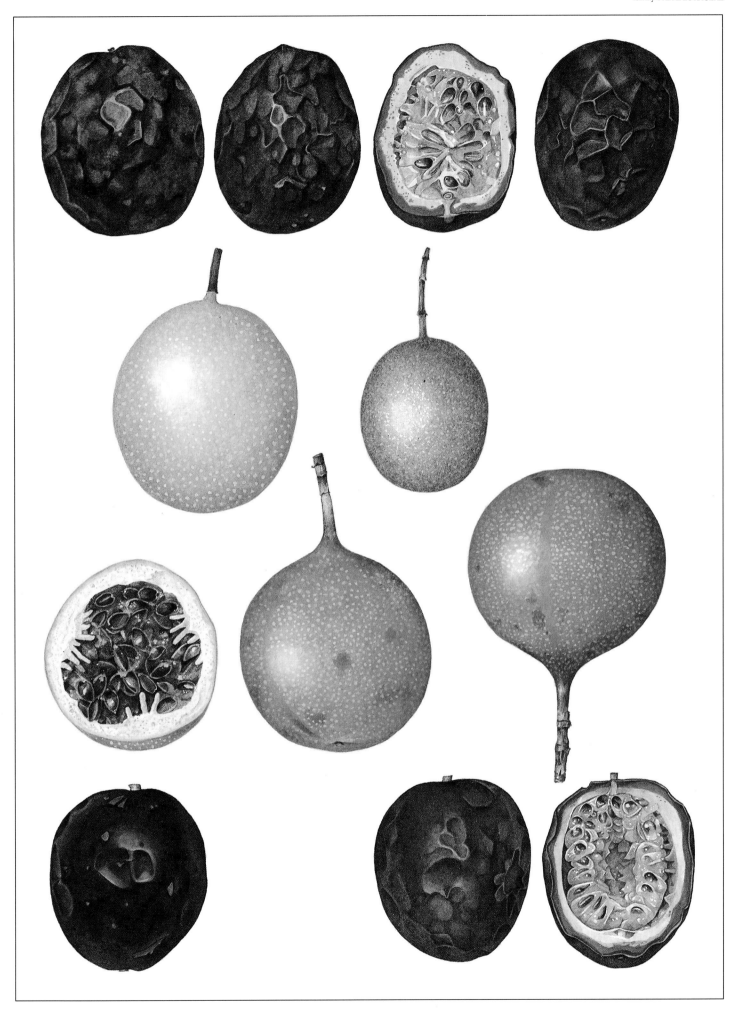

Giant Granadilla, Water Lemon, Banana Passion Fruit

family PASSIFLORACEAE

Note on nomenclature: the names of the species listed here sometimes overlap with names for passion fruit.

Other Names for *GIANT GRANADILLA*

French-speaking America: *barbadine*
Spanish-speaking America: *granadilla real, granadilla grande, parcha*
Brazil: *maracujá*
Malay: *timun belanda, markeesa*
Japanese: *ōminotokeisō*

Other Names for *WATER LEMON*

in English, the plant is sometimes called Jamaican honeysuckle, and the fruit referred to as sweet cup
Thai: *sawarot*
Malay: *buah susu*
Japanese: *mizuremon*
French-speaking West Indies: *pomme d'or, pomme liane, maritambou*
Spanish-speaking America: *parcha (de culebra)*
Portuguese-speaking America: *maracujá*

Other Names for *BANANA PASSION FRUIT*

in Latin America generally the common name is "curuba", sometimes with an epithet, such as "curuba sabanero blanco"
Ecuador: *tacso*
Venezuela: *parcha*
Bolivia and Peru: *tumbo*

Recipes

Banana Passion Fruit Jam: page 179

The **GIANT GRANADILLA**, *Passiflora quadrangularis*, is native to the hotter regions of tropical America, where it often bears names such as "granadilla real" to indicate its large size; it is the largest of the passion fruits. However, even with epithets meaning royal or large, the name granadilla is hardly appropriate. It is the diminutive form of the Spanish name ("granada") for pomegranate; so it means "small pomegranate". Even something called a "large small pomegranate" would not be expected to be as big as this fruit, which is up to 8 inches long. The delicate skin is of a pale greenish or yellow color, often blushing with pink and shading to brownish when ripe.

The giant granadilla is popular in many tropical regions, including the hotter parts of India and Southeast Asia. Besides being cultivated in many countries, it has been naturalized for some time in Indonesia, and runs wild in northern Queensland.

The fruit gives off a pleasing aroma, but is often bland in flavor. However, two parts of it are edible. Whereas the passion fruit itself is full of what looks something like frogspawn (seeds, each surrounded by a pulpy substance), and this constitutes the whole edible matter, this granadilla has a structure more like that of a melon; there is an outer layer of edible flesh, white or pink, plus a large inner space full of arils (seeds surrounded by pulp). The arils, whose color varies considerably, can be eaten raw without removing the seeds.

The giant granadilla is best combined with other fruits which have more flavor; and if it is cooked, for example to make a jelly, or as a pie filling, it benefits from added flavoring. In Indonesia it is made into a drink called markeesa which is available in bottles.

The **WATER LEMON**, *P laurifolia*, is also sometimes called yellow granadilla, or Jamaica honeysuckle, and is found in many parts of Latin America and the West Indies.

It has yellow or orange fruits, oval and about 3 inches long, which are eaten raw or used for juice. The pulp is sweet and pleasantly scented, just as good as that of the true passion fruit, *P edulis*. It is now grown in some regions of Southeast Asia where the climate is not right for the latter.

BANANA PASSION FRUIT in New Zealand and banana poka in Hawaii are two names for a yellow-fruited species, *P molissima*, which is of excellent quality. It is of special importance in Colombia, but grows also in Ecuador, Venezuela, Bolivia, and Peru. A popular fruit in the markets, it is eaten fresh, or used to produce a cool drink.

The pulp of the banana passion fruit is not quite as juicy and sweet as that of the purple passion fruit. Since the fruits are oval and long, it is usual to cut them in half lengthways and scoop out the pulp with a spoon, and then sweeten them to taste before consumption with ice cream or cream, or use in pies and the like.

Key to the Painting

top row: purple passion fruit;
center: giant granadilla, with seeds below;
center right: water lemon;
below: banana passion fruits

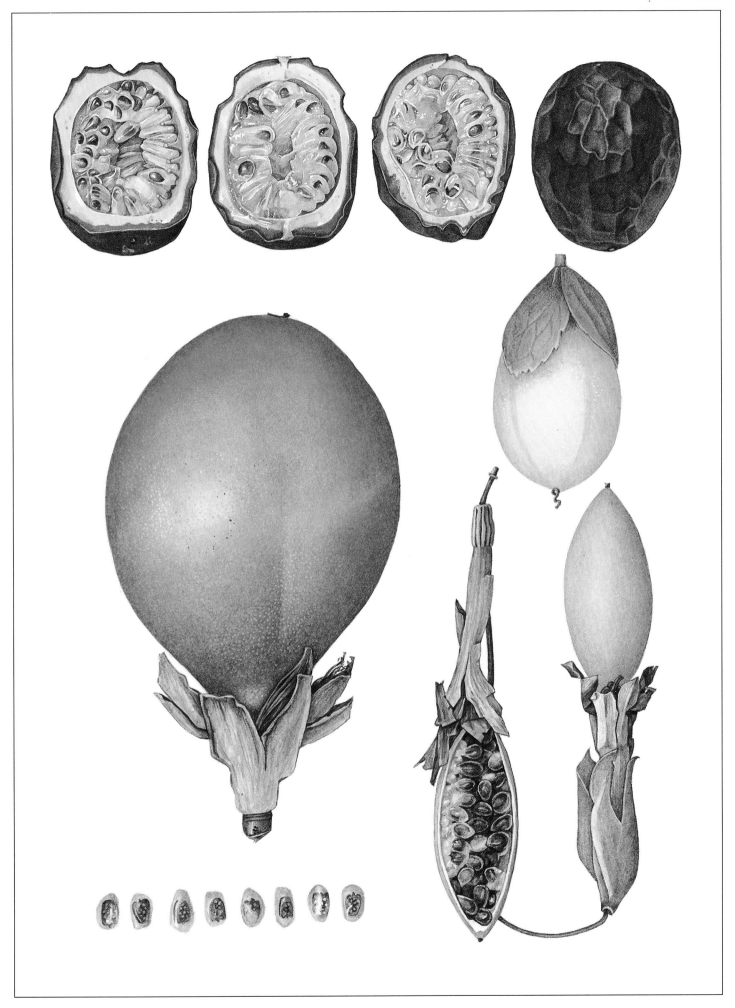

Red Granadilla, Wing-Stemmed and Blue Passion Flowers

The two preceding pages describe the principal passion fruits and granadillas of commerce. However, these are not all; there are others which bear edible fruits, including the three depicted here.

P coccinea, the **RED GRANADILLA** ("red" because of its vivid crimson flowers), bears the best fruits of the three. They are cultivated in Guadeloupe, for example, besides growing wild in parts of Brazil, Peru, Bolivia and Venezuela. The fruits are handsome; often attractively striped and mottled. They are green at first but usually become yellow or orange when ripe.

P alata, the **WING-STEMMED PASSION FLOWER**, grows wild in Brazil, where its fruits are available in local markets. It has, however, been introduced in many other parts of the world, mainly as a decorative plant; and it exists in numerous varieties, some of doubtful validity. The variety with the largest edible fruits (up to 12 inches long) is *P alata* var *macrocarpa*.

P caerulea, the **BLUE PASSION FLOWER**, is the hardiest and most widely distributed of these plants, but valued for its flowers rather than its fruits. The latter are about the size of a hen's egg, orange in color. They are often disregarded by gardeners, but are perfectly edible: somewhat insipid by themselves, but fine in combination with other more flavorful fruits.

Key to the Painting

left to right: red granadilla, wing-stemmed passion flower, blue passion flower

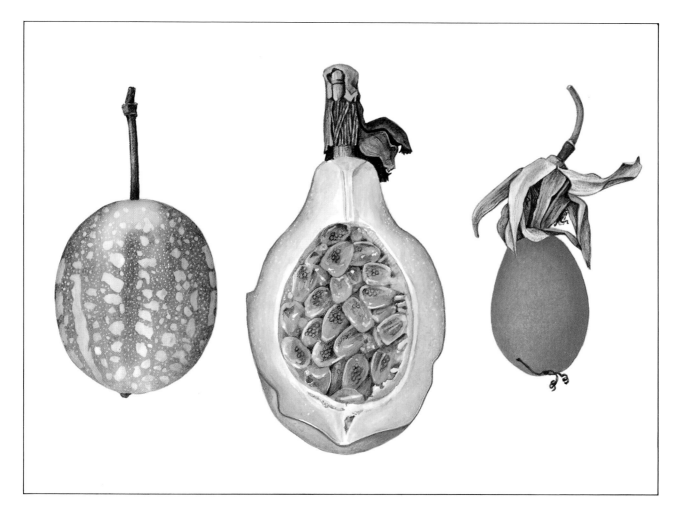

Introduction to Nuts

With the possible exception of eggs, nature provides no more perfectly packaged food than nuts. The elegance of an almond, for example, could hardly be surpassed. And there are few foods which provide such concentrated and instant nourishment, normally obtainable by merely cracking the nut and eating the kernel.

Yet the status of nuts in the human diet has not been stable; it has changed considerably over the millennia.

A long time ago, acorns, beech nuts and chestnuts were in the top rank of staple foods in the regions where they grow. In some places they are still eaten as staples, but the days when they were a major element in the diet of large populations have passed. It would be true, in a general way, to say that in the Western world and temperate climates nuts have been eclipsed in this respect by cereals.

The situation in the tropics is different. There the coconut and the groundnut (peanut) have retained their importance, partly on their merits and partly because they grow where cereals are not cultivated.

Returning to Europe, the place of nuts in the kitchen, that is to say as an ingredient, has also evolved. In the very distant past, cooking nuts (unless, in some instances, to rid them of toxins) would have been unusual. They do appear in recipes of classical Rome (see page 144), but without prominence. In medieval court cooking in Europe, however, we find the almond holding a place of real honor, especially as the basis of "almond milk". This came to Europe from the Arab world; but its importance in Europe depended on one factor which was of no interest to Arabs – the fact that it could be used on Christian fast days in place of milk.

It is strange to find that this almond milk occurred twice as often in English recipes of the medieval period as in French ones. Almond trees do not grow readily in England, but do in France. Professor Hieatt (1985) conjectures that this was in fact the explanation; almond milk had a snob appeal in England because the almonds had to be imported and were costly.

The almond is still, of course, an important ingredient, especially in confectionery, but the nature of its importance has changed.

Chestnuts have undergone a different metamorphosis, from staple food to delicacy (Marrons Glacés, page 175), as a result of the selection and breeding of new "super-chestnuts". One wonders what would happen if there were a parallel development of acorns.

Considered as delicacies in themselves, nuts reached an apogee in Britain in Victorian and Edwardian times, when the service of nuts at the end of a dinner became a considerable ritual. For connoisseurs such as Edward Bunyard (*The Anatomy of Dessert*, 1925), nuts had but one role, to go with the wine during dessert. He was strongly opposed to anything, such as the prior removal of the husks of filberts, which would diminish the leisurely enjoyment of the nut ritual, and proclaimed that the correct and unhurried handling of the dessert nuts constituted one of the prime virtues of the Victorian era.

In France there has been a different sort of connoisseurship, manifest mainly in the consumption of green (unripe) nuts. The world of nuts, as seen by the French, is dominated by just four kinds, all of which grow in France: walnut, almond, hazelnut, chestnut. And among these the walnut (whose name, "noix", is also the only general French word for "nut") reigns supreme.

Recently there has been another general change in the status of nuts. They are increasingly perceived as pure, innocent, and potent foods: pure because they are protected by their natural wrapping from contamination and additives; innocent because their consumption entails no apparent cost to the environment or penalty for other living creatures; potent because they contain so much in the way of nutrition. So nuts and nut products wear a new halo.

I do not underrate these considerations; but so far as I am concerned, nuts already had an adequate halo – their contribution to the pleasures of eating is so great.

Looking to the future, and bearing in mind the astonishing rise to fame, from a standing start in the last century, of the macadamia nut, one may surmise that a few other nuts which at present are of only local interest could become really important in the next century. Rosengarten, the distinguished American authority on nuts, thinks that international acclaim may be just round the corner for the oyster nut of Africa, which is comparable to the Brazil nut in flavor and superior to it in nutritional quality. He may be right. Certainly, the plant which bears these nuts tries hard enough. It is a vine of prodigious vitality which scrambles up and over trees and may cover an area the size of a parking lot – and even bring crashing to the ground the trees which support it and the weight of its huge seed-containers, each containing about a hundred of the oyster-shaped nuts.

Cycad, Ginkgo Nut, Acorn, Beech Nut, Chestnut

family GINKGOACEAE

Other Names for *GINKGO*

Japanese: *ginnan*

family FAGACEAE

Other Names for *ACORN*

French: *gland*
German: *Eichel*
Italian: *ghianda*
Spanish: *bellota*
Portuguese: *bolota*
Russian: *zholud*
Chinese: *xiang guo*

Other Names for *BEECH NUT*

French: *faîne*
German: *Bucheichel*
Italian: *faggiuola*
Spanish: *bayuco*
Portuguese: *fruto da faia*
Russian: *bukovyi oreshek*

Other Names for *CHESTNUT*

French: *châtaigne, marron*
German: *Kastanie, Edelkastanie*
Italian: *castagna, marrone*
Spanish: *castana, marrona*
Portuguese: *castanha*
Russian: *kashtan*
Chinese: *li zi*
Japanese: *kuri* (C crenata)

Other Chestnuts

The Chinese chestnut, *C mollissima*, has nuts of good flavor, with a relatively thin skin. This is now the main species cultivated in the USA.)

The Japanese chestnut, *C crenata*, has large, starchy nuts which are usually boiled, the result being not unlike potatoes.

Chinquapin, a name of Native American origin, applies to trees of the genus *Castanopsis*, related to the chestnut but smaller, and with smaller nuts.

Tip for the Cook

Chestnuts can be awkward to peel. The easiest method is to gash the shell of each chestnut, put them in a pan, sprinkle with a little water, and bake in a very hot oven until the skin splits away.

Recipes

Nesselrode Pudding: page 173
Candied Chestnuts (*Marrons Glacés*): page 175

Key to the Painting

top: ginkgo nuts, fruits and leaves; center left to right: chestnuts – wild Spanish, Japanese, French; bottom left to right: acorns of the holm oak with leaves, and above, acorns of the Californian black oak, then cycad, *Cycas revoluta*, and beechmasts and leaf

CYCADS are primitive plants which have been on earth since the time of the dinosaurs. A cycad looks like a palm tree with fern-like leaves, but proves that it is not by producing cones, often resembling those of a pine but sometimes far larger. The large, nut-like seeds found between the scales of the cones are no delicacy, being starchy and bland, but have provided food to many peoples after being processed to rid them of toxins.

The **GINKGO**, *Ginkgo biloba*, is the sole survivor of a group of primitive trees which grew all around the world in the very distant past; the "petrified ginkgo forest" near Ellenberg in Washington State is estimated to be 15 million years old.

The fruit is round, plum-sized, and brown. The nut, freed of the smelly flesh, has a soft pale yellow kernel, which becomes pale green on being cooked. In China, ginkgo nuts appear in any dish with the name "eight-jewelled"; and the Japanese also have culinary uses for them. Fresh ginkgo nuts appear in the markets in the autumn. I gather mine, with permission, from two trees in the Chelsea Physic Garden in London.

The **ACORN**, the nut borne by oak trees of the genus *Quercus*, is regarded in the main as animal fodder. However, man has eaten acorns since prehistoric times; and Smith (1929) suggests that over the whole of human history mankind may have consumed more acorns than wheat.

The oak which produces the best and sweetest acorns is the ilex (or holm, or holly) oak, which grows all round the Mediterranean and in western Asia. It is common in Spain and Portugal, and varieties of it are cultivated there for their acorns, the best of which are comparable to and eaten like chestnuts.

Several native American species bear acorns which constituted a food of some importance for Native Americans and early white settlers. Bean and Saubel (1972) provide an admirable essay on the use of acorns by the Cahuilla Indians, showing that these nuts were a staple food resource of great value, providing less protein and carbohydrate than barley or wheat, but much more fat.

Acorns themselves and cakes made from acorn meal have remarkable keeping properties. Acorn meal can be used in much the same ways as corn meal.

The **BEECH NUT**, a small nut of fine flavor, has been gathered from beech trees, of the genus *Fagus*, and used for human food since prehistoric times; but its main use has been for feeding animals, especially pigs. The nuts are often called beechmast, or simply "mast" (a term applied also to acorns).

In France and some other countries the practice of turning pigs and turkeys into beech woods to eat the fallen mast continues to this day.

Although humans rarely eat beech nuts now, the oil which can be obtained from the kernels is above average in keeping quality and flavor, and has been used by rural populations in Europe both for cooking and as a salad oil.

CHESTNUT is a name given to many nuts, originally and primarily to those of the European "sweet" or "Spanish" chestnut tree, *Castanea sativa*, and later to various Asian and American relatives. Chestnuts contain more starch and less oil than most other nuts and have had a special role as food for this reason. The European chestnut (of western Asian origin) was formerly a staple food of great importance, but has now become more of a luxury.

Many European languages have a different name for the finest cultivated nuts, for example "marrons" in French, as opposed to "châtaignes" for the wild chestnut or the ordinary cultivated kind. The biggest and best "marrons" are grown in the region of Lyon, where they (and imported chestnuts) are candied to make the famous marrons glacés.

135

Almond, Cashew Nut, Hazelnut

Key to the Painting

top center: Kentish cob with nut below;
left: white filbert with nut above;
right: purple filbert with nut above;
center: cashew fruit with nuts left and right;
below: calumpangs, Chinese almonds and in center, Indian almond;
bottom row: green almonds, almonds and almond kernels

The **ALMOND**, the nut borne by the beautiful almond tree, *Prunus amygdalus,* is delicately flavored and highly versatile. It grows only in warm temperate climates, but has been cultivated since prehistoric times, and is the most important nut in commerce. The USA (California) is the main producer, followed by Spain and Italy. Almonds are also grown in most other Mediterranean countries, and in Iran, Afghanistan, China, and Australia.

Both sweet and bitter almonds are cultivated. Sweet almonds are grown as dessert nuts and for use in many confectionery items. Bitter almonds are easier and cheaper to grow, but contain prussic acid and are suitable for use only after the removal, by heat, of this poison. They always retain a distinctive flavor different from that of sweet almonds. This apart, the main commercial distinction is between hard (or thick) shell varieties; softshells; and the extra thin papershells.

Well-known varieties include Jordan (nothing to do with the country of that name, but a corruption of the Spanish "jardin", meaning garden) and Valencia, both semi-hard-shelled Spanish types, and the Californian papershell Nonpareil and softshell Ne Plus Ultra.

Almonds were of great importance in early Arabic and medieval European cooking, partly as a source of the "almond milk" which was used in early versions of blancmange (and which is still current in refreshing drinks such as orgeat and horchata). Since then, although "green" (immature, soft) almonds are eaten in some places as titbits and many almonds are roasted and salted for consumption as snacks or with drinks, the main importance of the nut has been to the confectionery industry. Such products as marzipan, nougat (and its many relations) and macaroons all depend on it.

Because the almond is so well known and so highly esteemed, the name has been borrowed for application to other nuts. The "Chinese almond", *Prunus mume,* is a special kind of apricot grown in China for its kernels alone. The "Indian almond" is the kernel of the fruit of an Asian tree, *Terminalia catappa.* And the name "almondette" has been used for the calumpang nut, borne by trees of the genus *Buchanania* in the Indian sub-continent and Southeast Asia.

One of the strangest fruits of the world is the **CASHEW**, *Anacardium occidentale.* It has two parts: at the stem end a cashew "apple", and projecting from the other end a cashew "nut". Strictly speaking, the "apple" is the receptacle for the true fruit, which is the nut. Portuguese colonists, finding the cashew in Brazil, took it to Southeast Asia. Its cultivation is now widespread. The nuts are much used in Chinese cuisine, besides being eaten out of hand. The texture is delicate and the flavor something like that of almonds. Diana Kennedy (1986) has an interesting passage about the preservation of the "apples" in Mexico and recommends those in syrup ("maranónes en almíbar"); she found the flavor subtle, and couldn't relate it to anything else.

HAZELNUTS come from various trees of the genus *Corylus,* native to many temperate and warm regions of the world. Their cultivation began in southern Europe in antiquity.

North Americans reserve the name hazelnut for their wild species and usually refer to their cultivated nuts, which are of European origin, as filberts.

In Britain, the term hazelnut can be applied whether the tree is wild or cultivated, while the names cob and filbert indicate two sorts of cultivated hazelnut. Cobs are roundish nuts which are only partly encased by short husks. Filberts are longer and are completely encased by their husks, hence (some say) the derivation of the term from "full beard". There are now numerous named varieties of both cob and filbert. It is unfortunate that the variety most commonly offered for sale in Britain is called "Kentish Cob"; it is not a cob but a filbert.

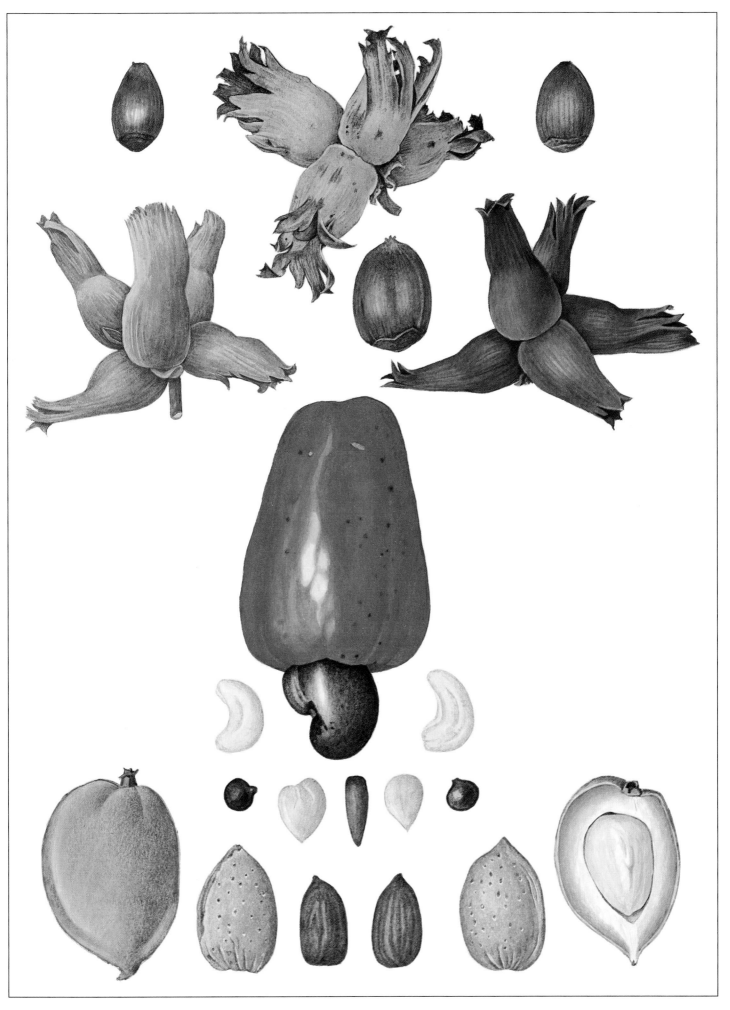

Brazil Nut, Macadamia Nut, Pecan, Walnut

family LECYTHIDACEAE

Other Names for *BRAZIL NUT*

French: *noix du Brasil*
German: *Paranuß*
Italian: *noce del Brasile / del Para*
Spanish: *nuez del Brasil*

family PROTEACEAE

Other Names for *MACADAMIA NUT*

Where these exist they are usually either transcriptions (Hebrew: egoz maqademya) or mean "Australian walnut" (Chinese: au zhou hu tao).

family JUGLANDACEAE

Other Names for *WALNUT*

French: *noix*
German: *Walnuß*
Italian: *noce*
Spanish: *nuez*
Portuguese: *noz*
Russian: *gretskiy orekh*
Greek: *karithis*
Turkish: *ceviz*
Arabic: *jawz*
Persian: *gerdoo*
Afghanistan: *charmaz*
Chinese: *hu tao*
Japanese: *kurumi*

Notes on Other Walnuts

The American black walnut, *J nigra*, belonged originally to the eastern half of the USA. The nut has a thick shell, blackish brown. The flavor is strong but pleasant. The same applies to the butternut or American white walnut, *J cinerea*, which also grows in the eastern States.

Among South American species are the Bolivian black walnut, *J boliviana*, which bears nuts of good quality, and the Ecuador walnut or "nogal", *J honorei*.

Native Chinese species include the Manchurian walnut of the north, *J mandshurica*, and the Cathay or mountain walnut, *Carya cathayensis*.

The Japanese walnut, *J sieboldiana* or *ailanthifolia*, bearing smallish nuts of fine flavor, is now also cultivated in the USA, sometimes called "heartnut" because of its shape.

Recipes

Miwa Naurozee (Afghan New Year Compote): page 156
Conserved Green Walnuts: page 177

Key to the Painting

top row: Brazil nuts with sapucaya in center;
2nd row: macadamia nuts;
3rd row: pecans;
4th row: walnuts;
bottom row from left to right: Japanese heartnut and section, butternut variety Craxezy and black walnut and section

BRAZIL NUTS are borne by the tree *Bertholettia excelsa*, which is enormous: up to 150 feet tall and with a crown as much as 100 feet in diameter. It grows in the dense jungle of the Amazon basin and, like most tall jungle trees, has branches only near the top. The nuts are harvested by waiting for the fruit which contains them to ripen and fall to the ground. The round fruit, about the size of a coconut, weighs up to $4\frac{1}{2}$ pounds and has a thick, woody shell, containing one to two dozen nuts, arranged like the segments of an orange, and each having its own woody covering. The fall of a fruit is a potentially lethal event.

Brazil nuts have a high oil content, shown in their unusually tender texture and rich, mild flavor.

Sapucaya nuts, also called paradise nuts or monkey-pot nuts, are superb, but available only in Brazil and Guyana. They come from trees of the genus *Lecythis*, closely related to the Brazil-nut tree.

MACADAMIA NUTS, from the trees *Macadamia integrifolia* and *M tetraphylla*, are the only example of an Australian food plant attaining international importance. They are native to north-eastern Australia, and used to be called Queensland nuts or Australian nuts. They did not receive their botanical name until 1857, when the Director of the Royal Botanical Gardens in Melbourne named them for his friend Dr Macadam.

Soon afterwards commercial cultivation began; and in the 1880s the macadamia was introduced to Hawaii, where it flourished. Hawaiian growers developed new strains so successfully that the nuts have become a major export.

The PECAN is the most important native nut of North America, borne by one of the hickory trees, *Carya illinoiensis*. The hickories, which are related to the walnut trees, include several other species with fine edible nuts. The kernels of all of them have a general resemblance to walnut kernels, but they are usually oilier and milder in flavor.

The native habitat of the pecan is the central southern region of the USA. The name comes from the Algonquin Indian "paccan", which referred not only to pecans, but also to other hickories and to walnuts. Pecans are now cultivated in many states, notably Georgia and Texas; and there are more than 500 named varieties. Yet, despite its excellence and the international fame which American pecan pie has won for itself, the pecan is still little known outside North America and Mexico.

The WALNUT, *Juglans regia* and related species, belongs to the same family as the pecan and hickories. Of the dozen species of walnut tree with edible nuts, the most important is the Persian walnut, *Juglans regia*, sometimes called English walnut in the USA, although its native region is south-eastern Europe and temperate Asia. It was not taken from France to Britain, where climatic conditions make its cultivation difficult, until the 15th century. Yet recipes for pickling walnuts, green and black, abound in English cookbooks of the 17th and 18th centuries, so it must have been grown extensively despite the difficulties.

Early settlers took the walnut to New England. Although there were several good native species in North America, the Persian nut achieved dominance, and is now the type most grown in the USA, currently the largest producer in the world. Walnut cultivation in France takes place mainly in the south-west; the varieties Corne and Marbot and the group known collectively as Grenobles are popular. In Italy, where walnut growing is concentrated in the region of Naples, the soft-shelled variety Sorrento is dominant.

Half-ripe "green" walnuts are preserved in syrup in the Middle East: to my mind the most delicious form these nuts take.

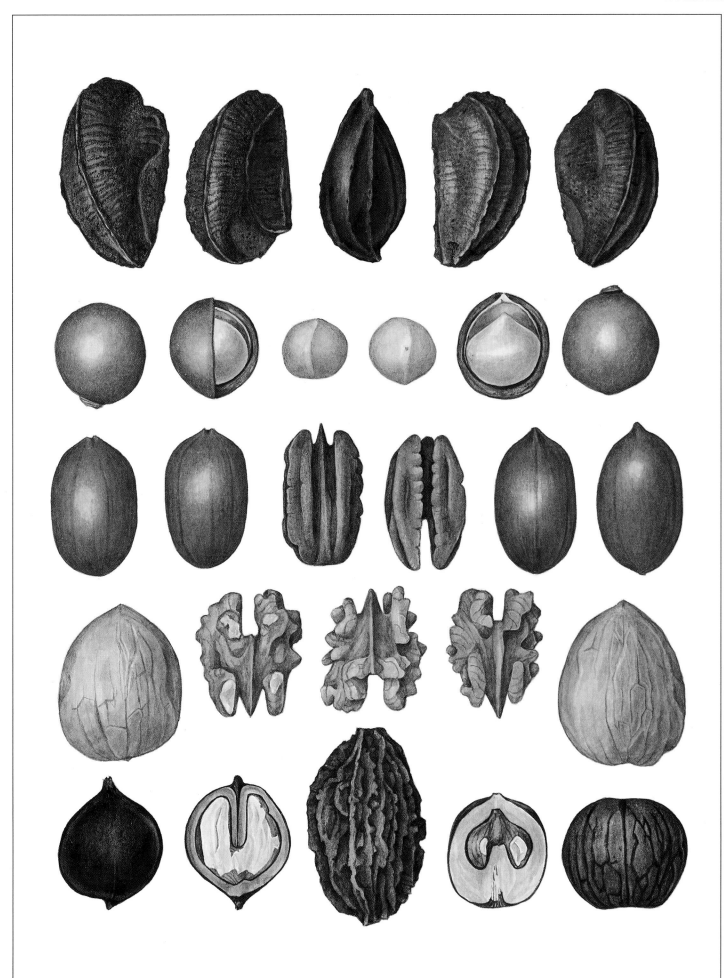

Groundnut, Pine Nut, Pistachio

Key to the Painting

top: pistachios;
center: pine nuts;
bottom: groundnuts

Many nuts have dual roles; they can be eaten fresh (or roasted), but they can also be used in cooking. This is particularly true of the trio described here.

However, **GROUNDNUTS** (often called peanuts) are not true nuts. The plants which produce them, notably *Arachis hypogaea*, are legumes like peas or beans, but thrust their flower stems into the ground after flowering, so that the fruit pods, with their nut-like contents, develop underground.

The groundnut, first grown by the Inca of ancient Peru, is now one of the world's major food crops. India is the main producer, Nigeria the principal exporter.

Groundnuts are rich in protein (about 30%) and oil (up to 50%). The skin may be white, cream, brown, red or even piebald (red and white).

In western countries groundnuts are most familiar as roasted or salted peanuts; or in peanut butter, made by roasting peanuts and grinding them to a paste, usually with a little salt. Peanut butter and jelly sandwiches have a hallowed place in the American diet; also in mine, for a lunch consisting of an open peanut butter sandwich topped with quince preserve or rose petal jam really suits me.

Elsewhere, peanuts are often more important in the kitchen. Thus in Indonesia and Malaysia peanuts which have been roasted and ground to a paste make satay sauce for meat grilled on skewers; fried and ground peanuts provide a salad dressing, gado-gado; and halved peanuts are used in "rempeyek kacang", a savory peanut brittle. Groundnut paste also features prominently in West African groundnut "chop", a kind of stew, usually made with chicken.

PINE NUT, piñón and pignolia are all names applied to the small edible seeds of many species of pine tree. The best of these are of high value, but are difficult to cultivate commercially. As Woodroof (1979) puts it, the trees "grow only under conditions that defy cultivation, fertilization, irrigation, and all kinds of mechanical spraying, harvesting and shelling. All operations are done by hand, in competition with rats, birds and insects." This may be an exaggeration, but is true for many species and regions.

The finest pine nuts, which are most in demand for Arab, Spanish and other dishes and confections, belong to the genus *Pinus* and to the northern hemisphere. Native Americans of the south-west have used pine nuts from time immemorial; and in the Old World their use goes back to Biblical times. The Mediterranean stone pine, *P pinea*, which grows at quite low altitudes, is a familiar feature of the landscapes of Provence, Italy and the Middle East. Its nuts are the finest and, imported to the USA, are the second most expensive nut on the market there, after the macadamia nut, with the pistachio third.

Some pine nuts are eaten out of hand, raw or roasted, but most are used as ingredients in cooking, notably in Turkey, the Middle East, North Africa, Sicily and other parts of Italy, and the Iberian peninsula. They work in both savory and sweet dishes. Tunisians add a few to their glasses of mint tea.

The **PISTACHIO** is the produce of a small tree, *Pistacia vera*, native to parts of West Asia and the Levant between Turkey and Afghanistan. The earliest traces of pistachios being eaten in Turkey and the Middle East date back to about 7000 BC.

The nut is the kernel of the pit of a small fruit which grows in clusters. When the fruit is ripe, the shell usually gapes open at one end to expose the kernel, a condition which in Iran is termed "khandan" (laughing).

The shell may be ivory or red (according to variety) or dyed red (for marketing reasons). The kernel is unique among nuts in being green, not just on the surface but all through. The green is due to the presence of chlorophyll, and varieties of pistachio differ markedly in this respect. The dark green kernels are the most highly valued and the most decorative.

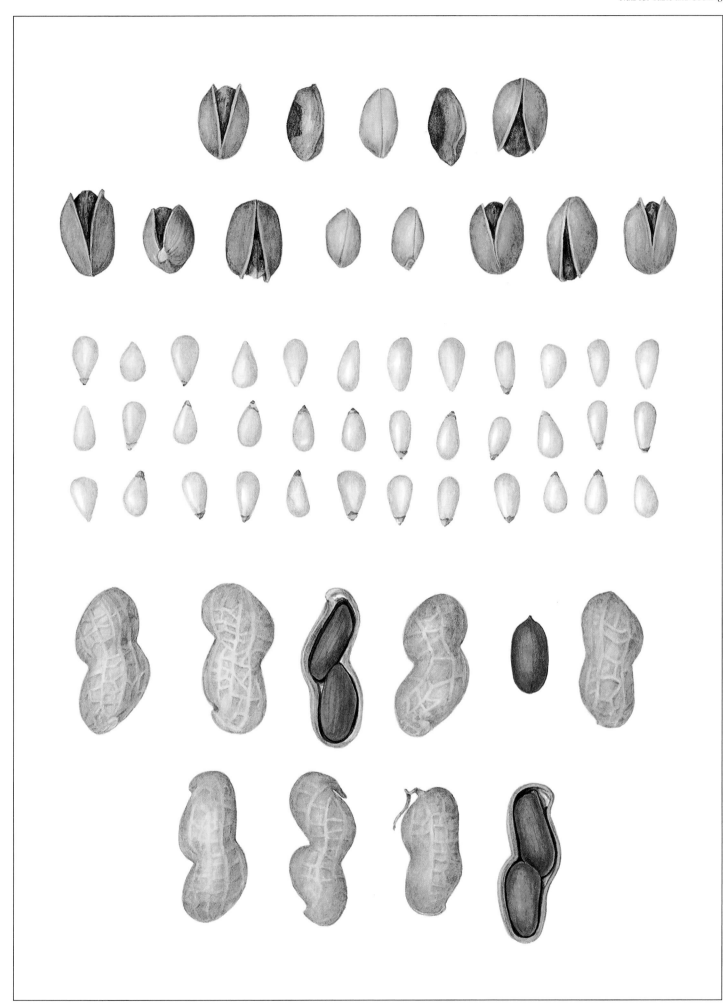

Coconut, Candlenut, Pili Nut, Water Chestnut

family PALMACEAE

Other Names for *COCONUT*

French: *noix de coco*
German: *Kokosnuß*
Spanish: *nuez de coco*
Arabic: *jawz al-hind*
Indian languages: *nariyal* (Hindi);
thenga (Tamil)
Thai: *ma phrao*
Malay / Indonesian: *kelapa*
Chinese: *yeh tzu*

Kinds of Coconut

The common, tall, coconut palms found in most commercial plantations fall into subgroups according to location, so that there is Jamaica Tall, West African Tall, Panama Tall (Choco), and so on.

Dwarf palms start bearing fruits sooner than the tall ones, but have a shorter economic life and their copra is of less good quality. One of the smallest-fruited kinds is the Cocos Nino of the Philippines. (The Maldivian coconut, which has evolved in an isolated position, has the smallest fruit of all: no bigger than an egg.)

The Macapuno coconut of the Philippines has no cavity occupied by liquid but is full of a gelatinous flesh which can be eaten with a spoon. Any given tree will bear only a few such nuts, the others being normal.

family EUPHORBICEAE

Other Names for *CANDLENUT*

Indian languages: *jangli akrot* (wild walnut) (Hindi); *nattu-akrotu-kottai* (Tamil)
Sinhalese: *kakkuna*
Thai: *phothisat*
Malay: *buah keras* (hard nut)
Indonesian: *kemiri*

family ONAGRARIACEAE

Other Names for *WATER CHESTNUTS*

French: *châtaigne d'eau*
German: *Wassernuß*
Italian: *castagna d'acqua*
Thai: *krajab*
Chinese: *bi qi*
Japanese: *hishinomi*

Recipes

Key to the Painting

top: candlenuts;
center: immature green coconut with Chinese water chestnuts (*Trapa bicornuta*) above and below;
bottom: Java almonds with pili nut in center

The **COCONUT** is the fruit of *Cocos nucifera*, the most useful tree in the world. It flourishes on seashores in the moister parts of the tropics. Botanists disagree about whether the species originated in the East Indies and Melanesia, as most think, or in tropical America, as a minority have vigorously argued.

The main growing and exporting countries are now the Philippines, Indonesia, India, Sri Lanka, Mexico, Malaysia, and Papua New Guinea.

A whole coconut, as usually sold, is only the kernel of the fruit, the husk having been removed before shipping. Inside the shell is a thin brown coat, the testa, covering the kernel, which is hollow and contains liquid. In a ripening fruit the kernel has a creamy gelatinous texture and the liquid in it makes a sweet and refreshing drink. (This liquid can conveniently be called coconut water. Coconut milk is different, as explained below.) In a fully mature fruit the amount of liquid is less, while the kernel is quite solid. Copra is the name for dried coconut meat.

Coconut "milk" or "cream" is a thick sweet liquid produced by pouring boiling water over grated coconut (fresh or shredded), leaving it to cool, and squeezing the liquid from the pulp through a cloth. Twice as much water by volume as there is grated coconut produces "milk" of normal thickness; half that amount of water will yield the thicker "cream".

Coconut milk is a standard ingredient in the cooking of southern India and Southeast Asia. It is an emulsion, as is cow's milk, but contains less protein and more fat. If it is left to separate, the fat rises to the top as coconut oil.

The **CANDLENUT** tree, *Aleurites moluccana*, is now cultivated from India to the Philippines and in the Pacific islands. Each nut contains either one or two waxy white kernels. These are widely consumed as a flavoring ingredient, after suitable preparation, in Southeast Asia and especially in Java. The usual practice there is to roast the nuts until they can be cracked open and then to sauté the kernels, crushed with other ingredients such as shallots, garlic and chili peppers, to produce an aromatic mixture for use in savory dishes.

The **PILI NUT** is the most important of a group of nuts borne by trees of the genus *Canarium*. Pili nuts proper come from *C ovatum* and *C luzonicum*, both native to the Philippines where "pili" is the local name, and where they are much cultivated. They have the highest oil content of any nut (well over 70%), and are comparable to almonds in texture, flavor, and uses. In Malaysia and Indonesia *C commune*, the Java almond or kenari nut, is the most important species.

WATER CHESTNUT is a name applied to three water plants of the genus *Trapa*, whose strangely shaped fruits each enclose a large white kernel bearing some resemblance to chestnuts. (Note: the "Chinese waterchestnut", *Eleocharis tuberosa*, is something quite different; a corm, not a seed or nut.)

The water chestnut best known in Europe is *Trapa natans*, often called "caltrop". (A caltrop is a military device consisting of four metal spikes arranged so that no matter which way it falls, one spike is pointing upward. Caltrops are still used by guerillas to burst car tyres.) This water chestnut bears four spikes and has a kernel of about the same size as an ordinary chestnut, to which it bears some resemblance in flavor and texture. It is usually eaten boiled or roasted.

In China, Korea and Japan there is a different species, *T bicornis*, with two large, curved "horns". This nut has been an important food in China since ancient times. Because of its starchiness it was counted as a grain rather than a nut; and it was generally consumed in the form of flour.

The singhara nut, *T bispinosa*, is an important food in Kashmir. The name is Bengali. The plant is cultivated in lakes or along river banks, and can be found over a wide area from Africa to Japan.

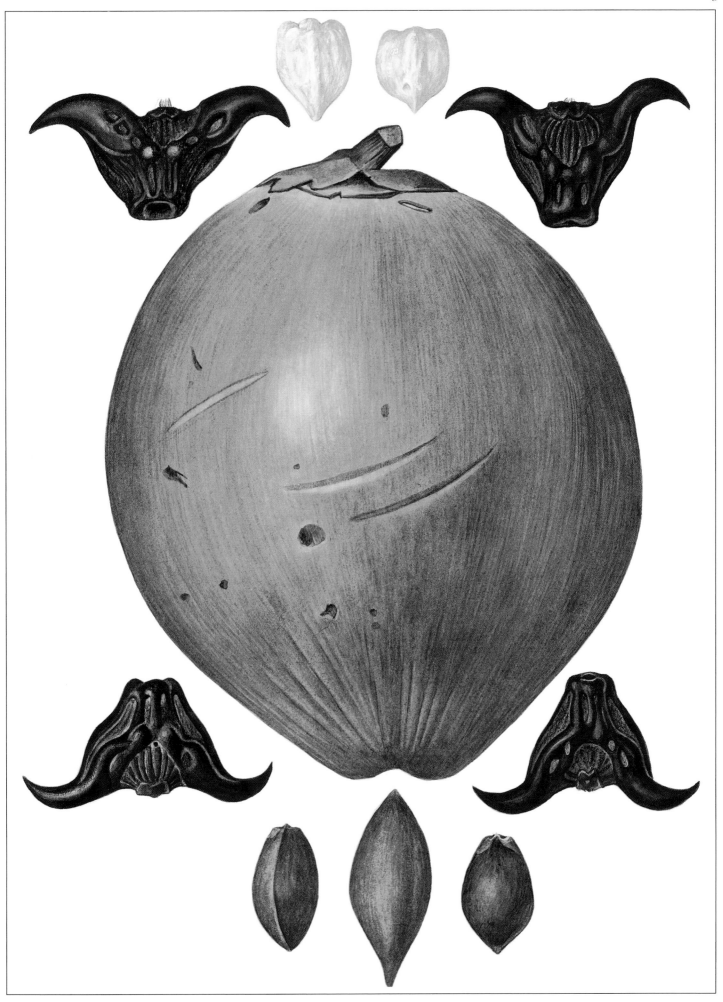

Pumpkin and Sunflower Seeds, Betel and Cola Nuts

family CUCUBURTICACEAE

Other Names for *PUMPKIN SEEDS*

Bengali: *kumdar dana*
Chinese: *nan gua zi*

family COMPOSITAE

Other Names for *SUNFLOWER SEEDS*

French: *graines de tournesol*
German: *Sonnenblumensamen*
Italian: *semi di girasole*
Spanish: *pipas*
Arabic: *lubb*
Indian languages: *surya mukhi* (Hindi);
suraj mukhi (Bengali); *surya-kanthi*
(Tamil)
Thai: *thaan tawan*
Malay: *bunga matahari*
Chinese: *kui hua zi*

family PALMACEAE

Other Names for *BETEL NUT*

French: *noix d'arec*
German: *Arecanuß*
Italian: *noce di areca*
Spanish: *nuez de areca*
Indian languages: *supari* (Hindi,
Bengali); *pakku* (Tamil)
Burmese: *kun*
Malay / Indonesian: *pinang*
Chinese: *bin lang*

PUMPKIN SEEDS. The name "pumpkin" is used of some varieties of *Cucurbita pepo* and its relations, usually ones which grow to a large size. Some have highly edible and nutritious seeds, which are enjoyed as a snack food, especially in Central Europe and the Balkans, and in Central America. They are eaten raw, or roasted, or fried and salted. They are normally have thin seed-coats, which are not eaten, but a variety of *C pepo* has been developed which has "naked" seeds and has wittily been called Lady Godiva.

SUNFLOWER SEEDS. The sunflower, *Helianthus annuus*, an annual plant, is grown mainly for the valuable oil obtained from the seeds; but the seeds are also a popular and nutritious snack food, raw or roasted and salted, and are used in confectionery. The plant has remarkably large flowerheads (the record is 30 inches each of which may contain several hundred seeds.

The name sunflower is probably derived from the resemblance of the flowerhead to the sun; but it may have to do with the plant's habit of keeping its maturing flowerhead turned towards the sun, so that it faces east at dawn and west at dusk. The French, Italian, Spanish, and Chinese names all suggest this.

Although the sunflower was introduced to Spain from North America in the 16th century, early attempts to utilize it in Europe were unsuccessful. In the early 18th century, however, Peter the Great took it to Russia, where a chance circumstance caused it to become an important food plant. The church banned the eating of oily plants on fast days, but the sunflower, being a recent introduction, was not on the list drawn up by the clerics. The laity, who were sharper-eyed, took to chewing the seeds and to extracting oil from them. Russia became, and the Soviet Union remains, the largest grower of sunflowers. The USA is the second largest producer.

The **BETEL NUT**, a popular stimulant in the Indian subcontinent and Southeast Asia, is the fruit of the areca palm, *Areca catechu*, which grows wild in Sumatra and the Philippines and is cultivated in other regions. The nut, which may also be called areca nut, contains a stimulating alkaloid (arecoline) and tannins which give it a pleasantly astringent taste.

The usual way of consuming betel nut is in the form of "pan". The nuts are gathered either green or ripe, according to taste. The dried nuts are crushed with lime and catechu, a scarlet and astringent extract made by boiling chips of wood from the areca palm. The mixture is wrapped in a betel leaf, which comes from a different tree, *Piper betle*, to make small packages. Elaborate equipment may be used for the various stages of preparation, and the provision of betel nuts for guests used to be an important element in hospitality. All this is now on the decline.

Packages of pan are chewed, not swallowed, and have a mildly stimulating effect. They sweeten the breath but stain the saliva bright red and eventually blacken the teeth. Indians believe that pan aids the digestion. No claim has been made for it as a source of nutrients.

COLA, or kola, is a popular stimulant in West Africa. Cola "nuts", not real nuts but the interior part of the fleshy seeds of tropical trees of the genus *Cola* (especially *C nitida* and *C acuminata*), are chewed fresh, or dried and ground to powder for making into a drink. They have a similar effect to tea or coffee, since they contain the same alkaloid, caffeine. They also contain smaller amounts of theobromine, as does the related cocoa "bean", and of kolanin, a heart stimulant.

The seeds may be pink, white, or purple, white being preferred. The taste is slightly bitter, but it is claimed that food eaten afterwards tastes sweet. A cola nut is often eaten before a meal for this reason, and because it is said to have digestive properties. The popular "cola" drinks of Western countries are presumed to contain cola, but the formulae are kept secret.

Key to the Painting

top left: sunflower and seeds;
top right: red and white cola nuts;
bottom left: betel nuts;
bottom right: Turk's Bonnet pumpkin
and pumpkin seeds

Cobnut, Gnetum Nut, Java Olive

family BETULACEAE
family GNETACEAE
family STERCULIACEAE

The term **COBNUT** applies not only to a type of hazelnut, but also to several nuts of the genus *Omphalea*, of tropical America, which have a flavor similar to that of hazelnuts.

There are three species of *Omphalia*, which play a minor role as food. *O diandra* and *O triandra* are both cultivated on a small scale. In Francophone islands of the West Indies these nuts are called "*noisettes*", ie hazelnuts; and in Santo Domingo the name is *avellana*, also hazelnut.

GNETUM is an Asian genus of tropical trees, none of which has an English name. They bear bunches of small fruits, dark red when ripe, with edible seeds which have local importance as food in parts of Southeast Asia. The most prominent species is *G gnemon*, grown and used to some extent in Malaysia and more so in Java, where the name for the nut is *malinjo*.

JAVA OLIVE is a name sometimes applied to a kind of pili nut (see page 142), but it belongs more properly to the seeds of *Sterculia foetida*, a tall tree common from Africa through India and Southeast Asia to Australia. The tree is called "foetid" because of the smell of its flowers. The seeds themselves smell and taste pleasant. They are the size and shape of olives, dark brown, and borne in a big, red, lobed pod. They are safe to eat only after being fried or roasted. Other Asian species with edible seeds include *S alata*, common in much of Southeast Asia and sometimes called "Buddha's coconut".

Introduction to the Recipes

Among all the broad categories of foodstuffs which human beings cook – game, meat, fish, milk products, cereals, vegetables and fruits – fruits are the most recent arrival in the kitchen, because of all these categories they are the one for which cooking is normally unnecessary.

The most primitive human beings just ate fruit from the bough, if it was edible, as birds and animals still do; and as Adam did when Eve passed him whatever fruit it was (not an apple, that much is sure). This is still the best way of enjoying many fruits, fresh from the tree or bush, eaten out of hand.

Although cooking fruit is not an ancient practice, drying it, to preserve it for use out of season, certainly is. Study of the practices of Native Americans, for example, shows that simple drying of fruit led naturally to more sophisticated processes, such as combining dried berries with fat and dried meat from game animals in pemmican. This sort of operation may be viewed as the precursor of fruit cookery.

In the earliest surviving collection of recipes (put together in the 4th and 5th centuries AD, but bearing the name of Apicius, a Roman gastronome who lived several hundred years earlier), fruits and nuts do appear, not only as flavoring ingredients and in sauces, but also as foods cooked in their own right. Apicius' recipes include dishes of peaches, pears, elderberries, and apricots. However, these are exceptional. If one analyses the whole collection, it is apparent that of all the fruits and nuts known to the Romans it was the pine nut which appeared most often, and in a supporting rather than a lead role.

In medieval Europe we find a larger number of real fruit recipes, a typical example of which is given in this book (Perys in Syrip, page 156); but still only a modest collection. If we think about the range of fruit recipes in use nowadays, and about the other ingredients which occur most often in them, we find that many of these other ingredients were lacking, or very costly, in the Middle Ages. A prime example is sugar, which was still an expensive rarity and was indeed treated as a "spice". Medieval cooks could of course use honey as a sweetener, and did. However, a more serious deficiency was in the realm of pastry. The history of pastry is complex, and stretches back further than one might think, but most of the kinds of pastry which are now used to such good effect in fruit cooking were unknown to medieval cooks.

It was when I began to group recipes for this book in categories that I fully realized the difference between then and now. Even with things like jams and jellies, great advances have been made in the last few centuries. The word jam itself (spelled "giam") did not enter the English language until the early part of the 18th century (see page 177 for a detailed introduction to the subject).

As for ice creams and all the associated iced desserts which we enjoy, it seems to have been only towards the end of the Renaissance period that water ices, which were naturally the first such confections to be made, began to achieve currency in Italy and France; and the first published ice cream recipe in the English language dates back only to 1718 (Mrs Mary Eales).*

These comments all pertain to Europe, and later to North America. The history of cooking and recipe writing in other parts of the world is more difficult to investigate. Although there are early Chinese documents, they do not tell us much about the use of fruits except for the eating of them fresh. Judging by the present, I would guess that in most parts of the world, especially the tropical regions where fresh fruits are available almost continuously, there is no ancient tradition of fruit cooking. In regions like the West Indies, what one finds of it seems to be largely derived from Spanish, Portuguese, French and even British practice. The exception is the coconut. In the regions where the coconut palm grows, cooking with coconut and its numerous products such as coconut milk can be presumed to stretch very far back in time.

The recipes given in this book are no more than a personal and small selection intended only to exemplify what can be done and to provide a stimulus for cooks. There are other books which give comprehensive collections of fruit recipes, including the use of fruits as ingredients in savory dishes. The outstanding one is *Jane Grigson's Fruit Book*, which covers all aspects of fruit cooking in that author's delightful style. For meticulous and fully illustrated information about techniques, one could not do better than consult the Time/Life books on *Fruits* and on *Cakes and Pastries* (see under Olney in the Bibliography). Excellent works on ice creams and related desserts are mentioned on page 171.

In choosing the recipes I have generally preferred ones which are easily made at home and in which not just one but any of several different fruits could be the main ingredient. It is, of course, a feature of fruit cooking that most recipes, even if they are traditionally associated with one kind of fruit, can be made with others.

---

* It is true, as Elizabeth David has pointed out, that we can probably assume that the recipe for ice cream in the manuscript recipe book of Grace, Countess Granville, was written several decades before then, and that in the latter part of the 17th century the art of using not plain ice but special freezing mixtures progressed to a point at which frozen creams of various sorts would have been familiar in the houses of the nobility. The French author Massialot, whose first book (1691) was devoted particularly to confectionery and allied arts, had much to say about freezing equipment, reflecting considerable advances made in France.

Using the Recipes

ENZYMES AND BROWNING

Enzymes present in certain fruits, such as most varieties of apple, cause the flesh to turn brown when exposed to the air. If such fruits have to be kept for a while after being peeled or cut, or if you are preparing a large quantity at one time, it is best to have a bowl of acidulated water handy in which to put the pieces. The acid, which can be lemon juice in the proportion of about a tablespoonful to two cups of water, inhibits the action of the enzymes and the flesh stays its natural color.

ENZYMES AND JELLING

Some fruits, notably pineapple and papaya, contain enzymes which prevent jelling. Cooking the fruits disables these enzymes. So for any jelly or jellied dish in which these fruits occur, they must be cooked first; or canned fruit, which is raised to the necessary temperature in being processed, should be used.

CARAMELIZING

Caramelized sugar, which is sugar heated beyond its melting point, above about 345° (the exact temperature varies according to whether the sugar is sucrose, the one we normally use, or another sort), has a remarkably tempting flavor, especially when mingled with the juices of cooked fruits. It is responsible, to take just one example, for the delightful flavor of a Tarte Tatin (page 160). Just a little caramelized sugar is enough, and a sprinkling of sugar on a pie or tart towards the end of baking will achieve this if the oven is hot enough. Caramelization can also be achieved by sprinkling sugar over a dish and then putting it briefly under a broiler.

BAKING

The oven should always be preheated to the temperature needed.

GLAZING

I had not been in the habit of keeping in my kitchen a supply of apricot glaze and redcurrant glaze, although well aware of the frequent use of these items by professional confectioners. Concentrating my attention on fruit recipes for this book has caused me to mend my ways. These glazes are so simple to prepare (see page 151) and have such a beneficial effect that they must count as almost essential.

EQUIPMENT

A blender or food processor greatly simplifies the task of extracting juice from fruit or turning fruit into a purée. If you have neither, and find a recipe referring to one or the other, you can manage perfectly well, although less quickly, with an old-fashioned juice squeezer and a strainer. Both these items are in any case required, since it is pointless to use machinery for very small quantities which you can produce just as quickly and less messily by hand. The importance of strainers is such that I recommend having several, of different capacities and mesh-sizes.

GELATIN

The use of gelatin is so important in fruit cookery, and the properties of gelatin so interesting, that the subject calls for special mention here.

Gelatin is a protein, closely related to and derived from another protein, collagen. Collagen has been described as the glue which holds animals, including the author and readers of this book, together, ensuring that they do not collapse into pools of liquid.

To make gelatin, for example from pig skin or other animal hides or bones, calls for what are quite simple chemical and cooking processes – so simple that many of them have been in use since antiquity. The result is gelatin in sheet form. This can then be cut into strips or broken up and granulated or powdered.

The form in which gelatin is presented does not really matter, although many cooks, no doubt with good reason, recommend leaf gelatin. However, it is necessary to know that the properties of any given batch of gelatin will depend to some extent on its origin and the method of processing which has been used. Commercial producers may blend different gelatins to ensure uniformity in the product they sell.

Plain gelatin in either leaf or powdered form should be soaked in cold water first to soften it, then dissolved in a warm liquid. It is soluble at around 86°. At temperatures above 150° it will be "denatured"; so the warm liquid should never be as hot as that.

When gelatin has been dissolved in a warm liquid and then cooled, it forms a sort of mesh which holds the liquid together in what will now become a jelly. If heat is applied again, the supporting mesh will unravel and eventually the mixture will again be liquid.

A little gelatin can deal with a lot of liquid. The packets in which gelatin is bought normally advise on proportions, and the simplest plan is to follow such advice. I should mention, however, that a comparison of the recommendations on different packets, or for that matter of what various cookbooks say, yields a rich crop of divergent formulae. An average formula would be that 2 tablespoons (or 2 envelopes) gelatin are enough to achieve a loose set in 4 cups of liquid or a firmer set in $2\frac{1}{4}$ cups.

Too much gelatin will produce an unattractively rubbery product. In this connection, remember that the effect of the gelatin will increase if the product is kept in the cold after setting. The protein chains will continue for some time building up further connections in the "mesh" they have created.

I have seen statements to the effect that gelatin may come from an animal source, collagen, or from seaweeds (agar agar) or other plant sources. Such statements are misleading. Gelatin comes from collagen and is always of animal origin. Certain products obtainable from plants or seaweeds have similar properties and can be used to produce a gel, but they are not gelatin. For those who are interested in fruit desserts, and who wish to avoid animal products, agar agar is perhaps the best alternative.

Techniques

The carving of fruits for decorative purposes is an art form in itself, practised especially in places such as Taiwan and Thailand. Most of us never aspire to activities of that sort, but we do need to know how to apply knives to certain fruits so as to prepare them with elegance and without waste.

The pineapple is such a fruit. As shown in diagram 1, one should begin by slicing off the skin with vertical cuts from close to the top of the fruit down to the bottom. The first such strip has been removed, and one can see the "eyes" which have been laid bare.

The secret of dealing with the eyes is to make diagonal incisions in the peeled fruit, angling the knife

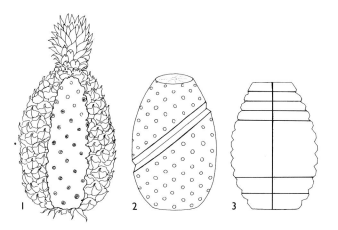

blade at 45° so that it carves out long triangular strips containing the "eyes" (see diagram 2). When these strips are flipped out and discarded, you will have rid the fruit of the eyes with minimum wastage.

Diagram 3 shows the prepared fruit ready to be sliced. You can halve or quarter it vertically, or cut it horizontally into thin (see sample cuts at the top) or thick (as at the bottom) slices. Or you can do both.

In the past, most pineapples had cores which were really too hard to be eaten with enjoyment. It is therefore common to come across instructions to remove the core when preparing a pineapple. But modern varieties, for the most part, have cores which are only a little harder than the surrounding flesh and which may be eaten. In my own experience, any doubt

on this score will be dispelled by slicing the pineapple thinly. This is anyway the most elegant procedure except for those few recipes which call specifically for pineapple chunks.

A mango, whether it is just ripe and still firm or riper and becoming a little squishy, is not easy to prepare unless you follow one of the approved techniques.

I prefer the one shown here. Using a sharp and flexible knife, make a cut right through the fruit from A, beside the stalk at the top, down to X, its lower tip, passing the knife as close as possible to the large pit

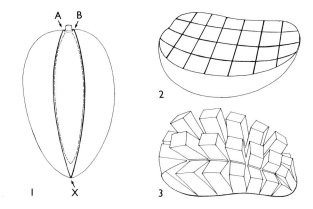

within (see diagram 1). (The pit is represented by a dotted line.) Repeat the process on the other side, from B to X.

This gives you two substantial pieces of fruit which between them contain most of the flesh. Make cuts in each as shown in the second drawing, cutting down to but not through the skin. Then grasp each in turn and push with your fingers from below to turn the fruit inside out, creating the effect shown in diagram 3. It will now be easy, holding the piece of mango over a bowl, to cut off the cubes.

When you have dealt in this way with both main pieces, return to the leftover piece which has the pit in it. Peel the two curving strips from each side and chop them into the bowl. Use your knife to chop off the pit such small slivers of flesh as can still be got from it.

It is well to remember when dealing with the last stage of mango preparation that in some varieties of mango the flesh immediately next to the pit is disagreeably fibrous, so that excessive zeal in cutting off every last gram of flesh may be misguided effort.

Recipes

Basic Recipes

Shortcrust Pastry

Quantities make 1 pound 10 ounces, enough for two single-crust 9 inch tarts or pies or one 10 inch double-crust pie.

$4\frac{1}{2}$ cups flour
2 teaspoons salt
$2\frac{1}{4}$ sticks butter
up to 4 tablespoons iced water

Sift flour and salt into a large mixing bowl. Add the butter, in small cubes, rubbing it into the flour with your fingers until you have a coarse crumbly texture.

While stirring the dough with a knife, begin sprinkling iced water onto it as sparingly and evenly as possible, and continue until the dough is beginning to bind. Then work the pastry into a ball, wrap it in foil or wax paper, and chill it for half an hour.

Sweet Shortcrust Pastry
(French Pâte Sucrée)

Quantities make 1 pound pastry, enough for two 10 inch tarts or single-crust pies or one 8 inch double-crust pie.

$1\frac{3}{4}$ cups flour
$\frac{3}{4}$ stick butter
$\frac{1}{2}$ cup superfine sugar
1 egg yolk
$\frac{1}{2}$ teaspoon salt
up to 3 tablespoons iced water

Proceed as in the Rich Shortcrust recipe above.

Suet Pastry

1 cup chopped suet
$2\frac{1}{4}$ cups flour
$\frac{1}{2}$ teaspoon salt
a little cold water

Knead the ingredients together lightly. Be sparing with the cold water; you don't want a wet batter. This pastry can be rolled out for immediate use.

Rich Shortcrust Pastry
(French Pâte Brisée)

Quantities make 1 pound pastry, enough for two 10 inch tarts or single-crust pies or one 8 inch double-crust pie.

$2\frac{1}{4}$ cups flour
1 tablespoon confectioners / superfine sugar
$\frac{1}{2}$ teaspoon salt
$1\frac{1}{4}$ sticks sweet butter, at room temperature
1 egg yolk

Sift flour, sugar, and salt onto a pastry board, and make a well in the center. Put the butter and egg yolks in the well and blend them lightly. Then use a spatula to work the dry ingredients gradually into the butter and egg mixture. If necessary to achieve the desired crumbly texture, add a few drops of water. Wrap and chill as in the first recipe.

Frangipane (Crème d'Amandes)

This is used in the French apple tart on page 159, and can also be used to coat pieces of fruit before making them into fritters. Fritter Dough is given on page 168.
This quantity makes 14 ounces.

$\frac{3}{4}$ stick butter
$\frac{1}{2}$ cup superfine sugar
1 whole egg, lightly beaten with 1 additional egg yolk
2 teaspoons Kirsch (optional)
generous 1 cup ground almonds
2 tablespoons flour

Cream the butter and beat the sugar into it. Add the egg and additional yolk, continuing to beat. Then put in the (optional) Kirsch, ground almonds and flour, and stir until everything is thoroughly mixed.

Coconut Cream and Coconut Milk

These can conveniently be prepared from commercial products, following the directions on the package. If you prefer to make your own from the grated white meat of a fresh coconut, mixed with water and squeezed through muslin, remember that cream is the first and thicker extraction you obtain, while milk is the second and thinner one which is got by repeating the process with the same lot of grated coconut. (See page 142)

Apricot Glaze

In a small pan, preferably enameled, melt 1 cup apricot jam (home-made or the best you can buy), 1 tablespoon lemon juice, and 1–2 tablespoons water (just enough to achieve a pouring consistency). Strain. If necessary, reheat to melt it again before use. You will have about $\frac{2}{3}$ cup of glaze.

Red Currant Jelly Glaze

In a small enameled pan, melt 1 cup red currant jelly (home-made or the best you can buy) with 2 teaspoons water, stirring very gently and cooking for only one minute after melting. You will have about $\frac{2}{3}$ cup of glaze.

Sugar Syrup

For a light sugar syrup, use generous 1 cup sugar to $2\frac{1}{4}$ cups water. For a medium syrup increase the amount of sugar to $1\frac{1}{2}$ cups.

For either kind, heat the water in a heavy saucepan, add the sugar, stir until the sugar is quite dissolved, and then boil rapidly for just a few minutes.

If the grated peel of half a lemon is added to the pan before the boiling, and a small amount of lemon juice stirred into the syrup after it has cooled, this will give it a lemon flavor which suits most fruits. Strain the peel out of the syrup before use.

Custard Sauce

An English tradition and well loved accompaniment for steamed puddings and stewed fruit and suchlike.

4 or 5 egg yolks
$\frac{1}{2}$ cup superfine sugar
$1\frac{3}{4}$ cups milk

Put the egg yolks in a mixing bowl and beat the sugar into them until pale in color and dribbling off the whisk in ribbons. Scald the milk, then add it little by little, stirring constantly.

Cook the custard without boiling in a heavy saucepan over a low heat until it is thick enough to coat a spoon.

Put the pan into a large bowl of ice cubes, to arrest the cooking. Strain into a warmed jug or sauce-boat. If the custard is to be served cold, leave it in the bowl of ice, stirring gently from time to time.

Fruit Salads, Jellies and other Summer Desserts

There is a notion that a fruit salad, to deserve the name, must comprise at least two and probably several different fruits. This idea is widespread; and certainly if one sees "fruit salad" on a menu in England one knows what to expect (including the statutory cherries artificially colored pink). But this is not really so; as is indeed apparent from the derivation of the word salad (from Latin "salata", meaning "seasoned"). A salad is a salad because it has a dressing, not because it embodies a variety of fruits or vegetables. To draw attention to this I have included one single-fruit recipe (Orange Medley, from the Dutch food historian Joop Witteveen).

However, the first recipe has many fruits; and it illustrates very well the importance of macerating (steeping) fruits in a flavored and sweetened liquid to produce a good salad.

An Italian Fruit Salad

The inspiration for our standard party fruit salad comes from Marcella Hazan and every time we make it, with whatever variations, we think of her with gratitude.

$1\frac{1}{2}$ cups freshly squeezed orange juice
3 tablespoons freshly squeezed lemon juice
grated peel of 1 lemon
6 ounces seedless green grapes
6 ounces cherries, pitted
flesh of half a small melon, diced
2 apples
2 pears
1 peach or nectarine
4 apricots or plums
1 banana
$\frac{1}{4}$ cup sugar
6 tablespoons maraschino liqueur (optional)

Put the fruit juices and grated lemon peel into a large serving bowl.

Wash the grapes and cherries. Put them and the diced melon into the bowl. Peel, core and chop the apples and pears into cubes or pieces measuring about $\frac{1}{2}$ inch each. Peel, pit and chop the peach (or nectarine) and apricots (or plums). Peel and slice the banana to a similar size.

Put each fruit straight into the bowl as soon as it is prepared, to avoid discoloration. Stir the contents of the bowl from time to time.

Finally, add the sugar and (optional) maraschino liqueur. Stir, cover, and refrigerate for 4 to 12 hours. Mix again before serving.

Tropical Fruit Salad

Combinations such as this one, which comes from Polynesia, are patently open to variation.

for the salad
1 cup papaya, diced
1 cup mango, diced
1 cup pineapple, diced
1 cup litchis, peeled
$\frac{1}{2}$ cup kumquats, quartered
1 cup shredded fresh coconut
1 tablespoon minced fresh ginger
2 tablespoons grated orange peel

for the dressing
1 cup orange juice
1 tablespoon lemon juice
1–2 tablespoons brandy (optional)
whipped cream for serving

Combine all the salad ingredients in a large bowl. Mix the dressing ingredients together, pour over the fruit and chill.

Spoon the salad into coconut shells or scooped-out pineapples. Serve with whipped cream.

Orange Medley

4 blood oranges
2 regular oranges
superfine sugar (see text for amount)
2 teaspoons orange flower water

Peel two of the blood oranges, reserving a little of the peel, and chop them very finely. Measure the pulp and add to it twice the amount, by volume, of sugar. Transfer to a jar and leave in a cool place for two days, with the top on.

Remove the pith from the reserved peel, cut a few short, thin strips and cover them with sugar and leave for a few days as well.

Peel the regular oranges, separate them into segments, remove pith and membranes, then cut each segment into three or four pieces and put them in a bowl.

Squeeze the juice of the remaining two blood oranges into the bowl and add the sugared peel; mix well; empty the jar of blood orange into the mixture; mix again; add the orange flower water and stir.

The medley is now ready to serve, but may be chilled in the refrigerator for a couple of hours if desired.

Strawberry and Elderflower Jelly

When my wife returned from sailing a sloop out into the Atlantic, her 1990 birthday treat, we had lunch at the Carved Angel restaurant in Dartmouth, England, where this wonderfully delicate dessert was my treat too. Joyce Molyneux kindly gave us the recipe afterwards.

for the strawberry jelly
$\frac{3}{4}$ pound ripe strawberries
juice of 1 orange
$1\frac{1}{2}$ tablespoons gelatin, soaked
scant 1 cup superfine sugar

for the elderflower jelly
4 heads of elderflower
$1\frac{1}{4}$ cups white wine
scant 1 cup superfine sugar
$1\frac{1}{2}$ tablespoons gelatin, soaked
juice of $\frac{1}{2}$ lemon

First, the strawberries. Warm the orange juice and dissolve the first quantity of gelatin in it. Purée the strawberries with the sugar in a blender, add the orange juice, blend again, then put aside.

Next, set the heads of elderflower, with $1\frac{1}{4}$ cups water, the wine and the sugar, over a gentle heat for five minutes. Strain the mixture, add the rest of the gelatin, stir to dissolve, then add the lemon juice.

When both mixtures are cold and almost set, put them into glasses in alternating layers. If you are using 1 cup glasses, you will have six of them.

Joyce Molyneux comments that these instructions produce a very light set, and that if you wish to mold the jellies you should use a little more gelatin for each.

Roselle Jelly

$2\frac{1}{4}$ pounds fresh roselles
generous 1 cup sugar
3 envelopes gelatin dissolved in a little hot water

Turn the roselle fruits into juice by boiling the washed calyces with 5 cups water and the sugar for about 30 minutes. Strain the liquid through a muslin cloth. This should produce about $3\frac{3}{4}$ cups.

Reheat the liquid and add the gelatin. Then pour into a 4 cup mold and leave to set.

The flavor is rich and floral, the color ruby red. If an accompaniment is desired, use crème fraîche.

Apples and Pears in a Sauternes Jelly

Much of Tom Jaine's *Cooking in the Country*, whence this recipe comes, reflects the time he spent at The Carved Angel restaurant in Dartmouth, Devon, England; and he comments that, although this jelly was successful, jellies are generally not popular on restaurant menus. "Perhaps there is a latent fear of the rock-set commercial jelly founded on artificial flavoring. Alternatively, people eat so much jelly at home, they never wish to see one when out. . ."

2 apples
2 pears
generous 1 cup sugar
1¼ cups Sauternes or similar wine
2 tablespoons gelatin
1–2 teaspoons lemon juice (optional)

Peel, core and slice the fruits. Make a syrup by bringing the sugar, 1¼ cups water and the Sauternes to a boil. Then poach the sliced fruit lightly in this.

Soak the gelatin in a little cold water.

Remove the fruit with a slotted spoon and set aside; measure into a bowl 2½ cups of the liquid, discarding the rest. Add the gelatin to this, stir until dissolved, taste, and add lemon juice if you wish.

Pour about half the liquid into a large bowl and put this in the refrigerator. When the liquid has started to set, add the fruit and pour on the remaining liquid. Return to the refrigerator and leave for at least four hours to set.

The jelly will be reasonably firm and have a delicious flavor.

Guava Tapioca

2 pounds guavas
½ cup quick-cook tapioca
1¼ cups sugar
a pinch of salt
1 teaspoon lemon juice
1 teaspoon grated lemon peel

Halve the guavas and scoop out the flesh. Push this through a strainer to remove the seeds and produce a purée.

Cook the tapioca gently with the sugar and salt in 1¼ cups water for five minutes until "clear". Then remove from the heat and stir in the lemon juice and peel and the guava purée. Heat through gently and serve hot, with or without dollops of whipped cream.

Swimming Melon

There are not many dessert dishes in Laos, but those which do exist are all very good and all feature sticky rice or coconut milk or both. This particular dish, whose name in Lao is Nam Van Loi Mak Teng, is very simple to make. Shredded coconut can, if necessary, be used instead of fresh coconut.

the grated meat of 1 coconut
1 melon
1 cup sugar

Begin by making two extractions of the coconut milk. The first will of course be creamier than the second (see page 142).

Cut the melon in half, remove the seeds, and scoop out the flesh in large pieces onto a chopping board. Cut the flesh into very thin strips, not much thicker than a matchstick, and cut these into lengths of about 1½ inches. Divide the strips into individual serving bowls.

Mix the sugar into the second (thinner) extraction of coconut milk and apportion this mixture into the bowls. Top each with a layer of the first (creamier) extraction of coconut milk, and serve.

Fresh Figs with Raspberry Cream

Geraldene Holt tells us in *French Country Kitchen* that she picked up this delightfully simple recipe in a locally produced booklet of fig recipes in the south of France, her "other home".

8–10 fresh ripe figs
¼ pound fresh raspberries
1 tablespoon superfine sugar
1¼ cups crème fraîche

Halve or, if they are large, quarter the figs and arrange them on a plate.

Push the raspberries through a strainer into a bowl and stir in the sugar. Mix in the crème fraîche, and you have your raspberry cream.

Spoon the raspberry cream over the figs and serve straight away or, if preferred, after chilling the dish for an hour.

Grape (or Berry) Dessert

We learned this one in Tunisia, not from Tunisians, but from the daughter of a much traveled army general – and it must be international, since we have since met similar preparations elsewhere. Other fresh fruits can be used, including berries; but the larger fruits must, of course, be peeled and cubed so that the pieces are about the size of grapes or berries.

If you use large grapes, they must be peeled, halved and seeded. Using small seedless avoids this chore.

$1\frac{1}{2}$ pounds grapes (see above)
2 cups light cream
$\frac{1}{2}$ cup brown sugar

Prepare the fruit as indicated. Butter the bottom of a shallow heat-proof dish measuring 7 × 10 inches or the equivalent. Strew the prepared fruit in this, pour the cream evenly over it and sprinkle the sugar on top.

Place the dish under the broiler for one to two minutes, until the topping has started to brown. Serve at once.

Cranachan
(Soft Fruit Brose)

Catherine Brown (1990) gives a number of enticing recipes for fruit broses. The Scots have produced many elaborations of the basic brose (which is just water or milk and oatmeal), and this particularly attractive one used to be a harvest-home dish.

quantities for 2 servings
6 heaped tablespoons medium oatmeal, toasted
scant 1 cup heavy cream / sour cream /
crème fraîche / yogurt
whisky to taste
honey to taste
soft fruit in season, prepared as necessary

Put the oatmeal into a large bowl, add the cream (or alternative) and leave for two hours to thicken. Flavor with whisky and honey and add as much prepared soft fruit as you please.

Pavlova

Passion Fruit Pavlova has been described as Australia's national dish, but is also claimed by New Zealand. The name was first recorded after the famous ballerina Pavlova visited both countries in 1926, and it was certainly named for her, although the dish itself seems to have existed earlier. Passion fruit is definitely the fruit to be used. However, as one can readily perceive, a pavlova (often abbreviated to "pav", which in turn gives rise to "afterpav cake", something you make to use up the egg yolks!) can be made with various berry fruits or with mixed fruits.

The meringue base must be home-made (it differs in composition and shape from the meringue "cases" available in European and American stores), and has to have a sort of chewy consistency in the center.

for the meringue base
4 egg whites
a pinch of salt
scant 1 cup superfine sugar
2 teaspoons cornstarch
1 teaspoon vinegar
1 teaspoon vanilla

for the topping
1–$1\frac{1}{2}$ cups whipping cream
1–$1\frac{1}{2}$ cups passion fruit pulp (or crushed berries, or a mixture of finely chopped or mashed fruits)

To make the meringue base, beat the egg whites and salt until stiff. Then beat in the sugar, a little at a time. Sprinkle the cornstarch, vinegar and vanilla over the mixture and fold these in lightly.

On a sheet of wax paper trace a circle of about 10 inches diameter. Pile the meringue mixture onto this, keeping it within the traced line and not flattening it out too much in the center (which is where you want the soft chewy part).

Place the meringue in the oven at 400°, reduce heat to low (290°) and bake for one hour 15 minutes. It should take on only a pale creamy brown color; if it looks like coloring too much, cover it with a sheet of wax paper.

Whip the cream, fold in the fruit pulp, cover the meringue base with this, and serve. (Note: the proportion between whipped cream and fruit pulp may be varied according to preference.)

I draw on a New Zealand author, David Burton, for some general tips, although he himself says that "the mystique surrounding the expert pav-maker is largely over-rated":

● The egg whites must be stiffly beaten, and to ensure a good consistency they must be firm and jelly-like, from eggs a few days old. Fresh egg whites are too thin.
● No more than a tablespoonful of sugar should be added at a time, and (more important) it must be completely dissolved after each addition or the end result will be a sticky, weepy pavlova.
● Once beaten, the mixture must be cooked immediately as it will not beat up again properly once it has settled. The cooking must be slow; to hurry it along causes the pavlova to crack and collapse after removal from the oven.

Strawberries with Orange

This is another brilliantly simple and good recipe from Raymond Sokolov.

1 "punnet" fresh strawberries
1 cup fresh orange juice
1 tablespoon Cointreau or other orange-based liqueur (optional)
1 tablespoon sugar

Rinse and trim the strawberries, then halve or quarter them, except any small ones, to finish up with pieces of suitable size.

Stir the orange juice with the Cointreau (if used) and the sugar in a bowl, until the sugar dissolves. Add the sliced strawberries and refrigerate for several hours, stirring occasionally.

Koshaf
(Iranian Dried Fruit Salad)

8 ounces mixed dried fruit (pears, prunes, figs, peaches, apples. . .)
$\frac{1}{2}$ cup pistachios
1 tablespoon rose water

Wash the fruit. Soak the fruit and nuts in $1\frac{1}{4}$ cups water and the rose water for at least 24 hours. Spoon into individual cups or bowls and serve with Greek yogurt.

Pineapple with Kirsch

Raymond Sokolov (1986), remarking that Pineapple with Kirsch has been a standard dessert in French restaurants for goodness knows how long, points out that the combination is apt, for the Kirsch, although made from cherries, has a flavor which is a fine partner for pineapple, while the pineapple softens the somewhat harsh "bite" of the Kirsch. The combination works best when fresh pineapple is used. If this is available, and you have Kirsch (also known as Kirschwasser), then you can create this classic French dessert with minimal effort.

1 fresh pineapple
1 cup Kirsh

Peel the pineapple as directed on page 149. Cut it into quarters lengthwise. If the core is woody, cut it out. Cut the flesh into neat wedges, place them in a bowl, pour the Kirsch over them, and leave them in the refrigerator for several hours, stirring occasionally to ensure that all the wedges receive their fair share of the liqueur.

Compotes and Stewed Fruit

Compotes

Fruit, water and (usually, but not always) sugar are the basis of any compote or stewed fruit dish.

In a compote, whose heartland is central and southeastern Europe (the best we ever had were in Yugoslavia) and the Near East, the fruits remain whole or in distinct pieces; whereas stewed fruits (not all, but some) are likely to lose their shape.

The best way of preparing a compote is to start by cooking the sugar in water to make a sugar syrup; and then to poach the fruit in that.

Compote of Pears

4 ripe but firm pears
$1\frac{1}{2}$ cups light sugar syrup (see page 151)

Peel, core and quarter the pears. Poach the pieces in the sugar syrup until they are tender. Allow to cool, then chill before serving.

Compote of Black Cherries and Nectarines

Proceed as above, but instead of the pears use 4 ounces black cherries and 2 nectarines.

Wash the cherries and remove their stalks. Peel the nectarines, remove the pits, and cut the flesh into bite-size pieces. Cook the prepared fruit in the sugar syrup until tender.

Litchis in Syrup

18 ounces fresh litchis
juice and peel of 1 lime (2 if very small)
generous 1 cup sugar
$2\frac{1}{4}$ cups water

Peel the litchis. Roughly chop the lime peel, put it and the sugar in the water, and bring to a boil. Add the peeled litchis and leave to simmer for 15–20 minutes.

Pour everything into a bowl, cover, and leave for 24 hours. Then remove the pieces of lime peel, and serve.

Stewed Feijoas

generous 1 cup sugar
2¼ cups water
1½ pounds feijoas
a pinch of grated nutmeg

Make a light sugar syrup as described on page 151 with the sugar and water. Peel the feijoas and cook them, with the pinch of grated nutmeg, for ten minutes in the syrup.

Serve chilled.

Ayva Tatlısı
(Turkish Quince Dessert)

A friend who worked in Turkey told me that he met this dish all over the place, but never found a published recipe for it until Nevin Halıcı's excellent book came into his hands.

1 large or 2 smaller quinces
¾ cup sugar
⅓ cup very thick cream (Turkish kaymak)

Peel, halve and core the quince(s). Heat scant ½ cup water and boil the quince halves in it for five minutes. Strain, reserving the liquid.

Add the sugar to the liquid and boil for one to two minutes, then add the quince halves and leave them over a low heat until they are soft (about 1–1½ hours) and have absorbed the syrup.

Let them cool, and serve them with dollops of thick cream in their centers.

Pears in Syrup

In *An Ordinance of Pottage* (1988), Professor Constance Hieatt presented, for the first time in print, one of the two most important collections of English culinary recipes of the 15th century. She added in many instances versions which can be followed today, including three for pears. As she explains, it is important when using medieval pear recipes to choose really firm fruits. (This is convenient since most of us have to buy pears in stores and most such pears have been picked unripe.)

The well known French dessert called Poires au Vin Rouge is, clearly, a descendant of this medieval dish. The differences include using more red wine nowadays; and in the version below we have adjusted quantities and ingredients to go some way in this direction without departing too far from the original medieval practice.

2 pounds firm, ripe pears
1 tablespoon cinnamon
1¼ cups red wine
¼ cup sugar
¼ teaspoon crushed or powdered anise
¼ teaspoon ground mace
⅛ teaspoon ground cloves
⅓ cup currants
⅔ cup chopped dates
½ teaspoon ground ginger

Peel and core the pears, quartering them lengthwise.

Dissolve the cinnamon in the red wine and strain the mixture into a saucepan. Add the sugar and other spices (except the ginger) and bring to a boil; cook until the sugar is well dissolved and the syrup has reduced just a little.

Add currants and dates, and poach the pears in this syrup, gently, over a low heat until done; then stir in the ginger.

Taste the syrup before you set the dish aside to cool: you may wish to add a little more cinnamon and/or sugar. Incidentally, you may wish to present this dish as "Perys in Syrip", the 15th-century spelling.

Miwa Naurozee
(Afghan New Year Compote)

The number seven is the motif of this unusual "fruit salad". It is traditionally made with seven fruits, including nuts; and seven passages from the Qur'an are read before it is served.

There is a similar dish (Khoshaf) in various Arab countries, and others in Iran, Armenia, and Bulgaria. In fact, they appear all over this broad region. This sort of dried fruit and nut combination is very popular among Moslems during Ramadan.

½ cup small, pale, dried apricots
⅔ cup dark seedless raisins
⅓ cup white raisins
½ cup walnuts
½ cup pistachios (with skins)
½ cup almonds (with skins)
6 cherries, fresh or conserved

Wash the dried fruit and put it in a bowl, adding enough cold water to reach 2 inches above them. Cover and set aside for two days.

Put the pistachios and almonds in a pan, scald them with boiling water, and peel off the skins as they soften. Discard the water and the skins.

Combine all the nuts with the soaked fruits, and add the cherries (pitted, if fresh). Refrigerate for a day or two, so that the juice becomes sweeter, then spoon into individual serving bowls or cups.

Appelmoes met Kweepeer
(Apple Sauce with Quince)

1 large quince
2 pounds apples (Reinette, or others which collapse
when cooked)
2 cups vanilla-flavored sugar
1–3 teaspoons lemon juice (adjust the quantity according
to the sweetness of the apples)

Peel and core the quince. Simmer the peel and core in a little water for an hour and a half, adding water if necessary.

In the meantime cut the flesh of the quince into very small pieces, and cook these in water to cover for an hour or more, until of a good red color and soft.

Now strain the peel and core, discarding them but keeping the liquid and adding it to the cooked quince.

Peel, core and slice the apples, add the slices to the quince, with the sugar, and stir well. Continue to cook until the apple slices are mushy (about five minutes), making sure that the mixture does not stick.

Finally, remove from the heat, stir in the lemon juice, continue to stir until the whole mixture is a mush, then leave to cool. (It is a good idea to refrigerate the dish for a while before serving it.)

The sauce has an interesting, slightly chewy texture and an attractive tawny rose color.

Claudia Roden's Stuffed Apricots

16 fresh apricots
juice of $\frac{1}{2}$ lemon
1 cup sugar (less if apricots are really sweet)

for the stuffing
$1\frac{1}{4}$ cups ground almonds
$\frac{1}{4}$ cup sugar
2 tablespoons rose water

Slit each apricot just enough to remove its pit. Put the apricots in a large pan with the lemon juice, 2 tablespoons water and the sugar, cover the pan and heat it very gently. Take the top off from time to time and carefully turn and baste the fruits (which are to stay whole). The juice of the apricots will form a syrup with the sugar. Once the apricots are soft, remove from the heat and allow to cool.

Meanwhile make a paste with the rest of the ingredients. Stuff some of this into each apricot. Set the apricots upright in a glass, or better still, in a crystal bowl, and pour the syrup over them.

Ginger, Apricot and Almond Pudding

2 cups dried apricots
$\frac{1}{4}$ cup almonds
$\frac{1}{2}$–$\frac{2}{3}$ cup crystallized ginger
1 tablespoon honey (or more to taste)
$\frac{3}{4}$ cup Greek yogurt
1–2 heaped tablespoons whipped cream (optional)

Wash and pit the apricots, cover them with water, bring to the boil and simmer for 15–20 minutes. Cool, and liquidize into a purée. Add the chopped almonds, ginger, honey and yogurt, and fold into the cream. Serve in individual glasses or bowls.

Summer Pudding

Not quite appropriate to this section, as the addition of bread takes it out of the normal compote and stewed fruit categories, but nevertheless a famous and delicious British dessert. Nowadays one meets little individual ones in restaurants, but the effect of a larger one, to be shared, is aesthetically more pleasing. For the quantities given here you will need a $4\frac{1}{2}$ cup ceramic bowl. The fruit should be a mixture of two or more sorts, with red fruits dominant.

butter
6 slices stale white bread
$2\frac{1}{4}$ pounds mixed fruit such as raspberries (or similar
berries), red currants and black currants
generous 1 cup sugar
thick heavy cream as accompaniment

Lightly grease the ceramic bowl with butter. Cut pieces of bread, with no crust, to cover the bottom and sides, and put them in place.

In a saucepan, heat the prepared fruit with a few tablespoons of water, add the sugar and continue cooking gently until the fruit is soft: no longer. Taste and add more sugar if necessary; this will depend on your choice of fruits.

When the fruit mixture has cooled a little, pour it into the bowl, taking care not to dislodge the bread lining. Check that the level of the fruit mixture is close to, but not brimming over, the top of the bowl. Cut some more pieces of bread to fit on top of the fruit mixture and put them in place.

Place a plate over the top of the bowl and weigh down the plate so as to compress the pudding. Leave overnight in a cold room or in the refrigerator.

To serve, remove the weights and plate, replace with a serving dish and invert. Carefully remove the bowl. Serve with thick heavy cream.

Pies and Tarts

There is no doubt about it: apple pies are the archetypal fruit pies. But there is more than one sort, and the subject also leads us into tarts.

The American version of apple pie, with pastry underneath and on top, may be derived from the medieval "raised" pies and various sweet or savory dishes completely enclosed in "coffyns" or pastry cases. If so, it could claim the oldest ancestry.

However, the British apple pie, normally baked nowadays in a deep pie dish with a crust on top only, can also claim a long history, since pies of this configuration had emerged as early as the 17th century. Old recipes often included quinces, which sharpened the flavor and gave an attractive pink color.

In France the classic dish is Tarte aux Pommes, which is topless, but otherwise subject to many variations. One recipe is given on page 159. To make such tarts, it is best to use the typical low-acid apples of the southerly growing areas, which retain their shape when cooked. Tarte Tatin is a variant: cooked with apples underneath pastry and served "upside down" to present a pastry base with apples on top (see page 160 for a version with pears).

Further east, the Apfeltorte (covered apple tart) and the well known Apfelstrudel of German-speaking regions return to the completely enclosed form, which is also found in Apple Dumplings (see page 166).

The standard accompaniment for apple pie is cream. A recipe of 1708, written in heroic couplets by the English satirist William King (one of the minor Augustans but possessed of a pleasing wit), cautions against tasting the pie until the cream has had an opportunity to "give a softness to the tarter juice". (His recipe sounds good. It includes quinces, brown sugar, cloves, and a little orange flower water.) It is a modern practice to serve the pie with ice cream, giving an attractive contrast of heat and cold.

One interesting thing about pies and tarts is that they remain essentially western items – oriental cooks have not adopted the genre. Indeed, many languages, and not only oriental ones, lack a truly equivalent word for pie, since pies, in the Anglo-American sense of the word, are indigenous to Europe, especially central and northern Europe, and occur elsewhere only as introduced dishes, notably in former colonial territories. But there is no reason why tropical fruits should not be used; not a new idea, as the 18th century recipe for Pineapple Tart (page 160) demonstrates.

Double-Crust Apple Pie

Use firm, tart apples such as Rhode Island Greening or Jonathan.

6 fairly large apples (see above)
1 teaspoon lemon juice
$\frac{3}{4}$ pound basic shortcrust pastry dough (see page 150, but make it with half shortening and half butter instead of all butter)
$\frac{1}{2}$ cup sugar
1 tablespoon tapioca
1 teaspoon grated lemon peel
$\frac{1}{2}$ teaspoon cinnamon
a pinch of grated nutmeg
$\frac{1}{4}$ stick butter
$\frac{1}{2}$ cup sour cream or crème fraîche

Peel, core and slice the apples (fairly thick, chunky slices) into water containing the lemon juice.

Roll out slightly less than half the pastry dough into a round which will line a 9 inch pie plate. Turn it into the well greased plate, press gently all round and on the rim, trim off excess. Roll out the remaining dough to become the top.

Combine the sugar, tapioca, lemon peel, and spices. Lift the apple slices out of the lemon water with a slotted spoon and add them to the sugar mixture, then put all this into the lined pie plate, dot it with the butter, and pour the sour cream or crème fraîche over all.

Moisten the edges of the pastry top and fit it into place, crimping the edges to seal them. Make three slashes across the center of the pastry lid.

Bake in the oven at 450° for 15 minutes, then lower the heat to 355° and continue cooking for a further 30 minutes, until golden brown.

Opinions vary on the question whether such a pie is best served warm, soon after it emerges from the oven, or cold the next day. If I prefer the former, it is not from any disrespect towards the latter.

Some would add a few cloves. And some would . . . Well, there is almost no end to the variations, as one can work out for oneself by recalling that Mom's apple pie is always best and that there are at least forty million Moms in America.

Tarte aux Pommes

This recipe, based on that given by Anne Willan in her brilliantly lucid *The Observer French Cookery School*, makes a tart for eight to ten people.

Of the four main elements in the tart, three can be prepared in advance; and these are all the subject of basic recipes on page 150. So operate from that page first, and then come back to this one.

I pound rich shortcrust pastry (see page 150)
10 ounces frangipane (see page 150)
¾ cup apricot glaze (see page 150)
3–4 ripe dessert apples
superfine sugar, for sprinkling

Wrap and chill the rich shortcrust pastry for at least half an hour. Roll it out and use it to line a tart pan of 10 inches (or slightly larger). Prick the dough lightly with a fork, then flute the edges and chill for some time until it is firm.

Set the oven at 400° and put a baking tray on one of the lower shelves.

Pour the frangipane into the chilled pastry case, spreading it evenly. Peel, halve and core the apples, then cut them into very thin slices and arrange them on the frangipane like the spokes of a wheel. Press them down gently so that they reach the pastry base.

Bake the tart on the hot baking sheet for 10–15 minutes until the pastry is beginning to brown. Then turn the heat down to 355° and continue cooking for another 15–20 minutes until the apples are tender and the frangipane is set. About ten minutes before you judge baking will be finished, sprinkle the sugar over the tart; this will melt and caramelize slightly.

When the tart is baked, remove it and leave it on a rack to cool. Then pour melted apricot glaze over it. Serve at room temperature.

Lemon Meringue Pie

I prebaked shortcrust pie shell (see page 150) for a 9 inch
pie plate
1¼ cups sugar
3 tablespoons cornstarch
6 egg whites and 3 egg yolks
grated peel of I lemon
juice of 2 lemons
a small pinch of salt
a pinch of cream of tartar

Combine and mix thoroughly in the top of a double boiler ¾ of the sugar, the cornstarch, egg yolks, lemon peel and all but 1 tablespoons of the lemon juice. Cook, stirring occasionally, until the mixture starts to leave the sides. Let it cool for a few minutes, then pour it into the pastry shell.

Beat the egg whites with the pinch of salt to soft peaks. Add the rest of the sugar, the remaining lemon juice and the cream of tartar. Continue beating until the whites are stiff. Spoon this meringue mixture over the lemon filling, smoothing it out with the back of the spoon.

Bake in the oven at 355° for 12 minutes or until the top of the meringue is golden.

Clafoutis
(Cherry Tart)

Clafoutis is a speciality of the Limousin region of France, and is traditionally made with the first ripe red cherries of summer. However, the idea – fruit embedded in a pastry base – lends itself readily to other fruits such as small plums and greengages, or prunes and raisins, and a mixture of fruits is often used in the Dordogne.

9 ounces rich shortcrust pastry made with: I cup flour; I
teaspoon granulated sugar; ½ teaspoon salt; ½ stick butter;
half a beaten egg; 2 tablespoons milk (see page 150 for
method)
¾ cup milk
½ vanilla pod (split lengthwise)
⅓ cup crème fraîche
3 eggs
⅔ cup sugar
3 drops orange flower water
14 ounces fresh cherries, pitted

Roll out the pastry and line a 9 inch pie plate or the equivalent with it. Refrigerate for at least an hour (as much as a day, if you like) before use. When the time comes, bake it blind in the oven at 400° for eight minutes only, in order to have it half-cooked.

Boil the milk with the vanilla pod for one minute, then remove from the heat and stir in the crème fraîche.

Beat the eggs and sugar together in a mixing bowl, then add the milk and cream mixture a little at a time, stirring constantly. Discard the vanilla pod. Add the drops of orange flower water.

Place the mixing bowl in a larger container of cold water and continue beating the mixture. Beat it until it is smooth and cold.

Dispose the cherries in the half-baked pie-crust, then pour the filling over them. (The filling should not come more than three quarters of the way up the sides of the pie-crust.)

Return the tart to the oven and bake for 20–30 minutes. Serve warm or cold.

Richard Bradley's Pineapple Tart (1726)

This recipe, from the first Professor of Botany at Cambridge University, is the earliest published recipe for pineapple in the English language; and it remains one of the very best. When the late James Beard, to use his own words, had "an instant love affair" with Bradley's book (to the delight of my family, as we were responsible for republishing it after two and a half centuries of obscurity), this was the recipe which he picked out for special attention.

In what follows, the charming text written by Bradley is preceded by my recommended quantities and followed by practical advice on making the pastry (for which Bradley had given measures and directions, acknowledged to Mrs Peasly), and on other aspects. Many of these echo what Jane Grigson worked out for herself when she used the recipe in *Jane Grigson's Fruit Book.*

for the pastry
½ stick butter
1¼ cups flour
⅓ cup sugar
a little cold milk
1 tablespoon brandy

for the filling
1 pineapple
½ cup Madeira wine
1–2 tablespoons sugar

for garnish
1¼ cups cream

"Take a Pine-Apple and twist off its Crown: then pare it free from the Knots, and cut it in Slices about half an inch thick; then stew it with a little Canary Wine or Madeira Wine, and some Sugar, till it is thoroughly hot, and it will distribute its Flavour to the Wine much better than anything we can add to it. When it is as one would have it, take it from the Fire; and when it is cool, put it into a sweet Paste, with its Liquor, and bake it gently, a little while, and when it comes from the Oven, pour Cream over it, (if you have it) and serve it either hot or cold."

Prepare the pastry as outlined on page 150, using the brandy in place of the cold water. Bake it blind in an 8 inch tart pan, until it is crisp and golden brown.

Madeira wine is not hard to find, whereas Bradley's "Canary wine" is difficult. So use Madeira.

When cooking the filling, add a little water at the start and cook gently until the trimmed pieces of pineapple are soft. Then add the sugar and turn up the heat, to produce a sticky marmalade-like mixture. Pour this hot onto the baked tart case, and gently pour the cream on top immediately afterwards.

Tarte Tatin aux Poires

Marie-Pierre Moine, in her engaging book *Cuisine Grand-mère* (her own grandmother, whose kitchen was a cave in the Loire valley), explains that you can make this in a tart pan, but that it is preferable to have a so-called *moule à manqué*, (see drawing below) which is strong enough to be heated directly on top of the stove.

1 stick butter
¾ cup superfine sugar
2½ pounds ripe eating pears

for the pastry
1¾ cups flour
1 tablespoon superfine sugar, plus extra for sprinkling
a small pinch of salt
1¼ sticks sweet butter, cut into small pieces
2 tablespoons crème fraîche

Prepare the oven at 430°. For the pastry, combine the flour (sifted), sugar and salt in a bowl and work the pieces of butter into the mixture with your fingertips; then work in the crème fraîche. Roll the dough into a ball and chill for half an hour or more.

Warm a 10 inch pie plate. Melt half the butter and pour into the plate. Sprinkle half the sugar over the butter and swirl it around, so that the whole inside of the dish is coated.

Now cook the fruit. Peel, core and quarter the pears, then arrange them in the plate, packing the pieces together tightly. Sprinkle them with the rest of the sugar and dot them with the remaining butter. Place on top of the stove over a moderately high heat for ten to 15 minutes until the butter and sugar look golden and lightly caramelized. Remove from the heat.

Finally, roll out the pastry so that it is about 2 inches wider all round than the breadth of the dish, then place it over the pears and tuck the edges in between the pears and the sides of the plate. Sprinkle a little sugar on top and prick it with a fork in a few places. Bake it in the oven for about 30 minutes, until the pastry is golden.

Having removed it from the oven, leave it to cool for a few minutes – Tarte Tatin is best served barely warm. Cover it with a serving dish larger than the plate, invert and unmold, tapping the plate sharply to make sure that nothing stays behind. Serve with crème fraîche.

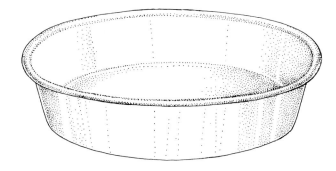

Blueberry Grunt

A famous dish of Newfoundland. This version is based on that given in the delightful book *Fish & Brewis, Toutens & Tales* by "Len Margaret" (pseudonym of a poetess).

for the dough
3 cups flour
1½ sticks butter
1 teaspoon salt
3 teaspoons baking powder
½ cup sugar
1 egg
3–4 tablespoons rice or barley (optional)

for the filling
1 pound blueberries, washed
1¾ cups sugar

Place the flour and butter in a bowl and work in the butter with the tips of the fingers until the mixture is like coarse crumbs. Add the salt, baking powder and sugar and mix lightly.

Whisk the egg with a fork in 2 tablespoons cold water until the yolk is broken. Add to the dry ingredients together with as little additional cold water as possible to make a soft dough.

Divide the dough into two equal portions. Turn out on a floured surface. Press the dough with the heel of the hand to about ½ inch thickness. Place over the bottom and sides of a greased pan 12 × 9 inches (or the equivalent) and 2 inches deep. Trim the dough to fit. To prevent the bottom pastry from becoming soggy, sprinkle it with rice or barley before adding the blueberry mixture.

Mix the blueberries with the sugar, and spread the mixture all over the pastry in the pan.

Roll out the remaining dough, lay it over the fruit mixture, trim, seal and flute the edges. Prick the center with a fork and bake in the oven at 430° until golden brown.

Cumberland "Plate Cake"
(A Fruit Pie)

One of the strongest culinary traditions in Cumbria, England is this "plate cake", really an enclosed fruit pie, thin but hearty. Numerous fruits are suitable for the filling: black currants, blackberries, gooseberries, plums, apples and rhubarb are all used in Cumbria. But if one is in the tropics one might just as well make the "cakes" with tropical fruits, choosing robust fruits rather than those with a delicate flavor or texture.

A number of cakes can be made ahead of time, frozen, and baked when needed. The quantities given make two.

for the short-crust pastry
2½ cups all purpose soft flour
1 teaspoon salt
¾ stick butter or margarine
½ cup shortening
4 tablespoons cold water

for the filling
1 pound fresh fruit (prepared as appropriate)
6 tablespoons superfine sugar, plus 2 more
flour to dust

Use the pastry ingredients to make a dough (see page 150). Let it rest for a while before rolling it out on a floured surface, so as to provide four pieces to fit your pie plates. Use plates of 8 or 10 inches.

Cover each of the greased plates with a sheet of dough. Arrange half the fruit on each, sprinkle the sugar over the fruit, and dust with flour (which helps to deal with the juices). Dampen the edges and put the pastry tops on. Trim the edges and pinch them together with your fingers.

Cut three slits in the top of each "cake" and bake them in the oven at 430° for about 30 minutes. Sprinkle the remaining sugar over them while they are still hot.

Lemon Mince Pies

for the pastry
2 cups flour
1 teaspoon salt
scant ¼ cup confectioners sugar
½ stick butter or margarine
¼ cup shortening
3 tablespoons cold water

for the filling
1 large lemon
2 medium apples, peeled, cored, finely chopped
1 cup shredded suet
1 cup currants
½ cup sugar
½ cup candied fruit, finely chopped

Make the shortcrust pastry as usual (see page 150), but incorporating the confectioners sugar with the flour.

Squeeze the juice from the lemon and reserve it. Quarter the squeezed lemon, cover with water and boil until it is completely tender, then drain and mash it. Add the chopped apple, suet, currants and sugar, and mix. Finally, add the lemon juice and candied fruit.

If you are using muffin pans you will have enough for 10–12; or you can make one 8 inch pie. Grease the pan(s) and then line with ⅔ of the pastry, fill with the mixture, and put pastry covers on them. Bake in the oven at 390°, 15–20 minutes for small pies, 35–40 minutes for a larger pie.

Greengage Frushie
(Scottish)

for the pastry
2 cups flour
pinch of salt
$\frac{1}{2}$ stick butter
$\frac{1}{2}$ cup shortening

for the filling
9 ounces greengages
2 teaspoons rose water (optional)
4 tablespoons clear honey

Sift the flour and salt into a mixing bowl, rub in the fats, then sprinkle on just enough water to make a stiff dough. Let this rest for ten minutes. Meanwhile, wash and halve the greengages and remove their pits.

Roll out the pastry slightly larger than a 10 inch round pie plate. Place it on the greased plate. Trim the edges, and roll the trimmings into strips. Spread the greengages over the pastry, sprinkle the rose water (if used) and pour the honey evenly over them. Decorate the top with the strips of pastry in a lattice pattern. Dampen and seal the edges.

Bake in the oven at 400° for 25 minutes. Serve hot, sprinkled with sugar and accompanied by cream.

Mango and Almond Tart

1 large ripe mango
18 ounces rich shortcrust pastry (see page 150)
1 stick melted butter
$1\frac{1}{4}$ cups ground almonds
generous $\frac{1}{2}$ cup sugar
$\frac{2}{3}$ cup sour cream
2 eggs

Peel and slice the mango thinly. Line a buttered 10 × 7 inch baking tray with the pastry, leaving a slight raised lip all around.

In a separate bowl, or a food processor, mix together all the other ingredients until smooth.

Lay the mango slices on the pastry and pour the almond mixture over them. Bake in the oven at 470° for 15 minutes, then lower the heat to 355° for a further 30 minutes, or until the top is golden. This is best served at room temperature or just warm.

The budding opera singer who furnished this recipe states that puff pastry, instead of the shortcrust pastry specified above, works well.

Blandford Gooseberry Tart

for the pastry
generous 1 cup flour
$\frac{1}{2}$ cup Graham flour
2 tablespoons butter
2 tablespoons superfine sugar
1 egg

for the filling
1 pound gooseberries
2 eggs, beaten
$\frac{1}{4}$ cup sugar
$\frac{1}{2}$ stick butter
grated lemon or orange peel
a pinch of nutmeg

Prepare and chill the shortcrust pastry dough (see page 148) as usual, then roll it out to line an 8 inch pan. Bake blind in the oven at 390° for 20 minutes.

Meanwhile bake the gooseberries in a single layer in the oven for about ten minutes until they are soft. Mix them with the beaten egg, sugar and butter, and add the grated lemon or orange peel and the nutmeg.

Turn the mixture into the pre-cooked pastry shell and bake it in the oven at 355° for 20–25 minutes.

Rhubarb and Egg Tarts

12 ounces rich shortcrust pastry (see page 150)
1 pound rhubarb, leaves discarded
2 eggs
$\frac{1}{2}$ stick butter
2 tablespoons sugar, or to taste
2 teaspoons grated lemon peel

First make the pastry and line one 8 inch tart pan or 10 muffin pans. Wash the rhubarb stems and cut into $1\frac{1}{2}$ inch pieces. Cook in as little water as possible and leave to cool. Whisk the eggs and then beat in the butter, rhubarb and lemon peel, and sweeten to taste.

Turn the mixture into large or small uncooked pastry cases and bake in the oven at 400° for 25–35 minutes.

Crumbles and the Like

There is no doubt about it: crumbles, whether called that or "frushies" or "buckles" or whatever, are almost ubiquitous. They don't make it into high-class restaurants, but otherwise they're all over the place in the western world. What accounts for their popularity? I suppose that one factor is that nothing much can go wrong with them. However, they're not only easy to make; they're a real pleasure to eat.

Our Almond Crumble

1½ pounds apples (choose firm and flavorful ones)
¾ stick sweet butter
¾ cup flour
scant 1 cup vanilla-flavored sugar
¾ cup almonds, chopped
½ teaspoon cinnamon
¼ teaspoon salt

Peel and core the apples, then chop them into a greased oven dish. Rub the other ingredients together to make a crumbly mixture, lay it over the apples, and bake in the oven at 390° for 25–30 minutes.

Apple Brown Betty

5 or 6 medium-sized tart cooking apples, peeled and cored
juice and grated peel of 1 lemon
1 cup soft light brown sugar
½ teaspoon cinnamon
½ teaspoon nutmeg
½ teaspoon ground cloves
2 cups dry breadcrumbs, moistened with a little melted butter

Cut the apples into small chunks and mix these with the lemon juice and peel. Mix the brown sugar with all the spices.

Place a layer of the buttered breadcrumbs in the bottom of a well-buttered 8 inch soufflé dish, then a layer of apples, then one of sugar. Repeat, ending with a layer of crumbs. Pour a little more melted butter and lemon juice on top.

Put the dish, covered, in the oven at 355°. After 15 minutes remove the cover and continue cooking until the top is crisp (about 40–50 minutes). Serve hot with whipped cream or ice cream.

Apple Tart with Crumble Topping

An interesting hybrid between tarts and crumbles. I have almost identical recipes for it from Germany and Normandy; the German name for "crumble" is, incidentally, Streusel. Suitable apples for this dish are fairly tart ones with plenty of flavor, such as Rhode Island Greening. If the apples are on the sweet side, use less sugar.

18 ounces rich shortcrust pastry (see page 150)
juice and grated peel of 1 lemon
4–5 apples (see above)
¼ cup raisins
3 pinches of ground cinnamon
¾ stick sweet butter
½ cup flour
⅔ cup brown sugar
crème fraîche or sour cream

Prepare the pastry and line a 9 inch tart pan with it.

Put the lemon juice in a bowl. Peel, core and slice the apples into the bowl and turn the slices occasionally to ensure that they are all protected by the lemon juice from browning.

Place the apple slices neatly in the pastry shell, with the raisins, and dust them with the cinnamon. Cut the butter into small pieces, put these in a mixing bowl and work in the flour, sugar, and lemon peel. Mix lightly, with your fingers, to obtain a crumbly effect. Spread this mixture over the apple slices.

Bake in the oven at 355°, until the topping is golden brown and crisp. Serve warm with a bowl of crème fraîche (whipped, if you like) or sour cream.

Apple and Banana Crumble

2 cups flour
1 cup brown sugar
1½ sticks butter
6 large tart apples
4 bananas
1 teaspoon cinnamon

Sift the flour into a mixing bowl and add the sugar. Cut the butter into small pieces and rub it in until the mixture is crumbly.

Peel, core and slice the apples into a buttered oven-proof dish, add the peeled and sliced bananas and the cinnamon and mix well.

Sprinkle the crumble evenly over the fruit and press gently to compact the mixture. Bake in the oven at 350° for about 35 minutes, or until the crumble is golden brown.

Serve hot with cream or custard.

Strawberry Rhubarb Crisp

Jo Marie Powers and Anita Stewart had a good idea when they decided to tour farmers' markets in Ontario and write *The Farmers' Market Cookbook*, and the (amazingly, to British eyes) enlightened Ontario Arts Council helped them. The book gives off a good farmhouse flavor.

This recipe came from Yvonne Thompson at the Kingston Farmers' Market. The combination of rhubarb with strawberries and the use of oats in the topping are distinctive and work well. Quantities given serve 8, or even 9.

$\frac{3}{4}$ pound fresh rhubarb, diced
$\frac{3}{4}$ pound fresh strawberries, sliced (not thinly)
scant 1 cup sugar
1$\frac{3}{4}$ cups rolled oats
1 cup flour
a pinch of salt
generous 1 cup brown sugar
1 teaspoon grated orange peel
generous $\frac{1}{2}$ stick butter

Mix the prepared rhubarb and strawberries with the white sugar and put it in the bottom of an 8 inch square baking dish.

Now mix the oats, flour, salt, brown sugar and orange peel together until the mixture is crumbly. Sprinkle it over the fruit.

Bake in the oven at 355° for 40–45 minutes.

Raspberry Buckle

This is found in Canada and New England.

The recipe can also be used for relations of the raspberry, such as the loganberry, and for blackberries and dewberries.

for the batter
$\frac{1}{2}$ stick butter
$\frac{1}{3}$ cup sugar
1 egg
a pinch of salt
1$\frac{1}{2}$ teaspoons baking powder
scant 1 cup flour
$\frac{1}{3}$ cup milk

for the filling
1$\frac{3}{4}$ pounds raspberries
scant 1 cup sugar
$\frac{1}{2}$ teaspoon cinnamon

for the topping
$\frac{1}{2}$ cup sugar
$\frac{1}{2}$ stick butter
4 tablespoons flour

Mix the butter and sugar until soft. Add the egg and beat well. Sift salt, baking powder and flour together, then add to the butter and egg mixture. Add the milk and blend well. Put this batter in a well buttered baking dish.

Mix the raspberries and sugar together and spread over the batter. Sprinkle with the cinnamon.

Rub the topping ingredients together until crumbly and sprinkle over the filling. Bake in the oven at 355° until the topping is slightly brown (about 30 minutes).

The sponge-like mixture below the raspberries "buckles" upwards during the baking.

Although the term "crumble" has spread more or less everywhere in the English-speaking world (and may even be met in France), there are many dishes which certainly are crumbles but do not bear the name.

The "buckle" above is one example, perhaps explained by the last sentence of the recipe. But what is one to make of the next item, called "Friar's Omelet"? As the American author Helen Cox remarks, in her good book about traditional English baking, it neither is nor resembles an omelet, but is a distinctive kind of apple crumble. It seems to belong to at least two English counties, Hampshire and Dorset. The lemon flavor should be clear and sharp.

Friar's Omelet

$\frac{3}{4}$ pound tart apples, peeled, cored and chopped
4 tablespoons sugar, plus 1 teaspoon
1 tablespoon lemon juice
2 teaspoons grated lemon peel
1 egg, beaten
2 cups soft breadcrumbs
1 tablespoon butter
2 pinches cinnamon

Put the prepared apple in a pan and add $\frac{1}{4}$ cup water, the sugar, lemon juice and grated lemon peel. Cook gently until the apple is soft, remove from the heat and stir in the egg.

Grease a 7 inch oven dish about 2$\frac{1}{2}$ inches deep and put half the breadcrumbs in the bottom, followed by the apple mixture.

In a small pan melt the butter and add the remaining breadcrumbs to it, with the teaspoon of sugar and the cinnamon. Spread this mixture over the apple.

Bake at 390° for 25–30 minutes. Serve with cream.

There are various fruit dishes which resemble crumbles in that they have a topping over the fruit, but are different in that the topping is not crumbly. I have two examples to offer.

Witnessing the Sainsbury Young Cooks of Britain Competition finals in London in 1990, I was struck by the calm demeanor of one of the youngest competitors, Matthew Nottingham of Caerphilly in Wales. His dessert was delicious, an ingenious marriage of the crème brûlée associated with Trinity College at Cambridge University (it was introduced there by a Scottish student in the 19th century) with the exotic fruits now so widely available.

Exotic Crème Brûlée

2 kiwi fruits
2 small bananas
8 litchis
2 passion fruit
8 tablespoons Greek yogurt
4 teaspoons clear honey
$\frac{1}{2}$ cup sliced almonds
$\frac{1}{2}$ cup sugar

Peel and slice the kiwis and bananas. Peel and quarter the litchis. Scoop out the flesh from the passion fruit. Divide the fruit between four custard cups.

Top the fruit in each cup with a tablespoon of yogurt, a teaspoon of honey and then another tablespoon of yogurt. Smooth the top surfaces and sprinkle them with the flaked almonds.

In a pan, dissolve the sugar in $\frac{3}{4}$ cup water and let it boil rapidly for five minutes, until it turns a rich brown color. Quickly pour a thin layer over the surface of each cup and leave to set as a brittle top.

Matthew garnished his presentation with "Cape gooseberries" in their papery husks, opened at the top.

Eve's Pudding
(with apple or feijoa)

just over 1 pound cooking apples, or feijoa fruits
90 g / 3 ounces sugar
grated peel of half a lemon
2 tablespoons pure apple juice or cider

for the topping
$\frac{1}{3}$ cup sugar
$\frac{1}{2}$ stick butter
1 egg
1 cup self-raising flour
a little milk
a little confectioners sugar

Peel, core and slice the apples, or feijoa; or indeed other fruit – this recipe works with any firm-fleshed fruit, although it isn't "Eve's pudding" unless made with apples.

Put the sliced fruit in a greased pie plate of suitable size and sprinkle the sugar over them, lemon peel and apple juice or cider.

For the topping, work the sugar into the butter, beat in the egg, work in the flour, and add milk (about 1 tablespoon should do) to produce a soft batter.

Spread the batter over the apples and bake the dish for 40 minutes in the oven at 355°.

Before serving, dust the top with confectioners sugar. Serve with cream.

Rhubarb Cobbler

A small area east of Sheffield is the home of early rhubarb in England; and this recipe is from the same county, Yorkshire.

$1\frac{1}{2}$ cups self-raising flour
a pinch of salt
$\frac{1}{4}$ stick butter or margarine
3 tablespoons superfine sugar
milk, as required
1 pound rhubarb
3 tablespoons soft brown (or other) sugar

Sift the flour with the pinch of salt, rub the butter or margarine into it, and incorporate the sugar. Use the milk to mix this to the consistency of a biscuit-like dough.

Wash and trim the rhubarb and cut it into lengths of about $1\frac{1}{2}$ inches. Place these in a pan with a little water (say, 3 tablespoons) and sprinkle the brown sugar over it. Bring to a gentle boil, cover, and simmer until cooked (just two to three minutes for young rhubarb, but five to eight minutes for thicker and older stalks).

Lay the drained rhubarb in the bottom of an ovenproof dish, spread the batter over it, and cook for 15 minutes at 400°.

Fruit Dumplings and Kindred Puddings

In this section the emphasis is on dumplings and steamed puddings, but room is found for fruit fritters and one remarkably good "cake" dessert.

Apple Dumpling

Many people make individual apple dumplings (each apple in its own pastry jacket), and will discuss in lively fashion whether to peel and core the apples; and, if cored, how to stuff (apricot jam, quince jelly, marmalade); and whether to steam or bake. Eliza Acton (1845) offered the charming advice that such apple dumplings look prettiest if they are boiled in cloths specially knitted for the purpose. However, I belong to a family in which the homely tradition of one large boiled or steamed dumpling, cooked in a ceramic bowl with a plain muslin cloth across the top, has always been maintained.

1¼ cups shredded suet
2 cups flour
¼ teaspoon salt
4–6 apples, peeled, cored, each cut into 8 slices
6 cloves

Butter the inside of a ceramic bowl. Mix the suet, flour and salt together, knead the mixture lightly with as little cold water as possible, roll it out, and cut out a segment (a quarter or so) of it to be used later for the covering. Line the bowl with what is left, bringing the cut edges together and ensuring that the dough overlaps the edge of the bowl slightly. Put in the apple and cloves. (Organize the top layer of apple pieces so that it is reasonably flat – if there are bits sticking up you will have problems covering them.) Cover with the rest of the paste, tie a muslin cloth firmly over the whole thing and set it in plenty of boiling water in a large covered pan. Simmer for an hour and a half.

We have never used any fruit but apple for this. However, the recipe adapts to many others: for example, a mixture of nectarines (quartered) and greengages (halved).

Serve with plain English custard (traditional) or spoonfuls of crème fraîche.

Pieroẑki with Blueberries

8 cups flour
pinch of salt
1 egg, lightly beaten
5 cups fresh blueberries, rinsed and drained
¾ stick butter melted

for serving
4 tablespoons confectioners sugar
1¼ cups sour cream

Prepare the dough by sifting the flour and salt, then mixing with the egg and just over ½ cup water. Knead well, then roll out thin and use an upturned glass to cut out rounds of about 3 inches. Put one tablespoon of the blueberries in the middle of each round, fold over into a half-moon shape, then moisten and seal the edges firmly.

Put the dumplings into plenty of boiling, salted water and cook them over a medium heat until they float to the surface. As they do so, take them out with a slotted spoon, rinse with warm water, drain, and place them on the plates, drizzling melted butter on top (this helps to prevent them from sticking together).

Mix the sugar with the sour cream and put it either in one common bowl (for family use) or in individual bowls (for company). The dumplings are to be dipped in the sour cream mixture as they are eaten.

It is a good idea to make double quantities so that the dumplings can be eaten hot and then, later on, cold.

Lemon Pudding

This is a simple version of what is often called "Sussex Pond Pudding", although it seems to belong also to Cumbria.

1 pound light suet crust (see page 150)
2 lemons (unblemished, thin-skinned, washed)
4–6 tablespoons dark corn syrup or sugar
½ stick butter

Mix your suet crust. Break off a piece big enough to make the single top and put this aside on greased wax paper. Roll out the remainder and use to cover the bottom and sides of a 6½ inch ceramic bowl.

Prick the lemons all over with a thin skewer. The pricks should go right in. Place the whole lemons in the middle of the suet crust in the bowl and cover them with the syrup or sugar, and the butter. Then place the single top of suet crust on top, and cover the bowl securely with greased wax paper.

Steam the pudding for three and a half hours. It will need no accompaniment when served.

Persimmon (or Sharon Fruit) Pudding

Quantities are for a pudding made in an 8 or 9 inch false-bottom tart pan.

$1\frac{1}{2}$ pounds ripe persimmons or sharon fruits
1 cup flour
a pinch of salt
$\frac{3}{4}$ teaspoon baking powder
$\frac{3}{4}$ teaspoon bicarbonate of soda
1 teaspoon cinnamon
$\frac{2}{3}$ cup sugar
3 eggs
$1\frac{1}{2}$ cups milk
$\frac{1}{4}$ cup light or whipping cream
1 tablespoon honey
$\frac{3}{4}$ stick butter
1 cup walnuts

Remove the pulp from the fruits and blend into a purée. Strain and mix the flour, salt, baking powder, bicarbonate of soda and cinnamon.

Combine the persimmon purée with the sugar, eggs, milk, cream, and honey. Stir this into the flour mixture, and let the resulting batter stand for a while to thicken.

Melt the butter, reserving enough to grease the pan. Toast the walnuts lightly, then chop them coarsely into the melted butter and work this mixture into the batter.

Grease the pan, pour the batter into it and bake in the oven at 355° for two hours or until the mixture is set and the top is brown. Serve hot, with crème Chantilly.

This recipe can be used with fresh figs, to which 1 tablespoon of lemon juice must be added.

Flan Périgourdin

$\frac{1}{3}$ cup raisins or white raisins
$\frac{3}{4}$ cup prunes (pitted) or dried apricots, chopped into large pieces
$\frac{1}{2}$ cup cognac
$\frac{1}{2}$ cup sugar
3 large or 4 medium eggs
a minimal pinch of salt
$\frac{1}{2}$ cup flour
$1\frac{1}{4}$ cups milk
$\frac{1}{2}$ teaspoon vanilla, or orange flower water

Put the dried fruits in hot water and leave overnight. Drain them thoroughly and place in a jar. Pour the cognac over them. Seal the jar and leave for eight hours or more, shaking the jar from time to time.

Beat the sugar, eggs and salt together in a mixing bowl. Sift in the flour, a little at a time, stirring with a whisk. Stir in the milk, the vanilla or orange flower water and the fruits from the jar.

Butter a suitable oven dish (about 8 × 6 × 2 inches), ladle the batter (which will be quite thin) into it. Bake in the oven at 390° for 20 minutes, until risen and brown on top.

Kue Talam Pisang
(Indonesian Banana Pudding)

Oriental fruit puddings are relatively rare. This one comes from Sri Owen's *Indonesian Food and Cookery*, the classic work in its field.

3 cups rice flour
$\frac{1}{2}$ cup cornstarch
a pinch of salt
$3\frac{3}{4}$ cups coconut milk (see page 150)
generous $\frac{1}{2}$ cup brown sugar
3 large bananas

Sift the rice flour, cornstarch and salt into a mixing bowl. Heat the coconut milk then transfer half to a smaller pan and in it, melt the sugar. Add the flours to the remaining coconut milk to form a fairly thick batter, then mix the coconut milk and sugar mixture into this.

Peel the bananas and cut them into thin rounds. Spoon the batter into well greased custard cups and top each with several rounds of banana.

Steam the little soufflés or puddings for 25–30 minutes until set and cooked. Serve warm or cold.

Steamed Rice and Banana Packets
(from Laos)

For the authentic flavor, wrap these packets in banana leaf; otherwise substitute foil.

3 cups sticky rice
$2\frac{1}{4}$ cups coconut milk (see page 150)
$1\frac{1}{4}$ cups sugar
$\frac{1}{2}$ teaspoon salt
5 medium bananas

Soak the sticky rice in water for at least four hours, then drain and add it to the coconut milk in a large cooking pot. Cook for five to ten minutes until the rice is half-cooked and still moist. Mix in the sugar and salt.

Halve the bananas lengthways and then cut each half into two across. Take 20 pieces of blanched banana leaf, or foil, about 6 inches square. Onto each, spoon 2 tablespoons of the rice mixture, place a quarter of a banana on top and wrap into a neat enclosed packet. Steam for half an hour and serve hot.

Orange and Almond Dessert Cake

I have based this recipe, which produces a moist cake suitable for use as a dessert, indeed almost like a cold pudding, on that given by Claudia Roden in her *New Book of Middle Eastern Food*, since it was in her house that I first ate the cake (and concluded at once that there could be no better version).

2 large oranges
6 eggs
2⅔ cups ground almonds
generous 1 cup sugar
1 teaspoon baking powder

Wash and boil the oranges (whole and unpeeled) in water to cover for one and a half hours. Let them cool, then cut them open and remove the seeds. Turn the oranges into a purée by rubbing them through a strainer or using a blender.

Beat the eggs in a large bowl. Add the ground almonds, sugar, baking powder and orange purée, mix it all thoroughly and pour into a buttered and floured cake pan with a removable base.

Bake in the oven at 390° for about an hour. Cool in the pan before turning out.

Although this cake is intended to be very moist, it should not be what one could call "wet". If it is still wet after the hour's baking, let it bake a little longer.

Fritters

There is a paradox here. To judge by the limited dessert menus of Chinese restaurants, fruit fritters occupy the place of honor in oriental fruit cookery. Yet in western countries fruit fritters are, generally speaking, uncommon.

However, they are well worth making. Although the recipe suggested here is a very simple one, producing a simple result, it can be elaborated into something much more sophisticated. For example, Richard Olney, in his *French Menu Cookbook*, suggests making fritters of cubes of pineapple which have been coated with frangipane. And there is a famous recipe for prune fritters which requires that the prunes be stuffed with marzipan. However, my own belief is that one should keep it simple, concentrating on having a really good batter, such as the one recommended here, and creating a pleasant contrast between its crisp coating and the succulence of the fruit within. Remember, though, that the fruit within, although it may have had the benefit of sitting in a marinade for a while to imbibe additional flavor, must be drained; otherwise there is a risk of finishing up with soggy fritters.

Peach/Banana/Pineapple/Papaya Fritters

Each fruit must be prepared in pieces of the desired size. Bananas, if large, would be cut in three lengthways and then halved crossways; but the very small bananas which are now more widely available can be left whole after being peeled.

Many cooks will have their own preferred recipe for a suitable batter. That given here has a distinguished author: Francatelli, who was for a time Chief Cook to HM Queen Victoria.

1⅓ cups flour
a pinch of salt
½ stick butter, melted
¼ cup Curaçao liqueur
3 egg whites
2 pounds fruit

Sift the flour and salt into a bowl, add the butter and liqueur, and mix with a wooden spoon. Then gradually add scant 1 cup water, continuing to mix until the batter has the consistency of heavy cream. (You may not need all the water, or you may need a little more.)

Whip the egg whites into "a substantial froth" and incorporate them in the batter, which is then ready for use.

Dip the prepared pieces of fruit into the batter until well coated, and then deep fry. Whether you pan-fry (as I do) or deep-fry, it is best to use a cooking oil which has no noticeable flavor of its own.

Apple Fritters

1½ tablespoons oatmeal
1 egg
½ cup ginger wine
2 Rhode Island Greening or similar eating apples

Medieval and later recipes for "fritters", nearly always meaning apple fritters, were often flavored with ginger and other spices, and sometimes used sack, or a fortified sweet wine, as the liquid. Here is a modern variation.

Grind the oats finely in a blender, add the egg and ginger wine and blend all three together to make a pleasantly nutty-tasting, mildly alcoholic batter.

Cut the apples into slices. Melt a little butter in a heavy skillet, arrange the apple slices in the butter and pour the liquid over them. Fry briskly for a minute or two on either side, cutting into sections as you turn the fritters over.

Thanks to Brigid Allen and her still-to-be-published study of ginger for this item.

Soufflés, Mousses and Fools

The distinguishing feature of this group of dessert dishes is that they have a light, aerated texture, usually achieved by the use of beaten egg-white. A cold soufflé or mousse may depend on whipped cream for the same effect.

Fools are different. They are achieved simply by combining fruit, in the form of a purée, with cream; and their texture is, naturally, quite thick and creamy.

Basic Soufflé Recipe

1 cup milk
3 eggs, separated
$\frac{1}{3}$ cup sugar
2$\frac{1}{2}$ tablespoons flour
flavoring (see below)

Scald the milk in a saucepan.

Put the egg yolks and half the sugar in a bowl, beat until you have a thick mixture, then stir in the flour. (Flavoring can be added at this point.)

Pour the boiling milk into this mixture, and whisk it in. Then return all to the saucepan, bring to a boil, and simmer for two to three minutes, stirring all the time. Remove from the heat. (Flavoring can also be added at this point.)

Whip the egg whites, add the remaining sugar to them and whip again until you have a glossy finish.

Stir about a third of the egg white mixture into the milk mixture, then take this new mixture and fold it gently into the remaining egg-white mixture.

Bake in a greased soufflé dish (or dishes) in the oven at 400°.

Hot Orange Soufflé

Proceed as above, but at the first flavoring opportunity add the grated peel of an orange; and at the second flavoring opportunity add $\frac{1}{2}$ teaspoon vanilla and 2–3 tablespoons of an orange liqueur such as Grand Marnier.

Hot Passion Fruit Soufflé

Proceed as above, but add nothing at the first flavoring opportunity, and at the second add 3 tablespoons of passion fruit sauce (see below).

Serve with more passion fruit sauce.

Passion Fruit Sauce

10 passion fruits
$\frac{1}{2}$ cup sugar
1 teaspoon cornstarch
$\frac{1}{4}$ teaspoon salt
a pinch of ground ginger
$\frac{1}{2}$ stick butter

Halve the fruits, scoop out the insides, push through a strainer and discard the seeds. Mix together the sugar, cornstarch, salt and ginger. Gradually add $\frac{3}{4}$ cup boiling water and cook over a medium heat until the sauce has thickened. Add the butter and passion fruit pulp. Bring back to the boil, then remove from heat and strain: rub the pulp in the strainer to get as much liquid as possible through. Serve hot.

The flavor of passion fruit is very strong. If you use less water, in order to have a thicker sauce, it will be stronger still.

Lemon Mousse
(from the artist's mother)

4 large lemons
4 eggs
1 cup superfine sugar
2 tablespoons powdered gelatin, dissolved in a little hot water
1$\frac{1}{4}$ cups heavy cream

for garnish
whipped cream
finely chopped walnuts

Have ready a 7 inch well greased soufflé dish; two heatproof bowls, one larger than the other; and a saucepan into which the larger bowl will fit, double-boiler fashion.

Grate the peel off all the lemons. Then extract all the juice. Separate the eggs: yolks into the larger bowl, whites into the smaller one.

Add the sugar to the yolks. Have several inches of hot water simmering in the saucepan. Place the larger bowl over it. Whisk the mixture until thick and light, add the lemon juice and whisk until thickened again. Remove the pan from the heat and lift out the bowl.

Whisk the egg yolk mixture occasionally, as it cools to lukewarm. Then whisk the gelatin into it, add the grated lemon peel, and whisk until creamy. In the smaller bowl, whisk the egg whites to floppy peaks.

Fold the heavy cream into the main mixture, then fold in the beaten egg-whites, working very lightly.

Pour the mixture into the soufflé dish, let it cool a little, then place it in the refrigerator for at least two hours. Before serving, decorate the top with whipped cream and chopped walnuts.

Soursop Mousse
(from the Seychelles)

Tess Conway, in her book *Seychelles Delights*, recommends using gelatin in this, as indicated below. However, when Stephanie Santich and I tried making the mousse in several different versions, we found that gelatin was not needed if the mousse was to be eaten right away, after its final chilling; it had a pleasant texture, mousse-like but more foamy and delicate than with gelatin added. So the gelatin is now labeled "optional", for use only if the dish is to be kept for a while after being made, when it would need some continuing support to prevent it from sagging.

I large ripe soursop
3 tablespoons superfine sugar
juice of I lime
I tablespoon powdered gelatin, dissolved in a little hot water (optional – see above)
2 egg whites
pinch of salt
½ cup whipping cream

Halve, peel and de-seed the soursop, then rub the pulp thoroughly through a strainer. Add 1 tablespoon of the sugar to the pulp and stir until it is dissolved. Next, mix the pulp with the lime juice and dissolved gelatin (if used). Leave the mixture for an hour to chill and thicken.

Beat the egg whites with the pinch of salt, adding the rest of the sugar gradually as you do so. Whip the cream to soft peaks.

Fold the egg whites and cream into the fruit mixture and leave it to chill.

Removing all the seeds from a large soursop is no light task. However, the delightfully refreshing result makes it all seem worth while.

Although chilling diminishes aroma, this particular dish will still broadcast a strong and delightful fragrance in the dining room.

Fools

In the 17th century a fool was "a kind of Custard . . . being made of Cream, Yolks of Eggs, Cinnamon, Mace, boiled: and served on Sippets, with sliced Dates, Sugar, and white and red Comfits, strewed thereon."

So fools have changed considerably over the centuries. One thing to remember about 20th century fools is that they contain dairy cream in the west but coconut cream in the orient.

A good oriental fool is made by combining strained papaya flesh with coconut cream.

Brompton Cemetery Blackberry Fool

The cemetery comes into this because it is where Hilary Hyman went blackberry gathering when she first made this dish many years ago. Now she gathers the fruit from Wimbledon Common, a little further away from central London.

I pound freshly picked blackberries
½ cup sugar
1¼ cups heavy cream

Wash the berries and add the sugar to them in a pan. Heat gently and, when boiling point is reached, leave to simmer for ten minutes. Then take a large measuring container and strain the berries into this, to get rid of the seeds. Measure the volume and add half as much of heavy cream. Blend thoroughly. Serve in individual glasses, with a swirl of heavy cream if you wish.

(The cooked and strained blackberry and sugar mixture can be frozen for use later on, if you wish.)

Elderflower and Gooseberry Fool

The National Trust, which owns and cares for many historic houses in Britain and much beautiful countryside, has published a number of cookbooks. Two by Sarah Edington are my favorites; the way in which she ties the recipes to the houses where they come from adds greatly to their interest. The present recipe is from Cotehele, "a jewel of a house" in Cornwall.

I pound fresh gooseberries
¾ cup sugar
2 tablespoons elderflower wine or cordial
1¼ cups heavy or whipping cream

Place the washed, topped and tailed gooseberries into a pan. Add no water. Simmer the fruit for about 15 minutes or until cooked and soft. Pour the gooseberries into a blender, add the sugar and purée. Allow this to cool, then add the elderflower wine or cordial, and divide the purée into two equal parts.

Whip the cream and fold it into one half of the gooseberry purée. In individual glasses, make layers of the gooseberry and cream mixture, the gooseberry purée and then the rest of the gooseberry and cream mixture. Chill before serving.

You can decorate the fool with mint leaves "frosted" with a little beaten egg white and a coating of superfine sugar.

Syllabub Trifle

1 pound strawberries, hulled and halved
$\frac{1}{2}$ pound green grapes, halved and seeded
2 cups macaroons
3 egg whites
$\frac{3}{4}$ cup superfine sugar
generous $\frac{1}{2}$ cup dry white wine
juice of $\frac{1}{2}$ lemon
2 tablespoons brandy
generous $\frac{1}{2}$ cup heavy cream
Amaretti or ratafias to decorate

Arrange the strawberries and grapes alternately to cover the bottom of a glass dish. Cover with a single layer of macaroons. Arrange the remaining fruit and macaroons in alternate layers on top of this, reserving ten strawberries and grape halves for the decoration.

Whisk the egg whites until stiff. Gradually add half the sugar and continue to whisk until the meringue holds its shape. Fold in the remaining sugar. Pour the wine, lemon juice and brandy over the egg whites and fold in carefully.

Whip the cream until it just holds its shape. Fold this into the frothy meringue mixture, then pour the result over the fruit and macaroons and allow to stand for several hours to let the macaroons become moist. Just before serving, decorate with the ratafias and reserved fruit.

Marjapuuro
(Whipped Berry Oatmeal)

Finns call this an oatmeal, although others would probably say "pudding". Anna-Maija Tanttu, who introduced me to it, describes it as "soft as a cloud, sweetly pink, light, but with a full-bodied flavor", and explains that it is so popular that it can be bought ready-made from Finnish grocery stores. It is a dish which can be made with juice from any of a large range of berries, although lingonberries are best.

generous 1 cup purée of lingonberries, cranberries or
other berries
$\frac{2}{3}$ cup sugar
2 pinches of salt
$\frac{1}{2}$ cup farina (ie flour or fine meal of a cereal, wheat, oats,
or other)

Add the purée to $4\frac{1}{2}$ cups water, bring to the boil, simmer for about four minutes, then strain.

Add the sugar and salt to the strained juice, bring to the boil, whip the farina into the boiling mixture, and simmer lightly for 20 minutes.

Cool in a water bath, then whip the mixture into a light, pink dessert, to be served cold with full fat milk.

Ice Creams

The accepted wisdom in our family is that the best ice cream we ever had was the peach ice cream we made in Tunisia, consulting Fannie Farmer and using an old hand-cranked machine which required cranking for half an hour. But the last two decades have seen great advances in domestic ice cream machines and those who have recent models assure us that there is no longer any merit in the old-fashioned technology. Since machines differ in the way they are used, and ice creams can anyway be made without them, I limit myself in the recipes given here to listing the ingredients and explaining how they are used to make the mixture. Readers can then follow their own techniques or the instructions which come with their machines, in freezing it.

The great 19th century books on ice cream etcetera were Mrs Marshall's *The Book of Ices* and *The Book of Fancy Ices*. One book which is important for anyone who wants to be "into" ice creams now is a descendant of these: *Victorian Ices and Ice Cream*, by Barbara Ketcham Wheaton. She is one of the few authors whose taste for historical research and whose skill in the kitchen are matched by an ability to write well. What she has done in this book is to reproduce a large number of Mrs Marshall's recipes, with marginal notes on how to adjust quantities (for example, because of the changed size of eggs). She and her family ate 65 of the ice creams in Concord, Massachusetts, deliberately including a number of oddities such as cucumber ice cream, and pronounced 60 of them to be excellent. One appears below, marked as Mrs Marshall's but incorporating the adjustments found advisable after all this testing.

A particularly valuable feature of *Victorian Ices and Ice Creams* is the introductory essay, which contains a clear exposition of the principles of ice cream making and thus equips the cook to carry out her or his own experiments with confidence (and, if need be, without any special equipment).

Other books highly recommended are: Philip and Mary Hyman's English translation and adaptation of the *Lenôtre's Desserts and Pastries* and Shona Crawford Poole's *Iced Delights*. For those who like to explore the physics and chemistry of the cook's activities, even in areas such as ice cream, there is now an ideal reference to consult, to wit chapter 10 of Harold McGee's *The Curious Cook* (1990).

For all these books, see the Bibliography. But the simple recipes which follow can be executed successfully, I hope, without any deeper study.

Basic Ice Cream Recipe
(Very Rich)
for about 4 cups

$1\frac{1}{4}$ cups heavy cream
$1\frac{1}{4}$ cups light cream
$\frac{3}{4}$ cup sugar
5 egg yolks

Make the basic ice cream custard by bringing the cream and sugar to a boil, allowing it to cool slightly, and then pouring it over the egg yolks in a bowl, and immediately mixing all thoroughly.

Next, return the mixture to the pan and stir it over a gentle heat until it thickens. Do not let it boil.

Strain the mixture and freeze it in your preferred way.

Basic Recipe 2
(Still Rich)
For the heavy cream, substitute milk.

Basic Recipe 3
(Less Rich)
For both kinds of cream, substitute milk.

This basic recipe, and the two less rich variations of it, will produce an unflavored ice cream. It could, of course, be plain vanilla ice cream if you put a piece of vanilla pod in the cream or milk when it is being boiled (or added a little genuine vanilla to the mixture before straining it). But there are scores of different flavors and textures which can be achieved on the basis of this initial preparation. Just a few are described in the following columns, together with some ice creams made by somewhat different procedures.

General Tips
● Freeze in a metal container – metal conducts the cold well.
● Move your ice cream or sherbet from the freezing compartment to the refrigerator about 45 minutes before serving.
● If in doubt, be generous with the flavoring, since the effect of freezing is to diminish our perception of flavors.
● Use only the best materials. For example, vanilla pods or real vanilla, not "vanilla flavoring".

Our Peach Ice Cream

Crush the flesh of 2 pounds ripe peaches. Sprinkle onto it a pinch of salt and 3 tablespoons sugar. Stir a little vanilla into $2\frac{1}{2}$ cups of cream with another $\frac{2}{3}$ cup sugar, let this start to freeze, then stir in the peach pulp, add a little more sugar if desired, and finish freezing.

Praline Ice Cream

When I first read Jane Grigson's book *Good Things*, back in the 1970s, I was struck by her forthright statement that this is just the best ice cream there is; not just the best nutty ice cream, but the best of all.

It is advisable to use home-made praline. All you need are 3 cups each of ground almonds and of sugar. Melt the sugar in $\frac{1}{4}$ cup water. When it is syrupy, add the almonds and continue cooking until the mixture is light brown in color. Pour it onto a sheet of foil, let it cool, break it into pieces, and store it in an airtight jar.

When you make the ice cream, prepare the rich custard as already explained, and in between the straining and the freezing stir into it $\frac{3}{4}$ cup powdered praline.

Pistachio Ice Cream

Follow the basic method, but incorporate a crushed cardamom pod in the cream or milk when it is boiled; and in between the straining and freezing stir in $1\frac{1}{2}$ cups of pistachios (shelled, blanched, peeled, and pounded).

The color of this ice cream will not be the vivid green to which one is accustomed in commercial establishments, but rather greenish-brown. That is as it should be. (Note, however, that you can reduce the amount of pistachio by, say, a third, and make up for that by the addition of 2 tablespoons of kiwi fruit flesh, finely chopped.)

Pistachio ice cream is often combined with other sorts to provide a multi-colored effect, for example in the Sicilian Cassata.

Black Currant Ice Cream
(Mrs Marshall)

Bring to the boil 1 pound black currants with scant 1 cup sugar dissolved in $1\frac{1}{4}$ cups water. Strain, and add to the strained liquid $2\frac{1}{2}$ cups Basic Ice Cream Recipe (page 172) and $\frac{1}{2}$ teaspoon lemon juice. Freeze.

(Mrs Marshall provides closely similar recipes for Cranberry Ice Cream and Gooseberry Ice Cream.)

Coconut Ice Cream

Follow one of the less rich Basic Ice Cream Recipes, but before you start put $\frac{1}{2}$ cup freshly grated coconut in the milk and let it stand for an hour.

Some experts advise you to strain out the grated coconut before carrying on; but others, including Lenôtre, prefer to leave it in, for the pleasing texture which it provides in the finished ice cream.

Nesselrode Pudding

This is called a pudding because "ice cream" seems inadequate; and Nesselrode because the cook of the 19th century Russian diplomat of that name is supposed to have invented it.

The ingredients and instructions are set out in two stages. The unsweetened chestnut purée can be made at home, but the French product in cans is fine.

I cup light cream
4 egg yolks
$\frac{2}{3}$ cup sugar

Bring the cream to a boil and pour it over the egg yolks in the top of a double boiler. Stir in the sugar. Set the top of the double boiler on the bottom part, in which water is simmering, and continue to stir until the custard thickens. Remove from the heat.

I cup unsweetened chestnut purée
$\frac{1}{2}$ cup whipped cream
$\frac{1}{4}$ cup white raisins, previously soaked for four hours in
$\frac{1}{3}$ cup Madeira or Malaga wine
$\frac{1}{2}$ cup candied cherries, chopped
$\frac{1}{2}$ cup candied citron (or orange or grapefruit) peel

Stir the chestnut purée into the custard mixture while it is hot, then fold in the whipped cream and add the fruit and wine mixture. Stir well and freeze.

The "pudding" can be served with a garnish of more whipped cream and marrons glacés (page 175).

Mango Ice Cream

2 large ripe mangoes
juice of I lime
$\frac{1}{2}$ cup confectioners sugar
$1\frac{1}{4}$ cups whipping cream

Peel the mangoes and cut the flesh from the pits. Purée this with the lime juice in a blender or food processor, or by passing it through a strainer. Stir in the confectioners sugar.

Whip the cream to soft peaks. Whisk the purée lightly into the cream, and freeze.

Lime Bombe
with Mango Sauce

Not strictly an ice cream, nor yet a sherbet, but a delicious confection nevertheless. A friend who made this recipe from Judy Bastyra's book *Caribbean Cooking* gave it the warmest praise. This is an adapted version.

4 limes
3 eggs, separated
a pinch of salt
$\frac{1}{2}$ cup sugar
$1\frac{1}{4}$ cups heavy cream

for the sauce
I large mango
juice of I lime

Cut the peel of one lime into fine strips, free of pith, and reserve these. Finely grate the peel of the other 3 limes, and combine this with the juice of all four limes in a bowl.

In a second bowl, whisk the egg whites with the pinch of salt until stiff. Then gradually beat in three quarters of the sugar. In a third bowl, whisk the cream with the remaining sugar, then add the grated peel and juice and continue whisking until firm.

Now fold the lime mixture into the egg mixture. Pour the result into a mold or ceramic bowl of 4 cup capacity, cover, and freeze.

To make the mango sauce, simply peel the mango, make a purée of its flesh and juice, and blend with the lime juice.

A quarter of an hour before serving, dip the mold for a few seconds into hot water, unmold the bombe onto a serving dish, decorate the top with the reserved strips of lime, letting some of the long pieces trail down the sides, then leave it in the refrigerator until you bring it to table. Serve with the mango sauce, chilled or at room temperature as you prefer.

Sherbets

The etymology of "sherbet" is complex, as I know from the 10,000 word essay which I am writing on it. It is enough here to say that the term is descended from an Arabic word meaning "cold drink".

The principle to be followed in making fruit sherbets is simple. Combine fruit juice or a well-strained fruit purée with sugar and water, or with a syrup already prepared from sugar and water. Then freeze.

Citrus Sherbet

Instead of the orange and lemon juice used in this example, you can use grapefruit, or grapefruit and lime, or other combinations.

$1\frac{3}{4}$ cups sugar
2 cups fresh orange juice
scant $\frac{1}{2}$ cup fresh lemon juice
1 tablespoon orange flower water

Boil the sugar in 2 cups water for five minutes, allow to cool, and then add the fruit juices and the orange flower water. Freeze. If not using a machine, take care to beat the mixture lightly every half hour while it is freezing.

Pear Sherbet

This is particularly delicate and refreshing. Use the best dessert pears you can buy, fully ripe. You need enough of them (about $1\frac{3}{4}$ pounds) to produce $2\frac{1}{2}$ cups of strained pear pulp.

Combine the pulp with $1\frac{1}{4}$ cups sugar syrup (page 151) and 2 teaspoons lemon juice. Freeze.

Other Fruit Sherbets

Take either of the recipes above as a model and substitute for the citrus juice or pear pulp either the juice or the strained pulp of other fruits, such as black currant, mango, soursop, red and white currants, etcetera – even durian.

Berry Sherbet
(Strawberry, Raspberry, Cloudberry, Blackberry, etcetera)

2 egg whites
$\frac{1}{4}$ teaspoon salt
$2\frac{1}{4}$ cups confectioners sugar
$2\frac{1}{2}$ cups fresh strawberries or other berries, mashed to a coarse purée

Whip the egg whites with the salt. Add the sugar gradually and continue beating until you have stiff peaks.

Fold the berry purée into the mixture, pour it into your freezing container and freeze it, without stirring.

Gélat D'Ametilla

This is described as an "ice cream" in Majorca, which is its home, but it is a water ice and the finest of the ices in the island.

The recipe, given by Elizabeth Carter, in her book *Majorcan Food and Cookery*, comes from Heladeria Ca'n Miquel in Palma de Mallorca.

$1\frac{1}{2}$ cups blanched almonds, finely ground
2 cups sugar
finely grated peel of one lemon
1 small stick cinnamon

Place all the ingredients together in a saucepan with $4\frac{1}{2}$ cups water and put this on a very low heat. Bring it slowly to the boil, stirring frequently. As soon as the mixture boils, remove the pan from the heat and leave to cool. Remove the cinnamon stick and either pour the liquid into a machine for making ice cream or freeze it in a metal container in the freezer, stirring from time to time as it is setting.

Conserved Fruits

Candied Fruits

Preserving fruits in jars gives you a bulk supply, to be used for many different purposes. Preserving them by candying them provides delicious sweetmeats, a selection of which makes a beautiful addition to the dessert table.

On the principle that things which lie within one's own experience are bound to be best, I sing the praises of the candied plums of Elva in Portugal. Seeing for myself the care with which the ladies of Elva attend to this task, using plums grown especially for the purpose (and peaches too), made it easy to understand why they have appeared for many decades as a favored Christmas delicacy in the best London shops.

The results of the process, if it is correctly done, will keep almost indefinitely. The sugar syrup will have penetrated into the very heart of the fruit and will guard it against going bad. But to achieve this total impregnation, the process has to be done in stages. Candied fruits may of course be prepared at home, but few people have the space and the patience to do this; the successive coatings with syrup and drying really call for a large workshop and a production line. Certainly, it would be a bold cook who would set out to candy whole large fruits, such as the candied grapefruit which are made in the island of Réunion and the candied whole pineapples which one London shop has been displaying recently.

Nonetheless I start this section with a full description of how marrons glacés are prepared, to serve as an interesting example of the technique required.

Marrons Glacés
(Candied Chestnuts)

Quantities given make 2 pounds. As the British Ministry of Agriculture, Fisheries and Food explains in one of its illuminating booklets, the use of glucose or dextrose (rather than plain sugar, which can be used in other candying operations) is advisable because the speed with which it is absorbed helps to guard against wrinkling of the nuts.

> 2 pounds chestnuts
> 4 cups sugar
> 1 pound glucose or dextrose
> 6 drops real vanilla

Make cross-shaped incisions in the rounded side of each chestnut, cutting through the shell only. Then blanch them, two or three at a time, in boiling water for two minutes. Lift them out and peel off both the shell and the inner brown skin.

Put the peeled chestnuts in a large pan of cold water, bring to a simmer, and continue simmering for 15 minutes, when the chestnuts will be cooked but still whole. Remove and drain them.

In another large pan, combine half the sugar with all the glucose (or dextrose) and $1\frac{1}{2}$ cups water, bring to a boil, add the chestnuts, bring back to a boil, then remove the pan from the heat and leave it, covered, overnight.

On the next day, bring back to the boil, remove the pan from the heat and leave overnight again.

On the third day, add the drops of vanilla and then reheat for the last time. When the chestnuts have cooled somewhat, lift them out and leave them to drain on a wire rack for several hours.

It remains to give the glacé finish. Dissolve the remaining sugar in generous 1 cup water and bring it to a boil to make a syrup. Keep this hot in a bain-marie or over a very low flame and a heat diffuser. Rinse a small bowl in very hot water, dry it, and ladle some of the syrup into it. Start dipping the chestnuts into it and transferring them back to a wire rack. As soon as the syrup in the bowl becomes cloudy, discard it and take a fresh supply from the pan.

The marrons glacés should be left in a warm place to dry and turned over after an hour and a half. In three hours they should be dry, and can then be stored in a covered container lined with wax paper.

Strawberry "Leather"

Apricot "leather" from Turkey (see page 26) is a familiar staple in our household, but I hadn't realized that berries can also be treated in this way – so long as you have good drying weather or a food dehydrator. Turner and Szczawinski's superb book on *Edible Wild Fruits and Nuts of Canada* alerted me to the possibility. By this means you can have something with the real strawberry flavor for use at any season of the year.

All you have to do is purée as many strawberries as you wish in a blender, then pour the purée out onto sheets of heavy-duty wax paper and leave to dry in the sun. Once it has dried to a tough and leathery consistency, peel it off the wax paper and store (indefinitely) in jars in a cool place.

A traditional Russian variation on this theme is to take freshly picked berries, smear them with honey, and dry them, to form a sweetmeat for use during the winter.

Peach or Nectarine Chips

Delicious morsels. The recipe is from Edward Lambert, the little-known author of *The Art of Confectionary* (1744). Alas for him, the whole content of his book was purloined by the more famous Hannah Glasse, without a word of acknowledgement, to constitute the bulk of her book, *The Compleat Confectioner* (*c* 1760).

Make a sugar syrup with $1\frac{1}{2}$ cups sugar and scant $\frac{1}{2}$ cup water boiled to 240°. Peel 2 peaches or nectarines, remove the pits, and cut the flesh into thin slices. Put the fruit into the syrup, return to the boil, and cook for two minutes. Take off the heat and leave to soak for 15 minutes. Bring back to the boil, and cook for two minutes. Leave to cool and soak overnight.

Next day, drain the fruit "chips" (on a wire rack, for example), then coat them in superfine sugar and let them dry.

Shackleton's Pickled Peaches

Elisabeth Luard scored a coup when she published (in *The Princess and the Pheasant*) this recipe for the pickled peaches which the explorer Shackleton took on the Nimrod expedition to the North Pole in 1907 and which, many years afterwards, were found by other explorers in his depot, still in perfect shape.

4 pounds perfect, scarcely ripe peaches
3 cloves per peach
2 cups wine vinegar
4 cups brown sugar
1 stick cinnamon
1 teaspoon allspice and pepper mixed

"Plunge the peaches into boiling water for a minute to loosen the skins. Peel them. Stud each peach with 3 cloves. Bring the vinegar and the sugar gently to the boil and add the spices. Simmer for five minutes and then slide the peaches gently into the syrup. Poach the fruit for five to ten minutes, depending on their size. Meanwhile put your jars to sterilize in a warm oven.

Remove the peaches from the syrup and pack them into the sterilized jars.

Continue to boil the syrup for another ten minutes to thicken it, then pour it over the peaches – they must be well covered. Seal when cool. The peaches will be ready to eat in a month."

Sir Kenelm Digby's Cordial Tablets

The most delicious sweetmeat I know. Sir Kenelm, writing in the 17th century, was sure that these confections were "good for you" and also had aphrodisiac properties.

Laura Mason, the expert on British confectionery, tried the recipe, using candied apricot instead of candied eringo root and omitting the powdered pearl, musk, amber, etcetera mentioned in the original.

for the first stage
$\frac{1}{4}$ cup candied apricot
$\frac{1}{4}$ cup candied lemon peel
scant $\frac{1}{4}$ cup candied orange peel
generous $\frac{1}{4}$ cup candied citron peel

Chop these together in a food processor, to yield pieces about $\frac{1}{4}$ inch square. (This takes time, as the peel is quite hard. Ready-to-use chopped peel is softer, and permits skipping this operation, but the flavor is less good.)

for the second stage
$\frac{1}{3}$ cup blanched almonds
$\frac{1}{3}$ cup blanched pistachios
$\frac{1}{3}$ cup pine nuts

Add the nuts to the food processor and process again. (If the peel has proved obstinate, the slightly damp blanched nuts will help soften it. Note that if the nuts had been put in at the start they would be reduced to an oily paste by the time the peel was ready, whereas one wants to retain some of their texture.)

for the third stage
$\frac{1}{2}$ teaspoon freshly ground cloves
$\frac{1}{2}$ teaspoon freshly ground mace
sugar syrup made by heating generous 1 cup sugar and $1\frac{1}{2}$ cups water to the "soft ball" stage (240°)
2 tablespoons orange flower water

Add the above to the food processor while the blades are running, and continue for a few moments until you have a paste. Spread this on a sheet of wax paper, about $\frac{3}{8}$ inch thick, and leave to set for about 24 hours in a dry place.

to ice and finish
1 cup confectioners sugar
a little more orange flower water

Make the icing by mixing the above ingredients to a spreading consistency. Spread it over the paste evenly and leave to dry. Then cut the confection into square lozenges of about $\frac{3}{4}$ inch.

Conserved Green Walnuts

This is a favorite preparation in the Balkans.

$2\frac{1}{4}$ pounds green walnuts

for the syrup
$2\frac{1}{4}$ cups sugar
4 cups water
4 teaspoons lemon juice
I vanilla pod (optional)

Peel the walnuts (a tricky job) and leave them to soak in several changes of cold water over a couple of days. Drain.

Melt the sugar in the water and cook until you have a moderately thick syrup. Allow this to cool to lukewarm, then add the walnuts and the lemon juice (and the optional vanilla pod), bring to a boil and simmer for 20–30 minutes. Remove from the heat and leave the walnuts in the syrup overnight.

Next day, bring it all back to a boil and simmer for another 20–30 minutes. Then put the walnuts, covered with syrup, in sealed jars.

Mirtilli Conservati
(Conserved Bilberries)

Visiting Patience Gray in Apulia, to work with her on her book *Honey from a Weed*, I became acquainted with this simple conserve.

Gather as many ripe bilberries (*Vaccinium myrtillus*, page 46) as you wish, rinse them and fill clean preserving jars with them, packing them well in. Keeping one jar of the fruit in reserve, filter sugar into each of the others, letting it trickle down between the berries. (If you are using jars of $2\frac{1}{4}$ cup capacity, you will need about half a cup for each jar.)

Let the sugared jars heat slowly on the bottom shelf of a very low oven (240°). The content of the jars will shrink a little while heating.

After 45–50 minutes, when the jars are thoroughly hot, remove them from the oven and top them up with more fruit, from the reserve jar, as necessary. Then pour boiling water into each jar, to fill it, cover and seal immediately.

The berries will need no cooking when you come to eat them in the winter. Other similar berries can be treated likewise.

Jams and Jellies

A gel. That is how scientists would classify the mixture of fruit and sugar boiled together, poured into jars and sealed to give a long-keeping preserve with a wet semi-solid consistency, which we call jam.

Jams, and related preserves such as fruit pastes, jellies and marmalades, are based on widespread and ancient methods of preserving fruit. Similar confections are made throughout Europe and the Middle East. Elsewhere in the world they derive mainly from European influences.

Successful jam depends on the interaction of three things in the correct proportions: sugar, pectin (long chainlike molecules occurring in the cell walls of plants), and acid. Fruit contains all of these, but the jam-maker always adds more sugar, and sometimes pectin and acid.

Sugar is usually added to the mixture in the proportion of 1:1 by weight of sugar to fruit pulp. It has two functions; it sweetens the fruit, and it plays an important part in gel formation. Sugar is highly attractive to water molecules and "binds" them in solution. This leaves less water available for the pectin to form bonds with. Instead, the pectin molecules link to each other, forming a network which traps the sugar and fruit pulp.

Acid encourages this process. Pectin molecules normally carry a small negative electrical charge in water and therefore tend to repel each other. The function of the acid is to reduce the electrical charge. The effect of reducing it (and thereby making the pectin molecules mutually attractive instead of repellent) is seen when a jam mixture cools; the chainlike pectin molecules bond affectionately with each other to form a network, holding the sugar solution and fruit pulp in what appears to be a solid mass.

Certain fruits are recognized by jam makers to need additional acid or pectin to produce a satisfactory result. Strawberries are a good example: they contain little acid and weak pectin, and are notorious for a "poor set". Extra pectin, extracted from apples or citrus fruit, can be added; and home jam makers are usually instructed to add lemon juice as well.

The optimum conditions for producing a good jam are: a sugar concentration of 60–65%; a pectin content of 0.5–1.0%; and a pH of 2.8–3.4. Stated like this, it seems remarkable that anyone should produce jam successfully outside a laboratory; but centuries of trial, error and experiment, especially with gluts of acid fruit such as gooseberries, have caused the emergence of countless family and published recipes which "work" because the simple instructions which they embody keep within the "rules".

It is often pointed out, and correctly, that the temperature to be reached by jam if it is going to set should be almost exactly 222°. The significance of this is that the boiling point of jam becomes higher and higher as the proportion of sugar to water in it increases; and, as one gives the jam its final boiling, water is progressively lost as steam until the correct proportion is reached. Temperature is not a separate requirement, but an index of the fundamental requirement that the proportion of sugar be right.

However, the preserve we now recognize as jam is a relatively modern descendant of all the rather solid fruit and sugar conserves, preserves, and marmalades of the 17th and 18th centuries. Even the word jam is a relative newcomer to our language, making one of its earliest appearances in *Mrs Mary Eales' Receipts* (1718).

The development which took jam from a solid confection to a soft spreadable paste was the increased understanding of hygiene, such as the necessity for clean processing and for sealing the jars, that developed in the 19th century.

Even then, jams were a luxury, as sugar was not cheap: Mrs Beeton observed, "It has long been a desideratum to preserve fruits by some cheap method . . . The expense of preserving them with sugar is a serious objection; for, except the sugar is used in considerable quantities, the success is very uncertain." (*Beeton's Book of Household Management*, 1861).

But to the cook and to the consumer, what is a jam? And what is a marmalade? Artemas Ward, the entertaining American writer on food history (not the same as the humorist of that name) put it well when he said that jam was:
". . . a title generally applied to that class of sweet preserve in which either the whole fruit or its pulp is cooked without regard to the preservation of the shape of the fruit . . . if the rind shows as such, the jam commonly becomes marmalade."

Neat. But not everyone will agree. Some jam makers prefer to have certain fruits, for example strawberries and cherries, retain their integrity.

In any case the corresponding terms in other languages don't mean the same. In France, for example, the difference between "confiture" (usually translated as jam) and "marmelade" is that the latter need only contain 55% solid matter (fruit and sugar) while the former must have 60%.

"Jam" only entered the English language in 1718. "Marmalade" has a longer history. It is derived from the Portuguese "marmelo", meaning quince, and "marmelada", meaning a solid quince preserve or paste. (The word "marmelada" also means "sex" in Portuguese. I once saw a second-hand book entitled *The Book of Marmelada* and thought I had stumbled on a historical treatise; but the pictures in it were so patently inappropriate to that theme that I gradually realized my error.)

From the Portuguese, the word passed into French as "marmelade" and into English as "marmalade", at first with reference to quinces only. However, in both languages it soon acquired a wider meaning. By 1609, Sir Hugh Plat was offering a recipe "to moeke marmalade of Lemmons or Orenges". Plat's marmalade was a solid paste, but such products soon

developed into the sort of marmalade now familiar to us; a story well told in Anne Wilson's *Book of Marmalade.*

As for jelly, the best descriptive definition is that of Goldthwaite in the *Bulletin of the Colorado Agricultural Experimental Station*, 1925:
Ideal fruit-jelly is a beautifully colored, transparent, palatable product obtained by so treating fruit-juice that the resulting mass will quiver, not flow, when removed from its mold; a product with texture so tender that it cuts easily with a spoon, and yet so firm that the angles thus produced retain their shape; a clear product that is neither sirupy, gummy, sticky, nor tough; neither is it brittle and yet it will break, and does this with distinct beautiful cleavage which leaves sparkling characteristic faces.

Canadian Peach Marmalade

A Canadian favorite for generations. It is sometimes called jam and sometimes conserve. Whatever the name, its constant features are oranges and peaches.

3 oranges
9 cups sugar
8 cups peeled, pitted, finely chopped peaches
I cup slivered, blanched almonds

Slice the oranges very finely and cut each slice into eight, removing the seeds. Put the pieces in a saucepan with 1 cup water, cover and simmer over a low heat until the peel is tender (about 20 minutes).

Empty the saucepan into a large preserving pan and add the sugar and peaches. Stir thoroughly.

Place over high heat, bring to the boil, reduce the heat and cook uncovered, at a good simmer, until the marmalade thickens, and the peaches are translucent. This takes about an hour. Stir often. About five minutes before the end, add the almonds.

Put in jars as usual. If you use 1 cup jars, you should have a dozen of them.

Many Canadian cooks add quartered maraschino cherries to the marmalade. These are stirred in after the almonds at the end of the cooking time.

Damson Cheese

2¼ pounds damsons
4 cups sugar

Cook the damsons, whole, in the upper part of a double boiler or in a slow oven until they are tender, then rub them through a coarse strainer to remove the skins and pits. Crack the pits, remove and blanch the kernels.

Heat the damson pulp in a preserving pan, add the sugar to it, bring back to a boil and continue boiling, stirring well, until the mixture starts to thicken. Reduce the heat, add the kernels, and let the cheese thicken further for a few minutes, stirring only occasionally.

Pour the mixture into pots or shallow molds and seal them when just warm. Dorothy Hartley advises keeping it for up to two years before use.

Banana Passion Fruit Jam

The banana passion fruit is less sweet than the purple kind, and less juicy, but well suited to making preserves.

1½ cups banana passion fruit pulp
juice of 2 lemons
1¼ cups sugar

Add the fruit pulp to the lemon juice in a pan, bring to a boil, and continue cooking until the pulp is really soft. Strain the mixture, to get rid of the seeds.

Add the sugar to the liquid and boil until setting point is reached. Allow to cool somewhat, stir, and put in your jars.

Kiwi Fruit And Pineapple Jam

10 kiwi fruits
juice of half a large lemon
1 cup fresh pineapple juice
½ cup fresh pineapple, crushed
3 cups sugar

Peel the kiwi fruits, chop them and put them in a pan with the lemon juice and pineapple juice. Bring to a boil, simmer for five minutes, then mash the fruit pulp lightly in the pan.

Add the crushed pineapple and sugar, bring back to the boil, and boil fast until setting point is reached (20–30 minutes).

Allow to cool somewhat, stir, and put in jars as usual.

My Marmalade

This began life as my grandmother's recipe, then became that of my parents (who were both marmalade-makers), and has since their time been progressively simplified by me in an effort to minimize the time I have to spend on making 75 pounds annually. Things I have cut out are: steeping the cut fruit overnight; fiddling around with the seeds in a muslin bag; preheating anything (sugar, jars, what have you); putting wax paper discs or melted paraffin wax on top of the marmalade before sealing it.

Yet I cling to cutting by hand.

Airing my views about marmalade, and in particular the apparent foolishness of incorporating Scotch whisky in it, led to an interesting discovery. A scientist at Cambridge University wrote to point out that, while whisky might interfere with the true flavor of marmalade, anyone who dispenses with the interior seal would do well to float a teaspoon of alcohol (which could be brandy or vodka) on top of it before applying the outer seal. This will stop mold from forming at the interface between the marmalade and the small amount of air trapped above it.

6 Seville oranges
1 lemon
sugar (for amount, see below)

Wash the oranges and the lemon. Remove the little rosettes at the stem end and clean out any foreign matter from that area. Chop the fruits, by hand or machine but, in any event, not too finely. Put them in a large pan with water to cover and to spare, bring to a boil and cook, uncovered, for 20–30 minutes or until reduced by a third.

Measure the result. For every 2½ cups, allow 2 cups sugar.

Bring the fruit and water back to a boil and add the sugar to it in several doses, stirring until it is dissolved. Have a candy thermometer in place, and let the temperature climb up to 222°; but it is worthwhile testing for setting just before this point is reached. Once the test shows that it is ready to set, turn off the heat, leave for five to ten minutes, stir, then ladle into your clean jars. Fill them very nearly full. Ensure that the top surface is level – no chunks of peel sticking up. Float a little alcohol such as brandy over the top if you wish.

Seal by whatever means you prefer – I just use screw-top jars and screw the tops on tight once the marmalade has cooled to just "warm".

Persimmon and Rhubarb Jam

10 ounces young rhubarb, leaves removed
2 sprigs of lemon balm or a large leaf of angelica
$1\frac{1}{2}$ pounds persimmon pulp
$5\frac{1}{4}$ cups sugar

Chop the rhubarb and cook it briefly with the lemon balm or angelica leaf in scant $\frac{1}{2}$ cup water, just until it is tender. Remove the herb and add the persimmon pulp and sugar, stir until the sugar is dissolved, then continue boiling until setting point is reached. The New Zealand orchardist and author Gilian Painter comments that this will take only five minutes.

Medlar Jelly

Hella van Schaik, the Dutch authority on the history of medlars, vouches for this.

$2\frac{1}{4}$ pounds ripe medlars
sugar (for amount, see below)

Cook the medlars in just a little water ($1\frac{1}{4}$–$1\frac{3}{4}$ cups) until they are soft.

Strain, weigh the juice, then add $\frac{3}{4}$ of that weight of sugar, stirring; and continue to boil until setting point is reached. Pot as usual.

Guava Jelly

$2\frac{1}{4}$ pounds guavas
2 cardamom seeds (optional)
sugar (for quantity see below)

Remove the blossom end from the fruits, then slice them into a large pan. If you have cardamom seeds, crush a couple and toss them in too. Add water just to cover, bring to the boil and continue boiling, gently, for ten to 15 minutes. Strain the contents of the pan through a fine strainer and then through a jelly bag – don't squeeze the bag, just let the juice drip through.

Measure the juice with a cup measure. For each cup of juice you will need just over a cup of sugar.

Restore the juice to the pan, heat it and let it boil for a few minutes, then add the sugar and boil vigorously until setting point is reached (about ten to 15 minutes).

Put in sealed jars as usual.

Pippin Jelly

Slightly adapted (by Laura Mason) from a recipe in Eliza Smith's book of the 1720s: a conservative compilation which generally reflects 17th century practice.

$1\frac{1}{2}$ pounds pippin apples
$2\frac{1}{4}$ cups sugar
$\frac{1}{2}$ cup candied lemon and orange peel, cut into fine slivers

Peel and core the apples. Cook them gently in $2\frac{1}{4}$ cups water for one hour, then extract the juice gently with a jelly bag. Add the sugar to the juice, bring to a boil, then add the candied peel. Boil rapidly until the mixture reaches setting point (222°), about 20 minutes.

This makes between three and four 1 cup jars of a very elegant, translucent pale gold jelly.

Prickly Pear Jelly

Behaving like a dutiful tourist, I bought a small jar of this in Santa Fe. Once I had tasted it, I wished I had bought a case of large jars.

Now that prickly pears are fairly easy to buy in London, I've made the jelly at home. It turned out to be another of the beautiful ruby red jellies.

18 ounces prickly pears
sugar (for amount, see below)

Wearing rubber gloves, peel the fruits. Slice the pulp into pieces, put these in a pan with almost enough water to cover, bring to the boil and simmer until really soft (about ten minutes).

Rinse your jelly bag under the hot faucet, hang it up and pour the contents of the pan into it. Let the juice drip for at least four hours (only a few drops will be gained by leaving it for the 12 hours often recommended).

Bring the juice to a boil and keep it boiling for a few minutes, uncovered, then remove it from the heat, take off any scum, and measure it.

For each cup of juice add a generous $\frac{3}{4}$ cup sugar and 1–2 tablespoons lemon (or lime) juice. Bring back to the boil and continue boiling fast until setting point is reached (about five to ten minutes).

Fruit Soups

Riley M Fletcher Berry (*Fruit Cookery*, 1907) is one of the relatively few authors who ruminates about the various categories of fruit dishes. Of fruit soups he observes that, for the prosperous readers whom he addresses, these will be served in very small china or glass bowls, or bouillon cups. Delicate fare. Yet, he admonishes, one should not forget that fruit soups "are *foods* and as such are used in many countries by even the peasants, though they may lack dainty table appointments".

Peasants would doubtless have used their biggest bowls for soups made according to some of his recipes, since he typically allows equal amounts of claret and fruit juice; or adds "half a pint of sherry".

Fletcher Berry's general guidance, alcohol apart, is that you should stew the fruit with enough sugar to sweeten it (this varies from fruit to fruit), then rub it through a strainer, add an equal quantity of water, thicken it with 2 teaspoons arrowroot (the quickest alternative) or sago or tapioca.

With this guidance, you can make a soup of just about any fruit; but the most popular are, naturally, familiar fruits such as apple, cherry, apricot, raspberry, prune, melon.

Apple Soup

just over 1 pound tart apples
½ cup sugar
juice and grated peel of 1 lemon
1–2 lettuce leaves, finely shredded
2 teaspoons cider vinegar
¼ cup cream of wheat

Set about 4 cups water to boil in a large pan.

Peel, core and slice the apples. Add them and the sugar to the boiling water. Stir until the sugar is melted, then add the juice and grated peel of the lemon, plus the shredded lettuce leaves and the cider vinegar. Bring back to the boil then turn down heat and leave to simmer.

When the apple is cooked, process the whole mixture in a blender. Then return it to the pan, stir in the cream of wheat, and cook gently for ten minutes or so, until the soup has thickened.

Serve either hot or, in summer, chilled. (A little sour cream or yogurt may be stirred into the bowls when they are served.)

Rødgrøt

½ cup red currants
1½ cups raspberries
2 teaspoons cream of wheat
2 tablespoons sugar

Cook the fruit lightly until the juice runs. Strain the whole and discard the seeds. Add the cream of wheat to the juice, bring back to the boil, and cook until thickened. Remove from the heat and add the sugar.

Serve with a swirl of heavy cream.

The Russian fruit soup called Kisel, and the Polish Kisiel and Bulgarian Kissel are effectively the same dish, but thickened with potato flour or buckwheat. The German version, Rote Grütze, is the same as the Scandinavian one.

If you prefer, you may use cornstarch as the thickener; but in that case, or if using potato flour, mix it to a paste with some cold water before adding it.

Sopa de Almendras y Piñones
(Almond and Pine Nut Soup)

¾ cup almonds, blanched
½ cup pine nuts
½ cup sugar
3⅓ cups full fat milk
1–2 teaspoons ground cinnamon

Soak the nuts in warm water for at least an hour. Then drain them, combine them in a mortar with the sugar, and pound the mixture finely.

Add the pounded mixture to the milk, bring it to the boil, remove from the heat and allow to cool slightly. Then serve, sprinkling each bowlful with a little cinnamon.

Cherry Soup

1½ pounds fresh morello cherries
3 pinches ground cinnamon
2–4 tablespoons sugar
scant ½ cup sour cream

Wash and pit the cherries, then cook them in 2½ cups simmering water until they are completely soft. Allow to cool a little, add the cinnamon, then taste and, guided by the taste, stir in the small amount of sugar.

Liquidize the mixture, chill it, and stir in the sour cream before serving.

Appendix I: Prunes

Some dried fruits, when reconstituted with water, have an unmistakable resemblance to the original fresh fruit. However, just as raisins seem different from grapes, so do prunes appear to be quite distinct from the plums from which they are made. For the cook and the consumer they are a fruit in their own right, and a remarkably good one; versatile, convenient, full of flavor. It is not surprising that the French authors Souyri and Glory entitled their book on the subject *Le Pruneau Gourmand.*

Not all plums can be dried to make good prunes. The varieties of *Prunus domestica* (see page 18) suited to the purpose are those which are firm of flesh, have a relatively high sugar content, and can be dried whole without fermenting. Such plums, incidentally, also have a higher nutritional value than the general run of plums.

The most famous prune plum is certainly the French Prune d'Agen, named after a charming town in Aquitaine in the south-west of France. When I went there, and extravagantly purchased a huge golden canister full of the prunes, I learned that Agen lies on the edge rather than in the center of the prune region, and that the prunes were named d'Agen because the Canal du Midi passes through the town, which therefore served as the main "port" for despatching them. Technically, the Prunes d'Agen are known as "Prunes d'Ente", and great care is taken over grafting and raising them.

It was this same French variety that was taken to California by a Frenchman in the 19th century and is prominent among those used in the Californian prune industry. Californian production is now so great that it dominates the commerce in prunes and indeed provides a high proportion of those sold in France itself.

Although the prunes of Agen are the top prunes in France, there are others whose rank is high. The Perdrigon plum is dried whole (in the shade, on an artisanal scale) to become a kind of prune called "brignole", after the town of Brignoles, whose speciality it is. If the same plum is pitted, dried in the sun, and flattened, it becomes a "pistole".

The Saint Catherine plum also makes a fine prune, and is the fruit used for producing the famous pruneaux de Tours (also called "pruneaux fleuris" because of a whitish bloom caused by crystallization of sugar).

Carlsbad "plums" are prunes: large ones. In Central Europe the small Quetsch plums are also made into prunes.

It takes approximately three pounds of fresh plums to produce one of prunes, the loss of weight being accounted for almost entirely by the removal of water. Yet prunes, as we enjoy them nowadays, are moist and succulent. The explanation is that their moisture content, reduced by the initial drying process to 23%, to ensure that they will keep satisfactorily in storage, is restored to a higher level (29% for "pruneaux secs", up to 35% for "demi-secs") before they are shipped to the markets. This "rehydration" is necessary if they are to have the attractive softness and sheen which we expect.

The uses to which prunes can be put, and the further treatments which they may be given, are numerous. Prunes of Agen are produced in close proximity to Armagnac, so are sometimes sold in jars containing this fine brandy, or steeped in a little of it before use. They may also be steeped in wine, or in tea, or of course in water; and they need not be steeped at all if they are to be incorporated in a dish which contains liquid, especially if the dish calls for long cooking. There are a number of meat or game dishes of this sort, notably Lapin aux Pruneaux (rabbit with prunes, a speciality in the Loire region and the north of France generally). A titbit or an English savory (Devils on Horseback) can be prepared by wrapping "demi-sec" prunes in half a strip of bacon and cooking them in a hot oven.

On the sweet side, it used to be fashionable to prepare prune mousses or prune soufflées, but nowadays, in France at least, prune compotes, prepared by stewing prunes in red wine, are much more common, and very good. So are prune tarts. Many delicious sweetmeats are prepared by stuffing prunes (for example, with marzipan) or coating them with a glaze of flavored sugar syrup, or both.

Appendix II: Further Varieties of Apple

Allington Pippin is one of the sweet and sharp varieties which exemplify the manner in which an apple's taste can change with age. As Dr Joan Morgan (1982) points out, it "can be almost bitter sweet in early November but mellows to a definite pineapple flavor by Christmas".

Api (Pomme d'Api) or **Lady apple**, a variety said to have originated in Roman times, is a very small, hard, winter apple. Lister, in *A Journey to Paris in the Year 1690* commented thus: "The Pomme d'Apis . . . is served here for show more than use; being a small flat apple, very beautiful red on one side, and pale or white on the other, and may serve the ladies at their toilets a pattern to paint by." The flavor, residing chiefly in the perfumed skin, is good, but the variety has the reputation of being indigestible.

Baldwin, a round, yellow- and red-striped American apple discovered in the mid 18th century, became popular in the 19th century in the northern states. First called Pecker or Woodpecker, it was later named Baldwin in honor of the Colonel who propagated it throughout Massachusetts. It has a good, medium flavor and stores well. Season: late winter.

Beauty of Bath, an old fashioned British apple once popular but now rare, is an early variety, bright pink and green, light-textured and a poor keeper, with a sharp and sweet flavor.

Ben Davis, a large yellow and red marbled variety of little flavor, was in the 19th century a popular variety in North America. It kept well, a virtue which ceased to compensate for its lack of taste when cold storage was introduced.

Blenheim Orange, one of the best apples of the Pippin family, was popular in England for a century after its introduction around 1818. It is large, dull yellow and red, and has crisp flesh and a flavor of unusually acid quality. It is the classic Christmas apple. Season: midwinter.

Bramley's Seedling or **Bramley**, the most widely-sold cooking apple in Britain, has a very long keeping season, from early autumn right through to next summer. It is usually very large and irregular in shape. It is harvested commercially as a green apple, or green with faint red stripes, but will turn yellow if left on the tree; and there are also crimson varieties.

Calville blanche d'hiver, an old French variety, is a connoisseur's apple. It is large, ribbed, golden, juicy, and scented. It needs a warm climate or a greenhouse and is in season in January and February.

Charles Ross, named after a 19th-century gardener in Berkshire, England, is a handsome dual-purpose apple, best used early in its season, when the juicy flesh still has a good flavor. The flesh is yellow when cooked.

Codlin is a family of British cooking apples of which new varieties have been appearing since the 16th century. They are elongated, pale green or yellow, sometimes with a reddish flush but never striped. They ripen in autumn and do not keep.

Cortland, a modern American variety bred from Ben Davis and McIntosh, is useful for fruit salads because its flesh hardly browns when cut. It is largish, yellow and red, and has a sweet, moderately acid flavor. Season: late autumn.

Costard, an extinct family of British apples, was one of the first types to have a distinct name, which was already in use in the 13th century. The costard was the first important kitchen apple, much used in pies until it began to disappear towards the end of the 17th century. The apples had a reputation for superior flavor and large size. "Costard" was medieval slang for "head". The name survives in the word "costermonger", although such a person may now sell any kind of fruit or vegetable.

Court pendu plat, an old French variety dating from before 1600, which may well be a survival from Roman times. It is small, flattened in shape, green with faint red stripes, and richly flavored. Season: midwinter to spring.

Cox's Orange Pippin, one of the best of the large family of Pippins (see Pippins, below). Since its introduction in the first half of the 19th century it has become the most popular British apple. It is a medium-sized, round apple, dull brownish green with faint red stripes and a red flush on one side. It usually has a matt brown russeted area around the stem. The texture is crisp, the flavor solidly acid but balanced by sweetness. The skin is strongly scented and should be eaten.

Decio, an Italian variety for which a very ancient origin, stretching back to late classical Roman times, is claimed. It is a small apple, crisp and refreshing but without remarkable flavor. Its great virtue is being a "late keeper"; best picked green towards the end of the year and eaten in the spring, when it will have turned cream and red.

Delicious, a red apple, which began as a chance seedling on the farm of Jess Hiatt of Peru, Iowa, in 1872 and was first marketed as Hiatt's Hawkeye. Stark Brothers, a large fruit-growing concern, bought out Hiatt and renamed the variety Delicious. Since the 1940s it has been the leading American apple. It is also widely grown abroad and has been developed to give new varieties: one familiar in Britain as an import is Starking (sometimes Star King). The fruit is large, red and elongated, with five projections at the bottom end. The texture, at first crisp, becomes mealy with storage. The flavor is sweet but insipid, lacking in acid. Delicious is eaten raw and is useful in salads, since it does not brown much when cut, but its lack of taste makes it unsuitable for cooking. Season: autumn to early winter.

Discovery, one of the first British apples to appear each season, is so named because it was a chance discovery by an amateur grower. It was first marketed on a large scale in the 1970s. The apple is bright green and crimson like a brighter version of a Worcester Pearmain, and the flesh often has a pink tinge on the sunny side. At first light and crisp, it softens quickly and must be eaten at once. The flavor is unique, with a hint of raspberries.

Flower of Kent, a large, green variety now almost forgotten, but said to be the apple whose fall inspired Sir Isaac Newton to formulate his law of universal gravitation.

Gascoyne's Scarlet is a dual-purpose apple. Pale greenish white, but with one side bright red. Fine, moderately juicy flesh, scant flavor. A French name, Cramoisie de Gascogne, suggests a French origin, but the variety was first raised by a Mr Gascoyne in England.

Gladpit, a large early summer apple of pleasing flavor and aroma.

Golden Delicious, an American apple which appeared as a chance seedling on Anderson H Mullin's West Virginia farm in about 1900, is now the most widely grown apple in many countries. It is not related to Delicious. The apple is elongated, tapering to five points, pale green becoming yellow and sometimes acquiring a faint flush. The flavor varies. When the apple is grown in a cool climate, so that a reasonable amount of acid is formed, it can be good; but in warmer regions it is insipid. The variety is popular with growers because the tree crops heavily. Because it lacks acidity, Golden Delicious retains its shape when cooked. It is therefore a good choice for dishes containing sliced apples which are exposed to view, such as the French Tarte aux Pommes.

Golden Noble, a cooking apple, one of those which disintegrates. Highly recommended for its flavor but rarely available in shops.

Granny Smith is unusual in being a brilliant, almost emerald, green even when fully ripe although a slight flush sometimes appears on one side. It is much grown in warm climates, notably in South Africa, Australia, Chile and France.

Gravenstein originated in North Germany or Denmark before 1800: no one knows exactly where or when. Scions were taken to California around 1820 and it soon became a popular American variety, especially for cooking; but it is also eaten by those who like rather acid apples. It is large, roundish and slightly lopsided, yellow with bright red and orange stripes.

Greening or **Rhode Island Greening**, a pale green apple first grown from seed in 1748 by a Mr Green at Green's End, Rhode Island, is crisp and sharp in flavor. Usually sold as a cooking apple, but a good dessert apple too. Long season: late autumn to spring.

Howgate Wonder, an outstandingly large cooking apple which disintegrates completely when cooked. Weak in flavor.

Idared, an American apple bred in Idaho in the 1930s-40s from the better known Jonathan and Wagener. A medium-sized, round, red and yellow apple with a sweet, moderately acid flavor; keeps and cooks well.

Jester, a recent English addition to the range of dessert varieties, has considerable merit.

Jonathan, an American apple dating from about 1825, is medium-sized with a yellow skin heavily overlaid with red stripes. The flavor is mildly acid, the texture crisp but quickly softening; so it must be used at once. It is good for both eating and cooking. Season: autumn.

Laxton apples, a large and important group, owe their name to Thomas Laxton (1830–90), who worked mainly on peas and strawberries but whose sons began in 1893 to experiment systematically in crossing apples. They produced thousands of cross-bred apples, from which many of the best British dessert apples are derived. A high proportion of them retain the name Laxton. They bear a general resemblance to Coxes (although they can usually be distinguished by their brighter color). The texture is crisp and the flavor light. The best-known late Laxtons include Laxton's Pearmain and Laxton's Superb. Laxton's Advance and Laxton's Leader are among the earlier varieties. Laxton's Fortune is a yellow- and red-striped mid-season variety.

James Grieve, wrote Bunyard, ". . . is one of the very few apples resulting from the marriage of a cooking and a dessert apple which is of dessert quality. One feels that like some of the recently ennobled we know of, it is a near thing, and untoward circumstances such as a cold and sunless summer reveal the humble origin. But given a fair chance we may welcome the newcomer, thankful for the melting, almost marrowy, flesh, abundant juice, and fragrant aroma."

Lord Derby, a cooking apple which does not disintegrate. Best while still green.

Macoun, a large, red American apple bred from McIntosh, which it surpasses in flavor. It also keeps better.

McIntosh, a popular American variety named for John McIntosh of Ontario, who discovered it as a chance seedling in about 1811. The apple is medium-sized, green or yellow heavily overlaid with red stripes. The area where it grows extends into Canada and is near the northern limits of apple country. Its texture is soft and juicy, the flavor a pleasing combination of tart and sweet; and it is aromatic. A good cooking apple, also eaten raw.

Mutsu, of Japanese origin, is now grown in Britain under the name of Crispin. A very late, long-keeping variety, developed from Golden Delicious but generally larger, with a more acid and more interesting flavor. Suitable for both cooking and eating.

Newtown Pippin, a fine, old established American variety, is little grown today because the tree is awkward to manage. Newtown was on Long Island, where Flushing now is. The original tree was found growing there soon after 1700. It produced a heavy crop of yellowish-green apples which were crisp but juicy, acid but sweet, and had exceptional keeping qualities. Ripening in midwinter, they kept in good condition till the following summer. The variety, spread by cuttings taken from the tree (which perished in 1805 as a result of excessive cutting), was soon grown over most of the settled parts of North America. The tree was unrivaled as an apple producer, but awkwardly sensitive to soil and climate. It lost popularity among growers towards the end of the 19th century because of its "crankiness".

Northern Spy, a large, yellow- and red-striped American apple resembling Baldwin but far better; indeed it was long considered the perfect specimen and became something of a legend for country people as well as urban gastronomes. It originated in the north-east of the USA in the first decade of the 19th century and was much grown well into the 20th, but is now less often seen.

Pearmain, the oldest English apple name, was recorded in a Norfolk document of 1204. It is derived from the old French apple name "parmain" or "permain", referring perhaps to a group of apples rather than a single variety. All that modern Pearmains have in common is the green and red coloring typical of many British apples. The best known is Worcester Pearmain, which has a good, sharp flavor with a hint of strawberry, and a crisp texture when fresh, but does not keep. Season: early autumn.

Pippin, originally meaning any apple grown from a pip, is a name derived from the French "pépin", meaning both "pip" and the apple. By the 16th century the term had come to denote a hard, late-ripening, long-keeping apple of acid flavor. The first pippins brought over from France to England were cider apples, but eating varieties were soon developed. London Pippin or Five Crown was known in Somerset before 1580, and is still grown in Australia. Golden Pippin, a well-flavored and juicy variety, enjoyed a high reputation throughout the 16th and 17th centuries. Later, Ribston Pippin became popular and from this the modern Cox's Orange Pippin was bred. Another good Pippin is Sturmer Pippin, a very late-ripening, hard variety which does well in the southern hemisphere and is grown for export in South Africa and Australia.

In America the name "Pippin" was used for different kinds of apple, the most famous being a purely American variety, Newtown Pippin.

Pitmaston Pine Apple, a small conical apple raised in Pitmaston, Worcestershire, England, in 1785. Rich in flavor.

Red Astrachan, a rosy Russian variety, is an early apple with a fruity, acid taste and plenty of character, but apt to fall off the tree before it is fully ripe.

Reinette, an old French apple name, originally meant an apple propagated by grafting (Latin "renatus", meaning reborn). The name soon came to denote instead a type of apple which was late-ripening and long-keeping, with a dull green skin, sometimes flushed and often "russeted". It had firm, slightly dry flesh, and a good, sharp flavor. Golden Reinette has been popular in France since before 1650. Orléans Reinette, an 18th-century variety which is unusually sweet, is generally regarded as better.

Reverend W Wilks, a mid-season cooking apple, first recorded in 1904. The crisp flesh cooks down to a yellow froth.

Rhode Island Greening (see Greening).

Rome Beauty, an American apple, is named for Rome, Ohio, near where it was discovered around 1820 by the farmer Joel Gillett. One of his grafted trees had shot from below the graft. The stray branch began to produce large, red-striped apples of handsome appearance and rock-like solidity. The variety became popular, especially among growers, for it is easy to manage and the attractive fruit sells well. It also keeps crisp for a long time; but the flavor is insipid. The apple is used for cooking, especially for baking because it keeps its shape well.

Russet is the name of a group of apples with distinctive matt brown skin, often spotted or with a faint red flush, and of a flattened lopsided shape. The flesh is crisp and the apples keep well from the late autumn, when they ripen until the following spring, although they may turn rubbery. The flavor is unusual and pearlike.

Russets are used both for eating and for cooking. Their size varies from tiny to very large. In Britain Egremont Russet and Golden Russet are the most popular kinds. An American variety, Roxbury Russet, is claimed to have originated in Roxbury, Massachusetts, in the early 17th century. If true, this would make it America's oldest named variety.

Spartan, a crimson apple of recent Canadian origin, is popular with growers and widely sold in Britain, though of inferior flavor and texture.

Wealthy, a large, bright-red American apple, grows well in northern climates. It was developed for that purpose in the 1860s by Peter Gideon, the first American to breed apples scientifically. The name was not bestowed to suggest opulence, but was Mrs Gideon's (Puritan) Christian name. The apple has a good, sharp flavor suitable for either eating or cooking, but the pinkish flesh softens quickly, so it should be eaten soon. Season: mid-autumn.

White Joaneting, an English apple known before 1600 (the Jenneting of Elizabethan writers), is still sometimes grown because it ripens before any other apple, in July. Its shiny skin is yellow, sometimes with a red flush. It has a good flavor and is juicy, but does not keep.

White Transparent, an early-ripening apple of Scandinavian or Russian origin, was introduced to Britain and the USA in the mid 19th century. As its name suggests, it is very pale with a transparent skin. The taste is mild but agreeable and the fruit should be used as soon as ripe, while still crisp, for cooking rather than dessert. Yellow Transparent is similar. Season: late summer.

Winesap is an American apple of unknown but early origin, so named because it was often used as a cider apple. It is generally of medium size, elongated, bright red with a little yellow on the shaded side, and with firm, aromatic flesh. Ripening in late autumn, it keeps well until early summer, although the texture softens. Good raw, and also for cooking, where its lack of tartness should be corrected with a little lemon juice.

Worcester apples form a group of which the Worcester Pearmain (see Pearmain) is the best known. Firm sweet flesh with a strawberry flavor is characteristic of them. They include Benn's Red, an old Cornish apple; Tydeman's Early Worcester; Duchess of Oldenbury; and Martin Worcester. By September they tend to be over-sweet.

Bibliography

Ackerman, E D, et al (eds): *Tropical Fruit Recipes*, Miami, Rare Fruit Council International, 1981

Acton, Eliza: *Modern Cookery for Private Families*, revised edn, London, Longman, Green, Longman & Roberts, 1860

Alexander, Agnes B: *How to Use Hawaiian Fruit*, Honolulu, Petroglyph Press, 1974

Alexander, D McE and others: *Some Tree Fruits for Tropical Australia*, Australia, CSIRO, 1982

Allen, Betty Molesworth: *Common Malaysian Fruits*, Singapore, Eastern Universities Press, 1965 (also in abridged form, Kuala Lumpur, Longman, 1975)

Ampleforth Abbey (monks of): *Cooking Apples*, York, Ampleforth Abbey, 1982

Babet-Charton, Henriette: *Fruit, 384 French Recipes*, London, Crosby Lockwood, 1949

Bacon, Josephine: *The Citrus Cookbook*, Boston, Harvard Common Press, 1983

Bailey, L H: *The Evolution of our Native Fruits*, New York, Macmillan, 1898

Bastyra, Judy: *Caribbean Cooking*, Leicester, Windward, 1987

Bazore, Katherine: *Hawaiian and Pacific Foods*, New York, M Barrows & Co, 1953

Beeton, Mrs: *Mrs Beeton's Book of Household Management* (1861), facsimile reprint, London, Chancellor Press, 1982

Berry, Riley M Fletcher: *Fruit Recipes*, London, Archibald Constable & Co, 1907

Bissell, Frances: *Sainsbury's Book of Food*, London, Webster's (for Sainsbury plc), 1989

Blakeston, Oswell: *Cooking with Nuts*, London, Pierrot Publishing, 1979

Bonnassieux, Marie-Pierre: *Tous les Fruits Comestibles du Monde*, Paris, Bordas, 1988

Bradley, Richard: *The Country Housewife and Lady's Director* (1732), reprint (ed Caroline Davidson), London, Prospect Books, 1980

Brooke, Justin: *Dessert Pears*, London, Rupert Hart-Davis, 1956

Brooks, Reid M & Hesse, Claron G: *Western Fruit Gardening*, Berkeley & Los Angeles, University of California Press, 1953

Brown, Catherine: *Scottish Regional Recipes*, Glasgow, Molendinar Press, 1981

Brown Catherine: *Broths to Bannocks*, London, John Murray, 1990

Brown Deni: *Aroids*, London, Century Hutchinson, 1988

Brown, Lynda: *Fresh Thoughts on Food*, London, Chatto & Windus, 1986

Brown, Lynda: *The Cook's Garden*, London, Century, 1990

Bruneton-Governatori, Ariane: *Le Pain de Bois – Ethnohistoire de la Châtaigne et du Châtaignier*, Toulouse, Eché, 1984

Bultitude, John: *Apples – A Guide to the Identification of International Varieties*, London, Macmillan, 1983

Bunyard, Edward: *A Handbook of Hardy Fruits – Stone & Bush Fruits, Nuts, etc.* London, 1925

Bunyard, Edward: *The Anatomy of Dessert*, London, 1933

Burkill, I H: *A Dictionary of the Economic Products of the Malay Peninsula*, vols 1 & 2, London, Crown Agents for the Colonies, 1935 (and reprinted for the Governments of Malaysia & Singapore, Kuala Lumpur, 1966)

Carter, Elizabeth: *Majorcan Food and Cookery*, London, Prospect Books, 1989

Castelvetro, Giacomo (translated and edited by Gillian Riley): *Di Tutte le Radici, di Tutte l'Erbe e di Tutti i Frutti*, London, Viking, 1988

Cavalcante, Paulo B: *Frutas comestíveis da Amazônia*, Manaus, Instituto Nacional de Pesquisas da Amazônia

Chamberlain, Lesley: *The Food and Cooking of Russia*, London, Allen Lane, 1982 (and Penguin since 1983)

Chamberlain, Lesley: *The Food and Cooking of Eastern Europe*, London, Penguin, 1989

Child, Reginald: *Coconuts*, 2nd edn, London, Longman, 1974

Chin, H F & Yong, H S: *Malaysian Fruits in Colour*, Kuala Lumpur, Tropical Press, 1982

Coley, Hilda M: *Our Heritage of Fruits*, London, 1937

Conway, Tess: *Seychelles Delights*, Seychelles, publisher (a women's organisation) and date (recent, certainly post-1975) not given

Cooper, William C: *In Search of the Golden Apple*, New York, Vantage Press, 1982

Corato, Riccardo Di: *838 Frutti e Verdure d'Italia*, Milan, Sonzogno, 1979

Coronel, Roberto, E: *Promising Fruits of the Philippines*, Los Baños, University of the Philippines, 1983

Couverchel, M: *Traité Complet des Fruits de toute Espèce*, Paris, 1852

Cox, Helen: *Traditional English Cooking*, London, Angus & Robertson, 1961

Darrow, George M: *The Strawberry – History, Breeding and Physiology*, New York, Holt, Rinehart and Winston, 1966

Dorn, Mabel: *Under the Coconuts in Florida*, South Miami, South Florida Publishing, 1949

Dowson, V H W & Aten, A: *Dates – Handling, Processing and Packing*, Rome, FAO, 1962

Draper, Jo: *Dorset Food*, Wimborne (Dorset), Dovecote Press, 1988

Duff, Gail: *The Fruit and Nut Book*, London, Sidgwick & Jackson, 1990

Eales, Mrs Mary: *Mrs. Mary Eales's Receipts*, London, H Meere, 1718 (and republished from the edn of 1733 by Prospect Books, London, 1985)

Edington, Sarah: *The Book of National Trust Recipes*, London, National Trust, 1988

Edlin, H & Nimmo, M: *Trees, Timbers and Forests of the World*, London, Salamander Books, 1978

Edwards, Graham & Sue: *The Guernsey Babaco Cookbook*, Gloucester, Allen Sutton, 1988

Eley, Geoffrey: *Wild Fruits and Nuts*, EP Publishing, Wakefield, W Yorks, 1976

Facciola, Stephen: *Cornucopia, A Source Book of Edible Plants*, Vista, CA, Kampong Publications, 1990

Farley, John: *The London Art of Cookery*, 8th edn, London, 1796

Farmer, Fannie Merritt: *The Boston Cooking-School Cook Book*, 8th edn, Boston, Little, Brown, 1950

Ficklen, Ellen: *Watermelon*, Washington DC, American Folklife Center, Library of Congress, 1984

Forsell, Mary: *The Berry Garden*, London, Macdonald Orbis, 1989

Francatelli, Charles Elmé: *The Modern Cook*, 9th edn, London, 1853

Fruit & Vegetable Facts & Pointers (78 reports), Alexandria VA, United Fresh Fruit and Vegetable Association, 1970s

Fruit Crops Fact Sheets, Gainesville, University of Florida, 1970s & 1980s

Garrett, Blanche Pownall: *Canadian Country Preserves and Wines*, Toronto, James Lewis & Samuel, 1974

Godfrey, T Crawford: *Hong Kong Fruits and Seeds*, Hong Kong, Urban Council, 1984

Gopalan, C et al: *Nutritive Value of Indian Foods*, Hyderabad, National Institute of Nutrition, 1984

Graham, Gladys R: *Tropical Cooking*, Panama, Panama American Press, 1947

Gray, Patience: *Honey from a Weed*, London, Prospect Books, 1986

Green, Joyce Conyngham: *Salmagundi*, London, Dent, 1947

Greenoak, Francesca: *Forgotten Fruit*, London, André Deutsch, 1983

Grigson, Jane: *Good Things*, London, Michael Joseph, 1971 (and reissued in new edn 1990)

Grigson, Jane, & Knox, Charlotte: *Exotic Fruits & Vegetables*, London, Jonathan Cape, 1986

Grigson, Jane: *Jane Grigson's Fruit Book*, London, Michael Joseph, 1982 (and Penguin since 1983)

Halıcı, Nevin: *Nevin Halıcı's Turkish Cookbook*, London, Dorling Kindersley, 1989

Hansell, Örjan Armfelt: *Bärboken*, Stockholm, P A Norstedt & Söners, 1969

Hartley, Dorothy: *Food in England*, London, Macdonald, 1954

Hazan, Marcella: *The Classic Italian Cookbook*, London, Macmillan, 1980

Heal, Carolyn and Allsop, Michael: *Queer Gear: How to Buy and Cook Exotic Fruits and Vegetables*, London, Century, 1986

Hedrick, U P: *Cyclopedia of Hardy Fruits*, 2nd (enlarged) edn, New York, The Macmillan Company, 1938

Hedrick, U P et al: *The Pears of New York*, New York Dep't of Agriculture, 1921

Hobson, Len: *Papino Papaws Please!*, Cape Town, Muller & Retief, 1972

Holt, Geraldene: *French Country Kitchen*, London, Penguin, 1987

Howes, F N: *Nuts – Their Production and Everyday Uses*, London, Faber, 1948

Hutchins, Sheila: *Grannie's Kitchen – Recipes from East Anglia*, St Albans, Granada, 1980

Hyman, Philip and Mary (translated, revised and adapted): *Lenôtre's Desserts and Pastries*, New York, Barron's, 1977

Hyman, Philip and Mary (translated and adapted): *Lenôtre's Ice Creams and Candies*, New York, Barron's, 1979

I C & R F Society Newsletter, nos 1–32, Los Altos CA, Indoor Citrus and Rare Fruit Society, 1980s

Iddison, Philip: "Leaves from a Turkish Notebook", in *PPC* (*Petits Propos Culinaires*) 34, London, Prospect Books, 1990

Jackson, Ian: "The Fruit Garden Display'd", in *Pacific Horticulture 47, 3*, California, 1986

Jackson, Ian: *The History of the Pear*, Not yet published

Jaine, Tom: *Cooking in the Country*, London, Chatto & Windus, 1986

Janick, Jules & Moore, James N (eds): *Advances in Fruit Breeding*, West Lafayette IN, Purdue University Press, 1975

Johns, Leslie, & Stevenson, Violet: *The Complete Book of Fruit*, Sydney, Angus & Robertson, 1979

Kennedy, Diana: *The Cuisines of Mexico*, revised edn, New York, Harper & Row, 1986

Kennedy, Teresa: *American Pie*, New York, Workman Publishing, 1984

Khaing, Mi Mi: *Cook and Entertain the Burmese Way*, Ann Arbor, Karoma Publishers, 1978

Kolesnikov, V: *Fruit Biology*, Moscow, MIR, 1964

Kranz, Brigitte: *Das große Buch der Früchte*, 2nd edn, Munich, Südwest Verlag, 1988

Lambert, Edward: *The Art of Confectionary*, London, 1744

Lanner, Harriette: *The Pinon Pine – A Natural and Cultural History*, Reno, University of Nevada, 1951

Leclerc, Henri: *Les Fruits de France*, Paris, Masson, 1925

Lemnis, Maria and Vitry, Henryk: *Old Polish Traditions in the Kitchen and at the Table*, Warsaw, Impress, 1979

Loewenfeld, Claire: *Britain's Wild Larder – Nuts*, London, Faber, 1957

Low, Tim: *Bush Tucker – Australia's Wild Food Harvest*, Angus & Robertson, North Ryde NSW, 1989

Luard, Elizabeth: *The Princess and the Pheasant*, London, Bantam Press, 1987

Lutes, Della: *The Country Kitchen*, UK edn, London, Bell, 1938

Maggs, D H: *An Introduction to Pistachio Growing in Australia*, Australia, CSIRO, 1982

Mann, Gertrude: *Berry Cooking*, London, André Deutsch, 1954

Martin, Franklin W and others: *Perennial Edible Fruits of the Tropics – An Inventory*, Washington DC, US Department of Agriculture, 1987

Massey & Sons: *Comprehensive Pudding Book*, London, Simpkin, Marshall & Co, c 1874

McGee, Harold: *The Curious Cook*, Berkeley CA, North Point Press, 1990

McPhee, John: *Oranges*, New York, Farrar, Straus & Giroux, 1967

Menninger, Edwin A: *Edible Nuts of the World*, Florida, Horticulural Books, 1977

Miller, Carey D; Bazore, Katherine; Bartow, Mary: *Fruits of Hawaii*, 4th edn, Hawaii, University of Hawaii Press, 1965

Ministry of Agriculture, Fisheries & Food: *Catalogue of British Pears – National Fruit Trials*, London, ADAS, 1976

Moine, Marie-Pierre: *Cuisine Grand-Mère*, London, Barrie & Jenkins, 1990

Morgan, Joan & Richards, Alison: *A Paradise out of a Common Field*, London, Century, 1990

Morton, Dr Julia F: *Fruits of Warm Climates*, Miami, Julia F Morton, 1987

Morton, Kendal & Julia: *Fifty Tropical Fruits of Nassau*, Coral Gables FL, Text House, 1946

Ochse, J J: *Vegetables of the Dutch East Indies*, Amsterdam, A Asher & Co, 1980

Oldham, Chas H: *The Cultivation of Berried Fruits in Great Britain*, London, Crosby Lockwood, 1946

Olney, Richard (chief consultant): *Cakes and Pastries*, Amsterdam, Time/Life Books, 1980

Olney, Richard (chief consultant): *Fruits*, Amsterdam, Time/Life Books, 1983

Orosa, Maria Y: *Maria Y Orosa – Her Life and Work* (ed Helen Orosa del Rosario), Quezon City, Philippines, R P Garcia, 1970

Ortiz, Elisabeth Lambert: *The Book of Latin American Cooking*, New York, Knopf, 1979 (and Penguin since 1985)

Ortiz, Elisabeth Lambert: *The Complete Book of Caribbean Cooking*, New York, M Evans, 1973

Ochse, J J: *Fruits and Fruitculture in the Dutch East Indies*, Batavia, Kolff, 1931

Owen, Sri: *Indonesian Food and Cookery*, 2nd edn, London, Prospect Books, 1986

Painter, Gilian: *The Home Orchard Cookery Book*, Auckland, Hodder & Stoughton, 1976

Payne, Selma and W J A: *Cooking with Exotic Fruit*, London, Batsford, 1979

Pétard, Paul: *Plantes utiles de Polynésie*, revised edn, Tahiti, Haere Po No Tahiti, 1986

Peterson, Maude Gridley: *How to Know Wild Fruits*, New York, Dover, 1973

Phillipps, Karen & Dahlen, Martha: *A Guide to Market Fruits of Southeast Asia*, Hong Kong, South China Morning Post, 1985

Phillips, Henry: *Fruits known in Great Britain – Pomarium Britannicum*, 3rd edn, London, Henry Colburn, 1823

Philpot, Rosl: *Viennese Cookery*, London, Hodder and Stoughton, 1965

Pijpers, Dick and others: *The Complete Book of Fruit*, London, Admiral Books, 1986

Poole, Shona Crawford: *Iced Delights*, London, Conran Octopus, 1986

Popenoe, Paul B: *Date Growing in the Old and New Worlds*, Altadena CA, West India Gardens, 1913

Popenoe, Wilson: *Economic Fruit-bearing Plants of Ecuador*, Washington DC, Smithsonian Institution, 1924

Popenoe, Wilson: *Manual of Tropical and Subtropical Fruits*, New York, Macmillan, 1932

Poulson, Joan: *Yorkshire Cookery*, London, Batsford, 1979

Powers, Jo Marie & Stewart, Anita: *The Farmers'' Market Cookbook*, Toronto, Stoddart, 1984

Radecka, Helena: *The Fruit and Nut Book*, New York, McGraw-Hill, 1984

Raffald, Elizabeth: *The Experienced English Housekeeper*, 3rd edn, London, printed for the author, 1773

Rare Fruit Council: *Tropical Fruit Recipes – Rare and Exotic Fruits*, Miami, Rare Fruit Council International, 1981

Rauch, George H: *Jam Manufacture*, London, Leonard Hill, 1952

Ray, John: *Historia Plantarum*, London, 1686–1704

Reuther, Walter (ed): *The Citrus Industry*, Berkeley, University of California, 1967

Reynolds, Philip Keep: *Earliest Evidence of Banana Culture*, Baltimore, American Oriental Society, 1951

Reynolds, Philip Keep: *The Banana*, Boston and New York, Houghton Mifflin, 1927

Riddell, Dr R: *Indian Domestic Economy and Receipt Book*, 7th edn, Calcutta, Thacker, Spink & Co, 1871

Roach, F A: *Cultivated Fruits of Britain*, Oxford, Basil Blackwell, 1985

Robinson, Jancis: *Vines, Grapes and Wines*, London, Mitchell Beazley, 1986

Roden, Claudia: *A New Book of Middle Eastern Food*, London & New York, Viking Penguin, 1985

Rosengarten, Frederic: *The Book of Edible Nuts*, New York, Walker, 1984

Round, Jeremy: *The Independent Cook*, London, Barrie & Jenkins, 1988

Roundell, Mrs Charles: *Mrs Roundell's Practical Cookery Book*, London, Bickers, 1898

Saberi, Helen: *Noshe Djan: Afghan Food and Cookery*, Prospect Books, London, 1986

Sahni, Julie: *Classic Indian Cooking*, New York, Wm Morrow, 1980

Sanders, Rosanne: *The English Apple*, Oxford, Phaidon, 1988

Schneider, Elizabeth: *Uncommon Fruits and Vegetables*, New York, Harper & Row, 1986

Shearn, W B (ed): *The Practical Fruiterer and Florist*, vols I–III, London, George Newnes, c 1930s

Shere, Lindsay Remolif (with preface by Alice Waters): *Chez Panisse*, New York, Random House, 1985

Shi Mingnan, Chen Guoxiong, Zhang Yikong (eds): *Fruits of Taiwan*, Taipeh, c 1980

Simmonds, N W: *Bananas*, London, Longmans, Green, 1959

Sing, Phia (eds Alan & Jennifer Davidson): *Traditional Recipes of Laos*, London, Prospect Books, 1981

Singh, R N: *Mango*, New Delhi, Indian Council of Agricultural Research, 1978

Slack, Margaret: *Northumbrian Fare*, Newcastle upon Tyne, Frank Graham, 1981

Smith, Eliza: *The Compleat Housewife*, 3rd edn, London, 1729

Smith, John: *A Dictionary of the Popular Names of the Plants which Furnish the Natural and Acquired Wants of Man*, London, Macmillan, 1882

Smith, Muriel W G: *A Catalogue of the Plums at the National Fruit Trials*, Faversham, Kent, Ministry of Agriculture, Fisheries & Food, 1978

Smith, Muriel W G: *National Apple Register of the United Kingdom*, London, 1971

So, Yan-Kit: *Yan-Kit's Classic Chinese Cookbook*, London, Dorling Kindersley, 1984 (also published as *Chinese Cooking* by Yan-Kit Martin, New York, Random House, 1984)

Sokolov, Raymond: *How to Cook*, New York, Wm Morrow, 1986

Souyri, Jean-Claude & Glory, Norbert: *Le Pruneau Gourmand*, Toulouse, Editions Privat, 1986

Sturrock, David: *Fruits for Southern Florida*, Florida, Horticultural Books, 1959

Switzer, Stephen: *The Practical Fruit-Gardener*, London, printed for T Woodward, 1724

Tanttu, Anna-Maija & Juha: *Food from Finland*, 2nd edn, Finland, Otava Publishing Company, 1988

Tate, Joyce L: *Cactus Cook Book*, 4th edn, Arcadia CA, Cactus and Succulent Society of America, 1978

Taylor, H V: *The Apples of England*, London, Crosby Lockwood, 1945

Taylor, H V: *The Plums of England*, London, Crosby Lockwood, 1949

Thorne, John: *Simple Cooking*, New York, Viking, 1987

Tolkowsky, S: *Hesperides – A History of the Culture and Use of Citrus Fruits*, London, Staples & Staples, 1937

Tsuji, Prof Shizuo: *Japanese Cooking – Simple Art*, Tokyo & New York, Kodansha International, 1980

Turner, Nancy J & Szczawinski: *Edible Wild Fruits and Nuts of Canada*, Markham ONT, Fitzhenry & Whiteside with the National Museum of Natural Science, 1988

Uphof, J C Th: *Dictionary of Economic Plants*, 2nd edn, Lehre, von J Cramer, 1968

Van Schaik, Hella: "The Medlar – Going or Coming Back?" in *Food in Motion* (Proceedings of the Oxford Symposium on Food History, 1983), Prospect Books, London, 1983

Vieira, Edite: *The Taste of Portugal*, London, Robert Hale, 1988

Wheaton, Barbara Ketcham: *Victorian Ices and Ice Cream*, New York, Metropolitan Museum of Art, 1976

Whiteaker, Stafford: *The Compleat Strawberry*, London, Century, 1985

Willan, Anne: *The Observer French Cookery School* (with an anthology of French cooking and kitchen terms by Jane Grigson), London, Macdonald, 1980

Wilson, Anne: *The Book of Marmalade*, London, Constable, 1985

Wickson, Edward J: *The California Fruits and How to Grow Them*, 2nd edn, San Francisco, Dewey, 1891

Wood, Beryl: *Caribbean Fruits and Vegetables*, Trinidad, Longman Caribbean, 1973

Woodroof, Jasper Guy: *Coconuts: Production, Processing, Products*, Westport CT, AVI, 1978

Woodroof, Jasper Guy: *Tree Nuts – Production, Processing, Products*, Westport CT, AVI, 1979

Wynne, Peter: *Apples – History, Folklore, Horticulture, and Gastronomy*, New York, Hawthorn, 1975

Zohary, Michael: *Plants of the Bible*, Cambridge, Cambridge University Press, 1982

Index